FORSYTH LIBRARY - FHSU
324.3M329i 1979
main   The last

2 1765 0004 3266 9

P9-EMB-846

The Isabella Beecher Hooker Project

The Isabella Beecher Hooker Project, consisting of the clothbound edition of the Guide/Index and the Microfiche, is distributed solely by KTO MICROFORM. All inquiries should be sent directly to:

KTO MICROFORM
A U.S. Division of Kraus-Thomson Organization Limited
Route 100
Millwood, New York 10546
Tel. (914) 762-2200

The Isabella Beecher Hooker Project

A Microfiche Edition of Her Papers
and
Suffrage-Related Correspondence Owned by The Stowe-Day Foundation

Edited and with an Introductory Essay by Anne Throne Margolis
Assisted by Margaret Granville Mair

The Guide/Index
Published by
The Stowe-Day Foundation
77 Forest Street
Hartford, Connecticut

*   *   *   *

The Microfiche
Published by
KTO Microform
A U.S. Division of Kraus-Thomson Organization Limited
Millwood, New York
1979

©Copyright 1979 The Stowe-Day Foundation

No part of this publication (or any portion of the Guide/Index, any individual fiche, or any image from a fiche) may be reproduced without the written permission of The Stowe-Day Foundation.

Permission to quote from any manuscript in this microfiche must be obtained by writing to The Stowe-Day Foundation or, in the case of manuscripts owned by other institutions, the repository so designated in the targets to the microfiche.

ISBN 0-917482-17-4 Guide/Index

324.3
M329i
1979

The National Historical Publications and Records Commission

This printed Guide/Index and the microform publication for which it serves as a finding aid were produced under the sponsorship of The National Historical Publications and Records Commission, General Services Administration. The Commission's Documentary Publications Program is designed to help achieve equal opportunities for scholarship.

TABLE OF CONTENTS

Three generations: L. to R., Alice Hooker Day, Isabella Beecher Hooker, Katharine Seymour Day, c. 1896–1902

FOREWORD

It is particularly fitting that the first major microform project of The Stowe-Day Foundation deals with the papers of Isabella Beecher Hooker, for she was the grandmother of Katharine Seymour Day, who established and endowed the Foundation. Mrs. Hooker epitomized many of the qualities that made the Beechers a unique and distinguished family: unflagging determination, a deep moral commitment to those principles that they perceived as just and essential to a true democracy, and an abiding faith that social changes could be realized through the sustained efforts of an enlightened citizenry. Miss Day likewise carried on in the Beecher tradition, first in her efforts for political reform and the suffrage movement, and later for the preservation of that most important portion of Hartford's nineteenth-century neighborhood, Nook Farm.

The scope of this project has been enlarged to include certain materials outside of The Stowe-Day Library, largely through the efforts of the project director, Anne Margolis. We wish to pay special tribute to Mr. Joseph K. Hooker, grandson of Isabella Beecher Hooker and a devoted trustee of the Foundation, whose gifts of many Hooker letters and photographs have greatly enhanced the collection. His enthusiastic and vivid recollections of his grandmother inspired all of us working on this reevaluation of her life.

Joseph S. Van Why, Director
The Stowe-Day Foundation

ACKNOWLEDGEMENTS

We wish to express our appreciation to the Director and Board of Trustees of The Stowe-Day Foundation, who have not only played a leading role in the preservation of the papers of Isabella Beecher Hooker but who have also recognized the need to make these papers known by and more accessible to the scholarly community. This goal has now been realized in the form of the present project, a microfiche edition of Mrs. Hooker's papers and other suffrage-related correspondence owned by The Stowe-Day Foundation. The project has been funded by The National Historical Publications and Records Commission and administered through The Stowe-Day Foundation. Thanks to the joint support of these two institutions, these manuscripts are now available to students of nineteenth-century American culture in microform for the first time, along with this printed Guide/Index, which is intended to serve as a finding aid for the microfiche.

We are indebted to Mr. Roger Bruns of The National Historical Publications and Records Commission for suggesting that we consider using microfiche rather than microfilm. Despite the unique technical problems that microfiche poses in both the preparation and filming stages, it is vastly superior to microfilm in ease of handling as well as indexing. Two articles by Thomas E. Jeffrey, Microfiche Editor of the Benjamin Henry Latrobe Papers, have served as a much needed guide to both the difficulties and advantages of this relatively new technique for preserving and publishing handwritten historical documents. (See "The Papers of Benjamin Henry Latrobe: New Approaches to the Micropublication of Historical Records," *Microform Review,* Vol. 6, No. 2 [March 1977] and "The Papers of Benjamin Henry Latrobe: Problems and Possibilities of Editing Historical Documents on Microfiche," *The Journal of Micrographics,* Vol. 10, No. 2 [November 1976].)

The Project Director was also able to benefit from the experience and advice of Lillian B. Miller, Editor of the Charles Willson Peale Papers. In the midst of her own hectic schedule, Dr. Miller took the time to explain the terminology of targets and control cards and to demonstrate the technique of using layout sheets. Although the procedures employed in the Hooker Project differ in several respects from those used by either the Peale or the Latrobe microfiche projects, we owe a substantial debt to both.

Librarians and scholars at the following institutions also deserve thanks for permitting us to include in the microfiche and printed guide copies of Mrs. Hooker's letters and/or original photographs of suffrage correspondents:

The Beinecke Rare Book and Manuscript Library (Yale University)

The Lucy Robbins Welles Library (Newington CT)

The Mark Twain Memorial (Hartford CT)

The Mark Twain Papers (The Bancroft Library, University of California, Berkeley)

The Morris Library (Southern Illinois University, Carbondale)

The Schlesinger Library (Radcliffe College)

The Seneca Falls Historical Society (Seneca Falls NY)

The Sophia Smith Collection, Women's History Archive (Smith College)

The Yale University Library*

Special appreciation is due to both Joseph K. Hooker, grandson of Isabella Beecher Hooker, and The Connecticut Historical Society for allowing us to film Mrs. Hooker's 1876 diary. It is the hope of all concerned that Mrs. Hooker will receive more even-handed treatment from scholars than has previously been the case when this diary (which may not be quoted from directly under an agreement with the family) is read in its proper context along with the rest of her papers.

The filming of this project, carried out by the Photographic Department at Yale University's Sterling Memorial Library, proved to be an educational experience for everyone involved. Lillian Pietruszka, Photographic Assistant, filmed the entire project and performed the painstaking task of mounting the fiche by hand. Friedrich Mueller, Head of the Photographic Department, and Daniel Ossorio, Chief Photographic Services Assistant, gave generously of their time, experimenting with various fiche formats and consulting with the Project Director concerning the filming of oversized, faded, or otherwise difficult to read documents. All three pooled their experience and expertise to come up with solutions to what often seemed to be insurmountable technical problems.

We also wish to thank the staff of The Stowe-Day Foundation for its supportiveness and for providing us with an enthusiastic atmosphere in which to work. Lillian Swanson and especially Lillian Peterson amazingly retained both their accuracy and their sense of humor while typing and proofreading our targets, transcripts, and the index. Olga Kuzyk and Earl French provided valuable assistance in the production and editing of the guide. Dorothy Mills, Secretary of the Foundation, proved willing to interrupt whatever she was doing to help smooth our way; while Ellice Schofield and Marion Carmichael shared with us their detailed knowledge of the Foundation's collections.

Special thanks go to Paige Savery, who was instrumental in helping us to locate and identify photographs, and to Diana Royce, Head Librarian, who advised, assisted, and encouraged us in ways too numerous to detail here. Finally, Joseph S. Van Why, Director of the Foundation, deserves credit for the continual moral support that he provided and for his commitment to achieving a first-rate project of which we could all be proud.

Anne Throne Margolis, Project Director

Margaret Granville Mair, Project Assistant

*When appropriate, specific collections are cited on the target of the microfiche.

The Lyman Beecher Family: L. to R., Isabella, Thomas K., Catharine, William, Lyman, Edward, Mary, Charles, Harriet, Henry Ward. Inserts, James, George, c. 1859

CHRONOLOGY OF ISABELLA BEECHER HOOKER
1822-1907

1822	On February 22 Isabella Homes Beecher is born to the Reverend Lyman Beecher and Harriet (Porter) Beecher, his second wife, in Litchfield, Connecticut.
1832	The Beecher family moves to Walnut Hills, Cincinnati, Ohio, where Lyman Beecher becomes president of the Lane Theological Seminary.
1835	Isabella moves to Hartford, Connecticut, to live with her half sister, Mary (Beecher) Perkins, and attend the Hartford Female Seminary, founded by another half sister, Catharine Beecher.
[1836-1837	Isabella returns to Cincinnati, where she attends the Western Female Institute, also founded by Catharine Beecher.]
1838	Isabella [returns to Hartford and] lives with Mary (Beecher) Perkins and attends the Hartford Female Seminary.
1839	Isabella becomes engaged to John Hooker, a law clerk in the office of Thomas Clap Perkins, her brother-in-law.
1841	On August 5 Isabella marries John Hooker. The couple resides with her in-laws in Farmington, Connecticut.
1842	On September 30 Thomas Beecher Hooker is born, the first child of Isabella and John Hooker.
	Thomas Beecher Hooker dies; his precise death date is unknown.
1845	On August 15 Mary Beecher Hooker is born, the second child of Isabella and John Hooker.
1847	On August 26 Alice Beecher Hooker is born, the third child of Isabella and John Hooker.
1853	Isabella and John Hooker finish building their new house at Nook Farm, Hartford.
1855	On February 26 Edward Beecher Hooker is born, the fourth and last child of Isabella and John Hooker.
1860	From April through August Isabella seeks medical treatment from Mrs. R. B. Gleason at the Elmira Water Cure in Elmira, New York.
1861	Anna Dickinson delivers a lecture in Hartford and visits the Hooker family, at which time she introduces Isabella to Harriet Mill's article, "Enfranchisement of Women," which had appeared earlier in *The Westminster Review.*
1864	Isabella travels to South Carolina and there meets Caroline Severance, who further interests her in the cause of woman suffrage.
1866	On October 4 Mary Beecher Hooker marries Henry Eugene Burton.
1868	Isabella visits Paulina Wright Davis in Providence, Rhode Island, and there meets Elizabeth Cady Stanton and Susan B. Anthony.
	Isabella joins in founding the New England Woman Suffrage Association.

During November and December Isabella's first pro-suffrage argument, "A Mother's Letters to a Daughter on Woman Suffrage," is published anonymously in *Putnam's Magazine*.

1869   The woman suffrage movement splits into two competing factions, the National Woman Suffrage Association and the American Woman Suffrage Association.

Isabella sponsors and organizes Hartford's first woman suffrage convention and presides over the founding of the Connecticut Woman Suffrage Association.

In June Alice Beecher Hooker marries John Calvin Day.

1870   "A Mother's Letters to a Daughter on Woman Suffrage" is reprinted as a tract of the Connecticut Woman Suffrage Association, becoming the first pro-suffrage argument published under Isabella's name.

Isabella introduces into the Connecticut Legislature a married women's property bill, drafted by John Hooker.

Isabella delivers a speech at the second meeting of the National Woman Suffrage Association in Chicago, Illinois, and gains her first national attention.

On May 8 Katharine Seymour Day is born, the first child of Alice (Hooker) and John Calvin Day.

1871   On January 11 Isabella meets Victoria Claflin Woodhull in Washington, D.C., on the opening day of the special woman suffrage convention that Isabella has planned when Woodhull makes an unexpected appearance before the House Judiciary Committee to testify in favor of woman suffrage.

1872   On January 3 Alice Hooker Day is born, the second child of Alice (Hooker) and John Calvin Day.

On September 11, before a convention of the Association of American Spiritualists in Boston, Massachusetts, Victoria Woodhull accuses Henry Ward Beecher of committing adultery with one of his parishioners (Elizabeth Tilton).

In November *Woodhull and Claflin's Weekly* publishes Woodhull's version of Beecher's alleged adultery, an incident that will become known as the Beecher-Tilton scandal.

1873   On November 2 Allen and Katherine Burton, twins, are born to Mary (Hooker) and Henry Eugene Burton.

1874   On August 15 Allen Burton dies.

1874-1875 From autumn through summer Isabella joins John Hooker in Europe for extended travel in order to escape the growing controversy caused by the Beecher-Tilton scandal and the resulting trial, which runs from January 11, 1875 through July 2, 1875.

1877   After after seven years of lobbying by Isabella and John Hooker, the Connecticut Legislature passes a married women's property bill.

1879	On September 18 Edward Beecher Hooker marries Martha Kilbourne.
1881	On November 8 Isabel Hooker is born, the first child of Martha (Kilbourne) and Edward Beecher Hooker.
1886	On January 20 Mary (Hooker) Burton dies.
	On July 20 Thomas Hooker is born, the second child of Martha (Kilbourne) and Edward Beecher Hooker.
1887	On March 8 Joseph Kilbourne Hooker is born, the third and last child of Martha (Kilbourne) and Edward Beecher Hooker.
1891	On August 5 Isabella and John Hooker celebrate their fiftieth wedding anniversary in Hartford.
1893	Isabella serves on the Board of Lady Managers of the Columbian Exposition in Chicago.
1901	On February 12 John Hooker dies.
1907	On January 5 Isabella dies of a cerebral hemorrhage at the age of eighty-five and is buried in Cedar Hill Cemetery in Hartford.

Isabella Beecher Hooker, c. 1873

A TEMPEST TOSSED SPIRIT
ISABELLA BEECHER HOOKER AND WOMAN SUFFRAGE

At the age of eighty-three, Isabella Beecher Hooker paused to take a backward glance at her life and work. In an autobiographical article that *Connecticut Magazine* aptly entitled "The Last of the Beechers," she reminisced about her early years as one of Lyman Beecher's eleven children and proceeded to chronicle her marriage to John Hooker and her subsequent activities in behalf of woman suffrage. Near the close of the article, after paying tribute to her "lover husband," who had only recently "passed to the Great Beyond," Mrs. Hooker permitted herself one last public lament regarding women's unenfranchised state. But, quite characteristically, she managed to close on a jubilant note. Addressing herself to her children and grandchildren as well as to the general public, she borrowed these "noble words" from "the sainted Whittier" to prophesize the ultimate triumph of the movement to which she had devoted so much of her life:

> Others shall sing the song,
> Others shall right the wrong,
> Finish what I begin,
> And all I fail of — win.[1]

Significantly, Isabella Beecher Hooker chose to present this late account of her evolving commitment to woman's rights within the all-encompassing framework of her family life, first as a Beecher daughter and sister and then as wife, mother, and grandmother to the Hooker family. It is worth noting that Mrs. Hooker's autobiographical sketch scrupulously avoids any reference to tension between these potentially conflicting social roles, thus implying that there was little or no friction between her family ties and her career as a reformer. Yet these private papers, many of which are published here for the first time, testify to the fact that Isabella Beecher Hooker's life was one in which private loyalties and public commitments, domestic duties and democratic responsibilities, often clashed. As these papers also make clear, the stress generated by this conflict prompted Isabella to adopt a theoretical framework that would enable her to envision the private and public realms as gradually evolving towards one harmonious whole. Yet, in practice, it was precisely during the moments when the conflict between these two spheres proved to be most intense that she succeeded in making her most significant contributions to the woman's rights movement and forging the unique amalgam of spiritualism and feminism that renders her life worthy of serious study by students of nineteenth-century American culture.

*　　*　　*

Born in Litchfield, Connecticut, on February 22, 1822, Isabella gained a marginal advantage in the family pecking order as the youngest daughter in the Beecher household and the only daughter born to Harriet Porter Beecher, Lyman's second wife. Fond memories of both Litchfield and Cincinnati, Ohio, where the family moved when Lyman Beecher became president of Lane Theological Seminary, remained with Isabella throughout her long life of eighty-five years. In Cincinnati Isabella continued her formal education in a school founded by her half sister, Catharine, who was twenty-two years her senior. Sometime after the death of her mother in 1835, young Isabella was sent back to Connecticut. There she came under the supervision of another half sister, Mary Beecher Perkins, who had settled in Hartford upon her marriage to an "eminent" local attorney.

Isabella was thus able to attend the prestigious Hartford Female Seminary, another school for women founded by her half sister. However, Catharine's intense commitment to the goal of equality in female education seems to have had little effect on their father. Although he saw to it that all of his sons were educated for the ministry, Lyman Beecher refused to invest in the higher education of his daughters. Years later, frustrated by her inability to clothe her "bare bones" of thought in the "flesh & drapery of historic literature," Isabella gave vent to her pent-up anger regarding this family practice. "At sixteen & a half, just when my brothers began their mental education, mine was finished — except as life's discipline was added with years & that we shared equally. Till twenty three, their father, poor minister as he was could send them to College & Seminary all *six* — cost what it might, but never a daughter cost him a hundred dollars a year, after she was sixteen."[2]

When seventeen-year-old "Belle," as she was then affectionately called, became engaged to a twenty-three-year-old law clerk who worked in her brother-in-law's office, her family had only one reservation. As his wife would later become fond of pointing out, John Hooker came from a distinguished family. "He was sixth in descent from Thomas Hooker, author of the first written constitution of the world, and founder of the Connecticut Colony."[3] With this impressive pedigree and his keen legal mind, the aspiring lawyer could look forward to a prosperous future; but in Lyman Beecher's household secular distinctions and rewards paled before the sacred glories of the ministry.

The letters that Isabella wrote to John from Cincinnati during their two-year engagement testify to the pressure that was brought to bear on the young couple by Isabella's family, especially by her father and her sister, Catharine, for they wanted John to forsake law and embrace a ministerial calling. In October of 1839, Isabella wrote: "I have felt for some weeks past in visiting my brothers — who are ministers, that they are the only class of men, that can accomplish any considerable amount of good without turning aside from their usual business — *all* that a minister does, is designed in some way to save the souls of his fellow beings. . . . Now it seems to me that it is not thus with a *lawyer* . . . he toils over (what you acknowledge to be most dry & uninteresting matter — writes & copies a world of waste words for the sake of living — & he must step aside — make an extra exertion to do anything for the immortal interests of their friends & acquaintances."[4]

Subjected to the persuasive pens of several Beechers, John Hooker vacillated at first; but he eventually adhered to his preference for the law, a field in which he would achieve distinction over the years. However, he was not the only one who was experiencing doubts regarding the future. As these same letters reveal, Isabella's impending marriage plunged her into a protracted state of tension and uncertainty. Describing herself as a "tempest tossed spirit," she continually asked herself (as well as John) not only whether she was worthy of so well-educated a husband but also whether she should marry at all.[5]

Commenting on a recent discussion she had engaged in regarding "the relative position of a wife — to her husband — her duty of submission etc.," Isabella was moved to complain to her intended "that while ministers & others insist most strenuously on the duties of the lady — the husband's fulfilment of his obligations is taken for granted. . . ." Although she hurried to assure John that she was ready to render him "the required obedience without being constantly reminded that such is the will of God & the expectation of man," Isabella made it clear to him that the prospect of compelled

John Hooker, 1878

submission was "galling to a sensible woman." She then went on to profess that "personally I fear nothing." Yet she was, in effect, laying out her own terms for their impending union when she roundly condemned all those "mistaken ideas of propriety" that dictated that married women "are to have no *will* of their own — except so far as it coincides with their husband's." As Isabella had made quite explicit earlier in the same letter, her misgivings about marriage itself intensified as a result of the close study of "the families of some even of my brothers & sisters ... but then I feel that there is a radical defect in their plan — one which can be avoided — they did not start rightly. ..."[6]

Her uneasiness must have been overcome by John's tenacious wooing, his tender concern for her feelings, and his frequent reassurances that they would begin their new life as equals, for the two became one before God on August 5, 1841. However, Isabella soon learned that she and John had also become one before the law, and that one was John. As she later recalled the incident, the young couple enjoyed passing their leisure time by reading aloud to one another, he from his lawbooks and she from a literary work. They were making their way through Blackstone's *Commentaries* when the chapter on reciprocal duties of husband and wife brought them to an abrupt halt. "I shall never forget my consternation when we came to this passage: 'By marriage the husband and wife are one person in law, that is, the very being or legal existence of the woman is suspended during the marriage, or at least is incorporated and consolidated into that of the husband under whose wing, protection and cover, she performs everything. ...'" All of Isabella's earlier anxieties resurfaced with these words; and "discussion after discussion" ensued, "till the subject was dropped as a hopeless mystery."[7]

In "The Last of the Beechers," Isabella presents this incident as a decisive moment in her conversion to the cause of woman's rights. However true this might have appeared in retrospect, it was only after the outbreak of the Civil War that Isabella made the key intellectual and social contacts that precipitated her entry into the inner circles of the woman suffrage movement. Although the twenty years between her marriage and the onset of the war were far from empty, they were filled with daily cares and frustrations such as any upper-middle-class wife and mother might have experienced: maintaining the household, disciplining her children (one of whom initially proved to be quite intransigent), and preoccupying herself with the health and happiness of her small domestic circle.

Although she lost a male child in infancy during the second year of her marriage, Isabella gave birth to three healthy children over the next thirteen years. After the infant Thomas's untimely death, she may have wished to lend these delicate and precious beings a further dimension of reality via pen and paper. Or perhaps she merely wished to confer upon her own efforts at maternal governance a consistency (and possibly even a status) that she feared they lacked. In any case, she proceeded to record and analyze her maternal interaction with Mary, Alice, and then Ned in a series of bound journals that she kept, for the most part quite faithfully, from August 1845 (the month during which Mary was born) through September of 1855 (shortly after the birth of Ned).

On the evidence of these journals, Isabella, who had herself been left motherless at a vulnerable age, took great pains to devote herself to the needs of her own children and the duties of motherhood. But this maternal devotion and vigilance could only have intensified her fear that the world of events, before which she and John had once stood as ostensible equals, was gradually becoming closed to her — not by the fiat of her husband, but by the all-absorbing demands of hearth and home. For a woman who had grown up in a large family circle in which "the United States Constitution, fugitive slave laws, Henry Clay and Missouri Compromise, alternated with free will, regeneration, heaven, hell and 'The Destiny of Man'" as topics of conversation,[8] life as a relatively isolated young wife and inexperienced young mother, first in the village of Farmington and then in Nook Farm, proved to be suffocating.

Although it eventually grew to be a fashionable literary and social colony, Hartford's Nook Farm then comprised one hundred acres of undeveloped land just outside the city limits. Isabella later insisted that her memories of this early period were "delightful," noting rather complacently that "we lived like a little society by ourselves."[9] At the time, however, she seems to have been preoccupied with the halt in her mental development. Isabella sensed an impending intellectual gap between herself and her lawyer husband that no amount of success in the domestic sphere could compensate for; and the resulting frustration, because it remained largely unexplored and unrelieved, aggravated her already delicate state of body and mind. While Isabella fought periodic bouts of neurasthenia, John, who had once left Yale and gone to sea in order to improve his own fragile health, now thrived on the stimulation provided not only by his law practice but also by the politics of his Free Soil party and antislavery reform. John's espousal of abolitionism, particularly at a time when it had not yet been made respectable, belied his conventional and soft-spoken exterior and shocked his wife's more conservative kin. At first, Isabella sided with her father, who advocated moderation and African colonization; but John's persistent arguments, augmented by a carefully chosen reading list, eventually won her over. By 1842, Isabella could register her dismay over the fact that her family took the antislavery cause as lightly as she *once* had.[10]

John Hooker's local reputation as well as his commitment to abolitionism were amply illustrated by the case of the Reverend James Pennington, pastor of a black Congregational church in Hartford. A runaway slave, Pennington was so alarmed by the passage of the Fugitive Slave Law in 1850 that he sought the legal advice of John Hooker, who suggested that the respected clergyman seek temporary refuge in Canada while negotiations proceeded with his former master. The price placed on his freedom proved to be so high that Pennington was forced to flee to the Continent until the death of his owner, at which time John settled with the estate by offering $150 for Pennington. On June 5, 1851, John Hooker, the minister's new "master," closed the books on this strange episode by legally setting his new "slave" free.[11]

According to Marie Caskey, "John believed that Isabella's conversion to the cause had capped their union." And, as Caskey also points out, Isabella did contribute occasional assistance with the planning and running of antislavery meetings.[12] But if such experience would eventually provide this future organizer of woman suffrage conventions with a valuable training ground, for the present, Isabella knew only that she was suffering from constant alternations in mood that she apologetically referred to as "nervous hypochondria," an accumulation of distressing dreams about her mother that refused to abate, and the unceasing demands of housekeeping and children, which she found to be an insurmountable obstacle to her most cherished goal, self-improvement.[13]

In a letter to John dated February 21, 1847, Isabella reiterated her dismay over her lack of formal education and cited the impressing case of an invalid schoolteacher who had made the most out of a long illness by reading up on all areas of learning before applying to Catharine Beecher for a job. With obvious envy, Isabella reported that the teacher's knowledge of law and medicine surpassed "those of most professional gentlemen." In yet another letter, the twenty-seven-year-old wife acknowledged to her husband that the improper advances of an old friend, advances that she had promptly repulsed, gave her great pleasure after the isolation of the past three years. "The fact is," she wrote, "I was engaged so young — I had little time to know my power — until after my destiny was sealed. . . ." She further admitted that this "glimpse into the world again" had helped to calm her fears of having become "dull and insipid even to you."[14] Such letters make it clear that Isabella was not content with basking in the reflected glow of her husband's professional and reform activities. She wanted to generate rather than merely register the respect and admiration of her contemporaries.

Isabella's discontent intensified in 1852, when her half sister, Harriet Beecher Stowe, achieved sudden financial and literary success with the publication of *Uncle Tom's Cabin*. While she publicly took great pride in Harriet's achievement and closely followed Catharine's efforts to renegotiate their sister's publishing contract, Isabella made the following confession in the privacy of a letter to her husband. "At first I was melancholy — in seeing the evidences of genius all around me here — my own littleness fairly stared me in the face — . . ." Forced to console herself with thoughts of her housekeeping and other capabilities, she insisted that her lack of brilliancy made her a good wife — "for one cannot do or be forty things at once."[15] It is precisely at this time that Isabella began to suggest that by skillfully managing her own motives she could control her children more effectively. When she wrote of withholding her "design" for this express purpose, she sounded like a woman who had made a private bargain with herself. If she could not successfully shape a space for herself within the public sphere, as two of her sisters had already done, she could at least rule over the lives of those who inhabited her own private realm, the home.

Such compensations formed the keystone of the nineteenth-century cult of domesticity, but Isabella's "design" evidently proved to be more difficult to execute than either she or contemporaneous theoreticians of femininity (such as Catharine) had ever imagined. As a result, her efforts at home management took a decisive toll on her delicate constitution; and she soon inaugurated a series of retreats to water cure establishments, first in Florence, Massachusetts, and later in Elmira, New York, in order to remedy her failing health. Occasionally, Isabella was joined at these establishments by John, who had health problems of his own and who found his stays at these resorts to be welcome respites from the pressures of the law. But more often she took advantage of such separations to improve her mind, not unlike the invalid schoolteacher whom she had described six years earlier.

Isabella also took advantage of her almost daily correspondence with her family to analyze her situation in some depth. These letters thus provide valuable insights into Isabella's views of herself and her marriage, as well as fascinating glimpses of the daily routine at a mid-century water cure. Writing from the Florence Cure in 1853, Isabella's self-assessment was bleak: "I do believe that I have less self reliance, in its best sense too, than I had six or eight years ago — You have more & I seem to lose as you gain." After lamenting about her waning mental powers and her "crippled mind," she nostalgically recalled the long talks that she and John used to have "on subjects *not* entirely domestic."[16]

As Isabella acknowledged with great candor, her stays at the water cure amounted to an escape, however temporary, from the current strain of domestic ties and the monotony of her daily routine. These cycles of invalidism also guaranteed her periods of enforced leisure in stimulating new surroundings where she could catch up on her reading and make new social contacts. In short, the water cure figured in Isabella's life (as well as in the lives of countless other nineteenth-century American women) as an alternative environment, a non-domestic yet respectable and safely "feminine" sphere in which she could salvage her sense of individual identity. To paraphrase Nathaniel Hawthorne, one of her favorite authors, it was a middle ground that enabled her to reopen her inter-course with the world.

There is some evidence that Isabella was beginning to perceive her private predicament within the wider context of the growing controversy over woman's "proper sphere." Writing from Hartford in January of 1859, she confided to a female friend that an anonymous article advocating equal education for women had raised her flagging spirits, despite her feeble health. She admitted that the piece, "Ought Women To Learn the Alphabet?," published in *The Atlantic Monthly,* had also set off a wave of envy: "What will you say when I tell you, I would rather have written these twelve pages, than any other twelve that ever I read. . . . There's not a vital thought there, but I have had for my own, & spoken it too, in a whisper & in my blundering way — & it is only my lack of this very Alphabet that has given this favored mortal (man or woman is it?) such precedence before the world." Recalling how her own formal education had been abruptly curtailed in her sixteenth year, she expressed her scorn for the popular idea that women were superior to men. Women "seemed to have more quickness of perception" because they had been "driven to their wits — preternaturally excited . . . by this *deprivation* of all *external* helps." She concluded by insisting that "when physical & mental training are similar, they will rank *with* men, — not *above* them — certainly not below."[17]

Isabella soon learned that the piece had been written by Thomas Wentworth Higginson, the well-known abolitionist and supporter of woman's rights. In a letter so forceful that Higginson could still remember it almost forty years later, she lavished praise on his article and vividly recounted the unequal treatment received by the sons and daughters in her father's household.[18] Higginson responded warmly to Isabella's praise, noting that "the history of the race has never been written — only of one sex . . . ." and encouraging her to be true to the cause of woman as represented *by* women. "Nothing makes me more indignant," he wrote, "than to be thanked by women for telling the truth, — thanked *as a man,* — when those same persons are recreant to the *women* who, at infinitely greater cost, have said the same things. It costs a man nothing to defend woman, — a few sneers, a few jokes, that is all; but for women to defend themselves, has in times past cost almost everything." Higginson went on to cite the example and influence of Lucretia Mott, Lucy Stone, and Antoinette Brown. Compared to them, he asserted, "the mass of women, especially educated women, are base: they revile their own bravest defenders; & their own aspirations become mere selfishness. There is much ignorance, much sensuality & some obstinacy among *men;* but *women* are a frightened garrison, seeking a mean safety by sacrificing those who have made a heroic sortie. Let me implore you to make it otherwise with you."[19]

His shrewd observations would prove to have a telling application to the postbellum history of the woman suffrage movement; but they hit their more immediate mark in Isabella, whose lack of self-confidence and conventional notions of respectability had prevented her from publicly espousing such "radical" sentiments. A year later, in February of 1860, she responded by sending Higginson her first attempt to express her own views in public. In "Shall Women Vote? A Matrimonial Dialogue," Isabella attempted to refute an editorial that attacked a recent speech by her half brother, Henry Ward Beecher, who had advocated woman suffrage as "'the cheapest, the easiest, [and] the most natural' way to reform politics."[20] Casting her ideas in the conventional form of a dialogue between husband and wife, the apprentice writer cautiously answered the question posed by her title in the affirmative, presenting arguments that had an obvious autobiographical origin. "Mrs. Smith" tells her husband that woman suffrage will improve as well as enlarge the electorate, for the politically educated woman will "imitate the wise procedure of a certain young gentleman ... who, having a spicy young girl that hated abolitionists more than she did slavery, begged her ... to read aloud ... 'The Life of Wilberforce' ... and surreptitiously laid on her table, 'Jay's View,' 'Thom. L. Kimball on West Indian Emancipation,' etc., etc., till in the course of months, she waked up a full-blooded Anti-slavery *woman* — and did not at once suspect the influence."

The theme of woman's influence was hardly an original one, but Isabella also evoked the more radical vision of "a very respectable Congress" drawn from the ranks of single women "and all who would be single if they did not fear the loneliness and ennui of such a life, all the widows and childless ones, and then the middle-aged mothers who have reared their brood and started them on their own independent flight ...."[21] When reading these lines, it should be kept in mind that Isabella herself, who turned thirty-eight that month, still had a five-year-old son at home. Although her eldest daughter, Mary, was barely fifteen, she seems already to have been anticipating the vacuum that would be created in her life by the departure of her children. Furthermore, Isabella's letters reveal that she was also experiencing intensified feelings of personal inadequacy during this period. Just weeks earlier, she had confessed to her husband: "I can't write a book — nor draw pictures — nor do any other productive work — I have always told you, that you overestimated your wife — I hope you are satisfied of it now."[22]

Gentle as it was, Higginson's assessment of the dialogue could only have had a demoralizing effect on an individual whose sense of self was so precarious. He informed her "that it is almost impossible for any one to get compensation for anything radical, unless with a reputation previously acquired, or else under very peculiar circumstances. One may make literature a means of earning money or a means of expressing one's most progressive views — but it is very rarely that any one can unite the two. To do great good & make money at the same time was the lot of Uncle Tom's Cabin, but a rare one." Isabella hardly needed to be reminded of this last fact, though she must have appreciated Higginson's willingness to forward her article to the *Atlantic* and his tactful mixture of praise and criticism. After advising practice and patience, he had urged that she not be discouraged if the article were rejected, "for you will only have failed in an attempt ... to make a first essay, & that a radical one, palatable to editors who are rather conservative & ought to be extremely critical." He closed his reply on a somewhat humorous note, promising that he would not exploit her praise of his recent article by printing it in an advertisement as "The opinion of an anonymous lady, of distinguished family."[23]

Ironically, it was precisely when she measured herself against the accomplishments of her distinguished family that Isabella felt herself to be most anonymous. A month later, propelled by growing self-doubt as well as increasingly poor health, Isabella left Hartford again to begin a prolonged stay at the Gleason Water Cure. She expressed her determination "to rove the woods — & do everything that I have no time & strength for *at home*."[24] Located in Elmira, New York, near the Congregational church of her brother, Thomas, the Gleason Cure provided Isabella with a much needed change of pace and another respite from her domestic responsibilities. "It is such a relief — to have nobody to care for — nothing that *must* be done," exulted Isabella, who was soon arranging to have a bloomer outfit made for her walks in the woods and her gardening at home.[25] But she quickly realized that once she ventured out of her small domestic circle, there was no escaping the Beecher reputation and example. Noting that "every where I go — I have to run on the credit of, my relations," Isabella arrived at the somewhat paradoxical conclusion that "no where, but at home can I lay claim to a particle of individuality — to any distinction of goodness, smartness or anything else whatever." Nevertheless, Isabella was becoming aware of the fact that she had "great power of personal influence — family name goes a great way no doubt — but there is a magnetism of heart & eye & voice, that is quite individual. ..." After weeks on her "tread mill of self analysis," she optimistically concluded that her strong "love of admiration" was indeed compatible with her even stronger desire to engage in benevolent activity. Both needs could be satisfied, if only she could exert her individual magnetism "on a broad scale" and "sweep people along in the right path."[26]

Yet Isabella's momentary glimpses of personal harmony and public influence were frequently interrupted by long periods of severe physical discomfort and depression that accentuated her sense of uselessness as well as her fears of premature death. As these water cure letters reveal, she was suffering acutely from dysmenorrhea and a prolapsed uterus. Given the widespread ignorance concerning the cause and treatment of "female diseases" in the nineteenth century, her anxieties were justified, if somewhat exaggerated. Victorian remedies were often more painful than the complaints that they were intended to cure; but for Isabella the alternatives, imminent death or a future of perpetual and hopeless invalidism, were equally unacceptable. She patiently underwent Mrs. Gleason's prescribed regimen, a quite typical treatment that combined a series of baths with local applications of silver nitrate.[27]

In a highly revealing letter, Isabella confided to John that her problems would not have been so dangerous if she were younger, but with "the crisis of my life which is approaching [menopause] — there was quite a possibility of flowing to death then — or if not that — an almost certainty of from five to ten years — of invalidism, severe & painful — & no certainty of any good health afterward — thro' life." She then tried to soften the blow of the necessity for their continued separation by inviting him to join her at the water cure, demurely informing him that Mrs. Gleason had given her assurances that she could make him "most heartily welcome & could do so, without detriment to health."[28]

It is greatly to Isabella's credit that she stubbornly resisted (and ultimately rejected) a social role that so many other Victorian women found convenient and even fashionable, that of the delicate invalid. While several contemporary historians have recently suggested that some women worked their invalidism as a desperate means of exerting a measure of covert control over their own lives (as well as the lives of their families), it is clear that Isabella was struggling to achieve a more direct understanding of and solution to her own sense of powerlessness.[29] Undoubtedly, the constant affection and continual supportiveness of her sensitive and gentle husband provided a real incentive for getting well. As she confessed to John, she had never properly appreciated him because of her tendency to overvalue "nerve — & muscle — & fortitude — & fearlessness." Now it seemed to her that "nothing very exquisite — can be very strong," for strength implied mere physical superiority, which was itself inferior to mental beauty.[30]

This radical bifurcation of qualities and the correlative belief in the superiority of all that was essentially mental or spiritual had traditionally functioned as a rationale for the ideology of separate spheres as well as for the argument against extending the franchise to women, who were thought to be too delicate and too refined to brave the coarseness and vulgarities of the public sphere. But these ideas would eventually be put to subver-

Lucy Stone

The Schlesinger Library, Radcliffe College

sive use by some members of the woman suffrage movement. Turning the tables on critics who considered their contact with politics to be unladylike if not unsexing, they would accept the idea that spiritual "superiority" compensated for woman's physical "inferiority" and use this "fact" to justify her entry into the public arena. In the hands of the more refined sex, the ballot would become a means of achieving social purity, or so the argument went.

On the eve of the Civil War, however, suffrage leaders preferred to base their arguments on the theme of political equality, framing their demands largely in language borrowed from two sources, the Declaration of Independence and the movement to abolish slavery. Yet the long-standing alliance between abolitionists and woman's rights activists had never been an easy one. Although women had helped to found, organize, and finance the abolitionist movement in America, their participation became a source of internal dissension in 1837, when Angelina and Sarah Grimke' became the first women to deliver public speeches against slavery before "promiscuous" (i.e., sexually mixed) audiences. When the Grimke' sisters, supported by William Lloyd Garrison and others, insisted on their right to speak in public, they were strongly opposed by those abolitionists who felt that the two causes must be kept discrete.[31] According to Elizabeth Cady Stanton, it was the abolitionists' refusal to seat the highly respected Lucretia Mott and other female delegates at the 1840 World Antislavery Convention in London, England, which prompted her to issue the call for the famous Seneca Falls convention. It was during this 1848 gathering that Mrs. Stanton launched her long campaign for a right that even Lucretia Mott initially considered to be too radical to support, the right to vote. Two years later, Paulina Wright Davis organized the first national woman's rights convention. Held in Worcester, Massachusetts, it attracted a galaxy of noted abolitionists, including Wendell Phillips, William Lloyd Garrison, and Thomas Wentworth Higginson as well as Lucy Stone, Lucretia Mott, Angelina Grimke', and Sojourner Truth.[32] The two movements thus became increasingly interdependent and increasingly identified in the public mind.

The outbreak of the Civil War was to change all this. In 1860, Elizabeth Cady Stanton, Susan B. Anthony, Lucy Stone, and other leaders reluctantly agreed to suspend suffrage agitation in order to concentrate their energies on the abolitionist cause and war-related activities. They assumed that in return for this act of loyalty, they would receive the unhesitating financial and organizational support of their fellow reformers when emancipation became a reality. After the war, when Republicans as well as abolitionist leaders such as Garrison and Phillips placed the political rights of the black male at the top of their list of priorities, claiming that "this is the negro's hour," many of the suffragists felt betrayed and abandoned. Some, like Lucy Stone and Antoinette Blackwell, ultimately proved willing to accept the logic and leadership of their male counterparts, who supported the insertion of the word "male" in the Constitution via the Fourteenth Amendment and who insisted that disinterestedness was (and should continue to be) the moral keynote of female reformers. Others, most notably Anthony and Stanton, refused to accept this rationale. They argued that the Fourteenth Amendment would legally sanction woman's second class status (and thus her oppression) and reminded their fellow abolitionists that black *women* were also entitled to equal rights before the law.

It was precisely during this period of postbellum dissension that Isabella took her first cautious steps towards publicly aligning herself with the woman suffrage movement. The war itself had helped her to gain a new perspective on her own capabilities for public service. As a Beecher, she had been able to claim ties of kinship with Harriet Beecher

Stowe and Henry Ward Beecher, the nationally known minister whom Lincoln had called upon to commemorate the return of the flag to Fort Sumter at the close of the war. In 1861, Isabella had felt it her duty to send Henry a long, closely argued letter attacking his stand against the constitutionality of emancipation. Not incidentally, this letter displayed and exercised her own quite considerable skill at arguing constitutional questions.[33] Yet Isabella's sense of her potential for influencing others paled before the forceful example of nineteen-year-old Anna Dickinson, a Republican orator who in the same year became the first woman to address publicly the citizens of "conservative and prejudiced" Hartford. The Hookers attended the event with "anxiety and apprehension," but "this new Joan of Arc" managed to entrance the entire audience with her antislavery speech.

It was Dickinson's eloquence rather than her message that spoke most directly to Isabella's suffocating soul. Although she was young enough to have been Isabella's daughter, Dickinson already embodied "the freedom denied to all women, except those known as Friends." Under her tutelage, Isabella "learned to trust as never before" the promptings of her innermost self. It was also Anna Dickinson who first introduced Isabella to Harriet Taylor Mill's "remarkable paper" on the "Enfranchisement of Women." In this article, published by *The Westminster Review* back in July of 1851, she had urged her countrywomen to note the progress of their American sisters, citing the 1850 Woman's Rights Convention held in Worcester as an example worthy of British emulation. As Alice Rossi has so forcefully argued, this essay takes a much more radical position on the social, legal, and economic status of women than even Harriet's husband, John Stuart Mill, was prepared to adopt. Insisting that even married women should seek employment in order to avoid financial dependence, Harriet Mill denied "the right of any portion of the species to decide for another portion, or any individual for another individual, what is and what is not their 'proper sphere.' The proper sphere for all human beings is the largest and highest which they are able to attain to."[34] Isabella would eventually christen this essay "a new gospel of individual responsibility" and announce that "a more comprehensive, logical, and unanswerable argument . . . was never made on any subject."[35] At the time, Harriet Mill's words must have read like a private exhortation, for Isabella was still searching intently for her own "largest and highest sphere."

In 1862, Isabella traveled to Washington, D.C., as the companion of her most famous sister, meeting various political dignitaries, including President Abraham Lincoln, and enjoying privileged (and perhaps demystifying) glimpses of the capital's great and near great as well as the higher echelons of the Union army.[36] Eager to aid in the war effort, Isabella subsequently joined the Women's Sanitary Commission; and by August of 1863, she could point with pride to the resolutions and circulars she had written for this organization. In 1864, as the war drew to a close, she journeyed to South Carolina, where she met Caroline Severance, the woman whom she credited with bringing her into the suffrage fold.[37] Yet it was not until 1868, two years after the marriage of her eldest daughter and just prior to the marriage of her second daughter, that Isabella took her first public steps in behalf of woman suffrage. While visiting the Severances at their home near Boston, she agreed to join William Lloyd Garrison and others in issuing a call to establish the New England Woman Suffrage Association; and in November and December of the same year, she saw her second pro-suffrage argument achieve an audience.

Although "A Mother's Letters to a Daughter on Woman Suffrage" appeared anonymously in *Putnam's Monthly*, it would be reprinted a year later as a tract under Isabella's

Anna Dickinson

Isabella Beecher Hooker with son, Edward, 1863

name. Its epistolary format, which exuded respectability and good taste, was shrewdly calculated to appeal primarily to the "high-minded, well-bred woman" who, suddenly facing a "half-forsaken nest," "finds it hard to realize that she is unfitted either by nature or education for the work of law making, on a broader and larger scale than she has ever yet tried." The author, identified in the original version only as "Mother," combined several of Harriet Taylor Mill's arguments with her own peculiarly American blend of domestic feminism, nativism, and patriotism. Idealizing "the blessed privilege" and power of motherhood as "the divinest agency" by which the human race was to be civilized, purified, and "preserved from utter destruction," she presented the family and maternal governance as the foundation of national glory and the goal of Christian training.[38] In somewhat altered proportions, this highly idiosyncratic variation on perfectionist, social Darwinist, feminist, and spiritualist thought would eventually characterize and dominate all of Isabella's ideas and activities. For the time being, however, she was to become embroiled in and increasingly preoccupied with the least spiritual aspects of the woman suffrage movement — its internal controversies and power struggles.

Tensions between suffrage activists and abolitionists had flared in the wake of the Kansas campaign of 1867. This concerted effort by leading suffragists to demonstrate the compatibility of the two movements by convincing Kansas citizens to extend the vote simultaneously to blacks and women had failed, largely because of Republican hostility to woman suffrage. During the heat of the hard fought campaign, Susan B. Anthony and Elizabeth Cady Stanton had responded to what they considered to be a Republican "betrayal" by agreeing to share the lecture platform with a flamboyant Democrat, George Francis Train. An effective if eccentric speaker, Train scandalized abolitionists and suffragists alike by his frequent recourse to racial slurs and by his advocacy of woman suffrage as an *alternative* to black suffrage. Despite mounting pressure from their fellow reformers, Anthony and Stanton refused to dissociate themselves from Train, the only man willing to provide them with consistent strategic and financial support. He not only took it upon himself to pay the two women's expenses when funds ran low, but also offered to bankroll Anthony's dream of a pro-suffrage journal in exchange for their continued presence on his return lecture tour to the East. In what seems like an obvious victory of expediency (or rather survival) over principle, both women accepted the offer, insisting on their "right to accept proferred aid without looking behind it for the motive." It was not the last time they would have to engage in such a defense.[39]

Contemporaneous letters testify to the fact that the Kansas campaign symbolized and increased the tactical and ideological differences not only between abolitionists and suffragists but also with the suffrage movement itself. As Ellen DuBois has recently asserted, "it demonstrated, first, the length to which Republicans would go to keep woman suffrage out of their plans for Reconstruction, and second the degree to which abolitionists had accepted Republican leadership and abandoned woman suffrage."[40] When abolitionists loyal to the Republican party mounted an attack on the suffragist alliance with Train and began to raise questions about Anthony's management of Kansas campaign funds, she and Stanton retaliated by using their new Train-funded paper, *The Revolution*, as a mouthpiece for their divergent views and as a public forum within which to air their internal grievances. In editorials that repeatedly attacked Republican duplicity, they chided Garrison and Phillips, two of Boston's most idolized abolitionists, for abandoning the cause of woman's rights.[41]

If the substance of *The Revolution* had proved unacceptable when judged according to

23

Boston notions of propriety, the outspoken personal style of its New York editors struck many of their New England sisters as just short of scandalous. Internal disputes came to a head in May of 1869, when Anthony and Stanton broke with the abolitionists and further alienated the Boston suffragists by founding the National Woman Suffrage Association, an organization that opposed the Fourteenth Amendment and sought federal legislation to secure the enfranchisement of women. Faced with a strategy and a leadership that they considered to be a political as well as a social liability, the Bostonians responded later that year by forming a rival organization. The American Woman Suffrage Association embraced the Republican/abolitionist approach and adopted a policy of lobbying for woman suffrage on a state by state basis.

It should come as no surprise to learn that Isabella Beecher Hooker, whose two main contacts with the suffrage movement were a Bostonian (Caroline Severance) and a Republican (Anna Dickinson), shared in the prevailing prejudice against (if not animosity towards) Anthony and Stanton, whom she had never met. But Isabella had fallen "in love" with Paulina Wright Davis, a woman "whose mere presence upon the platform" of the '68 convention she found to be "a most potent argument in favor of woman's participation in public affairs." At Davis's request, she soon agreed to meet Stanton and Anthony socially at the Davis estate in Providence, Rhode Island; and, according to her own testimony, Isabella underwent a conversion experience sitting at Anthony and Stanton's feet. From this appropriately humble vantage point, she confessed that while she had secretly mourned "over the degradation of woman, you have been working through opposition and obloquy to raise her to self-respect and self-protection through enfranchisement, knowing that with equal *political rights* come equal social and industrial opportunities."[42] Here were two women such as Higginson had once described, pioneers attacked and ostracized by the majority of their own sex, who sought to secure "a mean safety by sacrificing those who have made an heroic sortie." Isabella was determined to seek the truth rather than ignoble safety. After three days in their presence, she decided that the two women had been grossly maligned and pronounced Stanton "the truest, womanliest woman of us all."[43]

So began a friendship that would outlast the vicissitudes of over thirty years of periodic controversy and crisis. At first, Isabella used her family name to attempt to gain a prominent foothold within the New York wing. She hoped to act as a mediator and, not incidentally, she wished to satisfy her long-standing craving for personal influence exercised on a broad scale. When Susan B. Anthony asked Isabella to contribute to *The Revolution*, she countered by offering herself and her famous half sister, Harriet, as associate editors of the journal on the condition that Susan agree to pay them for their services and change the paper's name. Sensing that "what our movement now needs most is an accession to our numbers of *The Literary Women*," Anthony was sorely tempted, in spite of a serious shortage of funds. As she confided to Paulina Davis, ". . . if *Cash will bring Mrs. Stowe* to The Rev. with her *deepest holiest woman, wife & mother Soul struggle* — clothed in her *inimitable story garb* — then *it is cash that must be* — Mrs. Stowe — even — has never *yet given to the world her very best* — for she nor any other woman can, until she *writes direct* out of *her own souls experiences*."[44]

When Anthony proved to be unable to overcome a "maternal" reluctance to rechristen her literary child, the Beecher sisters withdrew their offer; but Isabella lost no time in demonstrating that she had more to offer the woman suffrage movement than a well-known name.[45] At her own expense, she not only organized Hartford's first suffrage convention but also managed to seat the "notorious" New Yorkers on the same platform

William Lloyd Garrison, Sr. with daughter, Fanny

Sophia Smith Collection, Smith College

as their Boston detractors and several of Hartford's conservative elite. Her famous sisters, Catharine and Harriet, also agreed to attend. As an attempt to effect a lasting truce between the two wings of the movement, this 1869 convention was ultimately a failure. But as a display of Isabella's formidable executive abilities and as a means of focusing statewide attention on the suffrage question, the fall convention was a resounding success. The Connecticut Woman Suffrage Association, launched during the convention and presided over during most of its existence by Isabella, was to educate women and lobby in their behalf into the early twentieth century.[46]

Suddenly, Isabella became sought after. Her undeniable family and social "pull" as well as her demonstrated capacities as an organizer and speaker made her the object of ardent wooing by both wings of the movement, especially the American, which would soon make Henry Ward Beecher its president. Caroline Severance and William Lloyd Garrison, among others, felt it their duty to warn and wean Isabella away from the "compromising" New Yorkers, whose ideas on marriage and divorce were pronounced "loose" and whose motives and methods were questioned and roundly denounced. As Severance explained to the initiate, "it is *no quarrel*, — but a radical difference in character & methods," a difference so serious that the Bostonians refused to meet the New Yorkers either in private conference or on the platform.[47]

Henry Blackwell, one of the leaders of the Boston wing, joined in this effort to capture Isabella's loyalty by rehearsing the A. W. S. A. version of the Kansas campaign as well as the subsequent split and charging both Anthony and Stanton with ambition, disloyalty to the Republicans, and improper views on "social questions." The series of detailed letters that he wrote to Isabella reveals as much about the character of the A. W. S. A. leadership as about their assessment of her potential value to their organization. Assuring her that "by your tastes, principles & social position, you belong to our phase of this Movement . . .," Blackwell urged Isabella to make the Connecticut organization an auxiliary of the Boston wing. Isabella politely refused. Although she at first attempted to remain resolutely neutral and to play a strictly mediatory role, Isabella grew increasingly impatient with the Bostonians' lack of tolerance for their New York counterparts. Writing to Mary Rice Livermore, she pronounced the American wing's refusal to cooperate with Susan Anthony "a sign of moral weakness or infirmity" and countered with praise of Anthony as a *"gentle, wise, logical & convincing"* woman.[48]

Yet in a letter to Henry Blackwell, Isabella implied that spinsterhood was the source of Anthony's lack of caution and moderation and provided an interesting clue to her own motivation. Her preference for companions "of least wisdom, of least social power," as long as "I have these myself in any large measure" was hardly noble, but it was understandable. The notoriety of the New Yorkers presented Isabella with a perfect opportunity to make a unique contribution to the cause of woman suffrage: she would improve the reputation of its most notorious leaders. Given the inflexibility of the Bostonians, Isabella's refusal to repudiate Stanton and Anthony by word or deed effectively settled the question of her organizational affiliation. It also reflected her tacit agreement with Anthony's opinion of the American wing, which she had described as "sick unto death with propriety . . . ." Stanton's views on marriage and divorce may have been "far more trying to meet than any thing Susan says or does," but at least these two women did not behave like Lucy Stone, who falsely accused the officers of the N.W.S.A. of being "loose women or free lovers."[49]

Isabella's all but instantaneous transformation into a key N. W. S. A. leader with national clout and responsibilities was the result of several factors. As her correspon-

Henry Brown Blackwell   *The Schlesinger Library,*
                               Radcliffe College

Mary Rice Livermore   *The Schlesinger Library,*
                              Radcliffe College

27

dence documents, Stanton was looking for a replacement. Far from desiring total control of the movement, she found herself at this juncture to be exhausted, impatient with movement infighting, and eager to share the burden with more energetic newcomers like Isabella: "You are younger & have more leisure . . . I am too burthened with cares already."[50] Furthermore, Ellen DuBois has argued convincingly that when the vital links between abolitionism and suffrage were severed, the suffragists were faced with the tasks of developing an independent organization and "identifying a future constituency among women." Denied access to antislavery women and resources, the National wing sought to align itself with organized labor. Despite a brief period of collaboration with working women from late 1868 through the summer of 1869, this group failed to emerge as a new basis for the movement. Stanton and Anthony then turned to leisured women for support, women "who had begun to extricate themselves from the confines of domesticity or who were growing discontent with the proscriptions of ladydom . . . ."[51]

As Stanton seems to have recognized, Isabella Beecher Hooker had become just such a woman. Unable to bear the loss of her younger daughter's company in the house, she had unsuccessfully attempted to prevent Alice from marrying John Calvin Day. In June of 1869, when the pair married, only Ned, aged fourteen, remained at home: Isabella's nest was almost empty.[52] Later that year, Isabella learned that she would soon become a grandmother; her eldest child, Mary, was pregnant. Thus at the age of forty-seven, Isabella found herself for the first time at a stage in the life cycle that permitted and virtually required her to seek a nonfamilial outlet for her pent-up energies and ideas. Considering herself skilled in the laws of maternal governance, the one area of human endeavor in which she could claim any expertise, she became increasingly confident that she was destined to make what she now perceived of as the *natural* transition from motherhood to a national leadership role.

In retrospect, it is clear that the time was indeed ripe for Isabella's entry into the public sphere; and so it must have seemed to her when, in the fall of that very year, John Stuart Mill sent her a copy of his new book, *The Subjection of Women*. In her subsequent letter of praise to Mill, Isabella took note of his unprecedented public acknowledgement of his wife's influence and intellectual leadership and pressed him to elaborate on one particular point. Wasn't woman closer to the divine nature because of her capacity to create? "Add to this her more intimate fellowship with the child of her womb during the antenatal period, & the power of sympathy that comes through this, & you have given her a moral advantage that man can never have & for which he has no equivalent or compensation." In his reply, Mill acknowledged the "closer relationship of a child to its mother" and predicted "important consequences with respect to the future legal position of parents and children;" but he denied that this relationship in and of itself guaranteed moral excellence, a quality that he considered to be the result of education and cultivation. Yet his negative reply could not dampen Isabella's belief that "a mother is the only being in this world, who . . . . approximates the divine nature," nor her growing conviction that after "ages of subjection," woman was on the verge of "ages of exaltation." As she had confided to Mill: "I see such honor & power coming to woman as makes me tremble — for with power comes responsibility for the just use of it & who save He that seeth the end from the beginning is competent to this."[53]

Isabella's earlier insistence that the intellectual differences between men and women were primarily the result of unequal education seems finally to have given way before the increasingly popular contemporaneous view that woman was inherently superior to man.[54] Unlike Elizabeth Cady Stanton, who considered marriage and motherhood to be mere "incidents" of a woman's existence, Isabella's views had much in common with those of her conservative and unmarried sister, Catharine, who (somewhat paradoxically) regarded motherhood as the central fact of womanhood. However, Isabella vigorously opposed the antisuffrage position Catharine was to endorse publicly in her 1872 work, *Woman Suffrage and Woman's Profession.* Starting from similar premises, the two sisters arrived at opposite conclusions. While Catharine advocated what amounted to the professionalization of motherhood, housekeeping, and teaching through parallel but disparate forms of higher education for the sexes and specially endowed schools and professorships for women, Isabella now maintained that it was precisely woman's "professional" expertise as mother and chief educator of the race that qualified her to enter into (and eventually control) the affairs of civil government. Her thought thus represents a prototype of what Aileen Kraditor has identified as a species of late nineteenth-century Progressive era thought — the drawing of an explicit analogy between housekeeping on a private scale and government, which was conceived of as "enlarged housekeeping."[55]

Isabella's millennial visions of the coming exaltation of her sex, which constituted a unique variation on this theme, were to find embodiment in Victoria Claflin Woodhull. A highly controversial figure whose antecedents were somewhat mysterious, Woodhull was endowed with a personal magnetism which had already proved irresistable to a series of infatuated men, including her two husbands (both of whom shared her home at one time) and the financier, Cornelius Vanderbilt, who had helped make Woodhull and her sister the first women to operate a Wall Street brokerage firm. Unlike Stanton and Anthony, who advocated changing divorce and custody laws but who bridled at the erroneous label of "free lover," Woodhull delighted in shocking her lecture audiences by vehemently denouncing marriage and openly claiming the right of women as well as men to change lovers at will. The resultant notoriety made her unexpected testimony in behalf of woman suffrage before the House Judiciary Committee in January of 1871 not only a potential embarrassment to the entire movement but also an unwelcome disruption of Isabella's long-standing plans for a national convention on the same date. However, after reluctantly agreeing to listen to Woodhull argue that the Fourteenth and Fifteenth Amendments already enfranchised women, she was completely won over by the younger woman's persuasive combination of beauty, personal presence, and apparent purity of character.[56]

On the basis of this performance, Hooker and Anthony invited Woodhull to share the platform with them during the suffrage convention that followed. Isabella herself went on to deliver a forceful and eloquent reply to those congressmen who wished to restrict rather than expand the franchise. Concentrating on her belief in the key doctrine of "personal liberty and personal responsibility," which she regarded as God-given, Isabella contradicted her earlier nativist views by speaking out against those who would take the franchise away from foreign-born men. Still arguing from expediency, she warned that "a disfranchised class is always a restless class" and predicted that only when all men and all women were enfranchised would a stable and true Christian civilization be achieved.[57]

For reasons that still remain partially obscure, Isabella immediately began to court Victoria Woodhull's favor. Regarding (and privately referring to) Woodhull as the new "Queen" of the suffrage movement, she staunchly refused to listen to the many relatives, friends, and fellow suffragists who considered this new alliance to be a

Victoria Claflin Woodhull

Sophia Smith Collection, Smith College

dangerous one for both the movement and a "respectable" member of the Beecher and Hooker families. Kenneth Andrews and others speak of the "spell" that Woodhull supposedly cast on Isabella; but aside from functioning as an allusion to Victoria's proven powers as an orator and her undeniable magnetism (which would now be called "charisma"), such phrases explain virtually nothing. On the basis of the many letters written by and to Isabella concerning this relationship, it is possible to speculate that her admiration for and staunch defense of "the Woodhull" may have grown as much out of her revulsion against the bitter and often underhanded attacks on the antecedents and character of Victoria and her sister, Tennie C. Claflin, as they did from her genuine regard for Woodhull's eloquence and abilities. By refusing to abandon Woodhull to her critics, Isabella could not only assert the value of her own judgment over that of her family and friends but also could lend her wisdom and social prestige to another suffrage leader whom she considered to be conspicuously lacking in these advantages.

Furthermore, Isabella's friendship with Woodhull seems to have figured to her as a personal protest against the prevailing sexual double standard. The issue was being vigorously debated in America during this period not only because of Woodhull's outspoken attacks on the marriage bond, which were given wide circulation in her newspaper, but also as a result of two well publicized incidents that involved members of the Beecher clan. In late November of 1869, Daniel McFarland, furious about his wife's recent divorce, had taken it upon himself for the second time in two years to attack Albert Richardson, the man she planned to marry. Henry Ward Beecher and O. B. Frothingham agreed to officiate at Richardson's subsequent deathbed marriage to McFarland's ex-wife. When the affair received hostile publicity in the wake of the ensuing murder trial, Beecher himself came under heavy attack as a supposed supporter of "free love."[58]

Lawless passion if not precisely free love was also an issue in the furor touched off by the 1869 article in which Harriet Beecher Stowe revealed to the American public for the first time the precise nature of the accusations against Lord Byron. Refusing to be intimidated by the vicious denunciations of both herself and Lady Byron, whom she had eloquently defended in her article, less than a year later Harriet published Lady Byron Vindicated, an expanded version of both the charges of incest and her defense of Byron's widow. It seems quite likely that with the courageous example of her two revered siblings before her, Isabella felt that she could hardly maintain her self-respect if she caved in to unsubstantiated gossip or acquiesced to conventional notions that held Woodhull's alleged vices to be more contagious than her own proven virtue (although this gossip was taken quite seriously by members of Isabella's family, most notably by Catharine and Harriet herself). As she confided to Susan Anthony in the spring of 1871: "I shall always love her [Woodhull] — in private shall work for her redemption if she is ensnared — for I never saw more possible nobilities in a human being than in her." Isabella steadfastly refused to denounce her new co-worker in public, however guilty she might be, "till the time when men guilty of the same crimes are avoided & denounced."[59]

Yet this same letter reveals that the criticism aroused by Isabella's fellowship with Woodhull was already having adverse effects on her relationship with her family and her Nook Farm neighbors. Asking that Anthony pass her letter on to Stanton, Lucretia Mott, Martha Coffin Wright, and then to John, who was "keeping every hasty line I have written as historical matter concerning this remarkable campaign," she noted that she wanted to pursue her discussions with Woodhull regarding political and domestic economy; but she feared the effect upon the health of her husband, who "has been so harassed by my *three* sisters in N. York & by every friend we have in Hartford on my acc[oun]t that he is scarce able to exist." Less than two years earlier, John Hooker had braved censure and ridicule by defending Anthony and Stanton before the American public in a letter to the prestigious *Nation*. Likening their radicalism to that of the now respected William Lloyd Garrison, he argued that all reform movements depended upon "persons who are characterized by courage and energy and a disregard for conventionalities." Although he acknowledged that "there is almost always some bad taste" in the conduct of reformers, John nevertheless maintained that "good taste alone never wrought out a reform, and bad taste, though a hindrance and an offense, never ... defeated one."[60] Within two years, John would find himself publicly denouncing the judge who presided over Susan Anthony's trial for illegally voting on the grounds that Anthony had been denied due process. He was also willing to spend seven years drafting and submitting bills and articles in support of a then controversial issue, women's property rights. Yet Victoria Woodhull and her free love doctrines eventually proved to be the one thing that would threaten to come between John Hooker and his wife.

Isabella's letters in the fall of 1871 and the spring of 1872 reveal that she was struggling amidst great family pressure to maintain both her balance and her sense of humor. While she joked to a friend that Catharine Beecher's vituperous attacks on Victoria Woodhull's private life only resulted in larger lecture receipts for their intended victim, she could not conceal her intense dismay over having such a foe in her own household — "if you can escape that you can live." To her trusted friend and fellow state organizer, Olympia Brown, she confided that her husband and daughters had at last agreed to withdraw their opposition to the relationship, on the condition that she promise not to invite Woodhull to join in future campaigns. Isabella summed up her point of view when she wrote to Stanton, insisting that they could not ignore Woodhull's crucial contributions to the cause, her gifts of "money & brains & unceasing energy ... I verily believe she has sunk a hundred thousand dollars in Woman Suffrage, besides enduring tortures of soul innumerable — let us never forget this ...."[61]

The loyalty of the N. W. S. A. leadership to Woodhull was soon to be sorely tried. During the 1871-72 period, Isabella continued to work tirelessly for the cause, which she was fast coming to regard as a "holy war." In January of 1872, she joined Susan Anthony in testifying on behalf of a federal suffrage amendment before the Senate Judiciary Committee. But Isabella's efforts to canvass her state and lobby on a federal level for Congressional action in support of woman suffrage were interrrupted in the fall of 1872 by a scandal of national proportions that had special repercussions for the Beecher family.[62] Prodded largely by the public attacks made on her character by several Beechers, especially Catharine, Victoria Woodhull decided to retaliate by giving voice to rumors that had been circulating in New York City for some time. After using her presidential address to the September convention of the Association of American Spiritualists in Boston as an opportunity to hint at the existence of secret free lovers in high places, Woodhull publicly charged Henry Ward Beecher with adultery in the November 2nd issue of *Woodhull and Claflin's Weekly*. The paper, which rapidly sold out at black market prices, identified Elizabeth Tilton, one of Beecher's parishioners and the wife of one of his closest friends, as the partner in this adulterous relationship (which Woodhull pronounced sinful only by virtue of its lack of candor). Despite incriminating evidence unearthed during subsequent ecclesiastical and civil trials, Beecher not only maintained his innocence but also joined in the fray, counterattacking with the charge that it was Theodore Tilton, rather than himself, who was the real free lover, the object of Tilton's unlawful affections having been none other than Victoria Woodhull.[63]

Isabella Beecher Hooker shocked and further alienated many of her family, friends, and acquaintances first by refusing to denounce Woodhull as a liar and then by publicly entertaining the possibility that her brother might not be innocent and might even benefit from an open confession if he were indeed guilty. On the basis of confidences that the Tiltons had shared with their close friends, Stanton and Anthony, as well as her own intimate knowledge of her brother's unhappy marriage, Isabella had good reason to doubt the reliability of Henry Ward's version of the story as offered in his private letters, newspaper accounts, and ultimately his sworn testimony in court. Yet those around Isabella were unwilling to grant her the right to approach the question of her brother's guilt legalistically and impartially. There was an unspoken assumption that she was not an individual free to make up her own mind but a sister who owed her brother a blind trust and unswerving loyalty, regardless of the facts of the case.

Cast in these terms, the scandal can be seen as a kind of identity crisis for Isabella, for it forced her to make a choice between being a Beecher first and foremost or her own person. However, general cultural issues were also involved. Several aspects of Woodhull's denunciation of the nation's most prominent clergyman and the scandal that ensued deserve closer attention from historians of nineteenth-century American culture, most of whom have virtually ignored the affair, leaving it to figure as a quaint Victorian episode in biographies of the principal figures involved. Yet the volume as well as the substance of the unprecedented public reverberation set in motion by the trial suggest that, far from being an isolated event of limited consequences, it raised issues crucial to an understanding of contemporaneous anxieties regarding the family and extramarital sex as well as the power structure and economic base of postbellum America.

Elizabeth Cady Stanton's analysis, based on her inside knowledge of the affair and a cousin's investment in Beecher's literary enterprises, provides a succinct (if somewhat one-sided) assessment of what was at stake. As she explained to Isabella, "the Christian Union — Ford & Co — who publish the Life of Christ [Beecher's biography] & Plymouth Church had too much money at stake to see B. [Henry Ward] sacrificed," so "the 'lie' as they called it was to be saddled upon us women." Though Victoria's story was "exaggerated," "the main facts corresponded with what Susan & I had heard." She went on to charge that "the outrageous persecution of Mrs. Woodhull in our courts [she had been jailed for obscenity] shows money & power behind" and concluded "I have been crucified in this matter as much as you .... But through it all I see one thing, we must stand by each other. Women must be as true to women as men are to men."[64]

Isabella heeded this plea: she publicly stood by Woodhull, Stanton, and Anthony instead of her brother, who enjoyed more than his share of powerful and influential friends. Privately, she defended her position by arranging for her husband to speak directly with Anthony so that he could "get his fill of satisfaction at her hands." Isabella could "think of nothing that will tend to calm his fears more than Susan's sterling honesty — good sense, faith & courage." To her daughter, Alice Day, she complained about her son-in-law's self-righteous attitude and counterattacked by blasting the double standard. Men defended their sexual passion "as righteous & God sent," yet they "lose all confidence in womanhood when a woman here & there betrays her similar nature & gives herself soul & body to the man she adores." Questioned by her son, Isabella referred to the "wretchedness" of his uncle's inner life due to an "uncongenial marriage" and attempted to temper her brother's guilt by reminding Ned that the stories might have been "fearfully exaggerated" and admitting that she did not know the exact truth.[65]

Isabella's siblings did not prove so charitable. When Henry Ward and Harriet went so far as to question publicly their half sister's sanity, Isabella began to realize that she would be asked to pay, and pay heavily, for her independence of mind and her sexual solidarity. For insight into her activities and state of mind during the next six years, years of terrible suffering that she glossed over quite rapidly in her autobiographical reflections (from which she understandably omitted any mention of Victoria Woodhull or the scandal), one must look first to her correspondence and then to the two intimate journals that she kept during 1876 and 1878. Isabella's correspondence reveals that she at first attempted to avoid the growing controversy regarding the scandal and escape the bitter resentment of her relatives and Nook Farm neighbors by joining John in the autumn of 1874 for an extended European tour. But the Atlantic Ocean did not provide an adequate buffer, for letters and newspaper articles concerning the affair caught up with her at every stop.[66]

It is worth noting that before Isabella left the country, she published *Womanhood: Its Sanctities and Fidelities,* a pioneering work in which she supported Josephine Butler's campaign to abolish Britain's hated Contagious Diseases Acts and defended woman's right as a mother to speak out on "delicate" social questions such as prostitution, birth control, abortion, and sex education for children. This published plea for sexual self-restraint on the part of men and a spirit of "divine love" on the part of women towards their most "degraded" sisters can be interpreted as a private as well as a public document. While it overtly represented a broad Anglo-American outlook in its vigorous support of the British campaign against the double standard, it covertly figured as a highly personal statement, for it justified Isabella's refusal to condemn Victoria Woodhull and Elizabeth Tilton and her inability to condone her brother's actions.[67]

As a private message, *Womanhood* fell on deaf ears. Unable to escape the mounting pressure and animosity even in Europe, Isabella suddenly experienced a vision of her mother in her Paris hotel room. Harriet Porter Beecher offered her daughter unconditional acceptance and loving counsel.[68] Although Isabella kept these "visits" to herself, she was soon writing home about her meetings with several reform-minded mediums and providing enthusiastic accounts of the various "personations" they were able to achieve.[69] On the evidence of these letters and her 1876 diary (from which direct quotations are no longer permitted), it becomes clear that Isabella underwent a conversion to spiritualism while in Europe. This experience has been variously attributed to the influence and example of Victoria Woodhull, who considered herself to be a medium of rare powers and who claimed to receive private messages regarding her high destiny, and to the devastating effect that social and family "ostracism" had upon Isabella's troubled spirit. While both explanations are certainly convincing, they seem somewhat oversimplified. Neither takes into account the fact that Isabella's antebellum correspondence betrays an early affinity for and disposition towards a spiritualist-type belief in the gradual evolution of civilization from coarse and materialistic matter towards more refined and ethereal (and hence more "feminine?") form. Nor do such explanations entirely square with the fact that her fervent belief in spiritualism, which John eventually came to share, grew stronger rather than abated with the passage of years, long after the resentment against her had subsided and all direct contact with Woodhull (who eventually recanted her radical ideas, remarried and settled in England with her titled husband) had ended.[70]

Josephine Butler

Sophia Smith Collection, Smith College

Part of the difficulty of interpreting Isabella's conversion lies in the fact that spiritualism still awaits a penetrating and evenhanded treatment from historians of nineteenth-century American culture. While R. Laurence Moore's recent book on the subject treats the field as an area worthy of serious study, his work focuses primarily on professional mediums, many of whom were charlatans, and thus it tends to emphasize the more sensational and commercial aspects of the movement. Furthermore, Moore has difficulty sustaining a sympathetic stance towards the multitude of sincere spiritualists, many of whom confined their activities to "home circles" presided over by strictly private mediums. As Sydney Ahlstrom has remarked, "Spiritualism was not merely commercialized entertainment . . . . It was a religious force — for some it was a religion . . . ." He also stresses the fact that spiritualism was "a form of theological liberalism in which such eminent thinkers as Alfred Russell Wallace, Victor Hugo, and William James were seriously interested."[71]

As her papers reveal, Isabella Beecher Hooker made contact at some point with all three: she read the works of investigators like Wallace (as well as the memoirs of well-known mediums such as Emanuel Swedenborg), attempted to meet with Hugo in Paris, and conducted a brief correspondence with James. As in everything else that she became committed to, Isabella consulted the experts and closely studied every major book on the subject. It is also worth noting that these papers, especially the suffrage correspondence, reveal that many of her friends, co-workers, and even several of her Beecher siblings shared this intense interest in spiritualism, while not a few considered themselves to be mediums.[72] Given both this social milieu and Isabella's ample knowledge of the literature on the subject, it seems quite likely that her mediumship was essentially a *learned* behavior. Isabella's receptivity to the spiritualist movement can also be approached in terms of Moore's observation that spiritualism served to "console" the misunderstood and his assertion that it helped to sustain reform zeal. Yet he leaves the deeper ties between the woman's rights movement and spiritualism (the modern versions of which both began in the same state, New York, and in the same year, 1848) largely unexplored.[73] Furthermore, while Isabella certainly experienced herself during this period as a martyred and misunderstood individual, her case was complicated by the fact that her overwhelming sense of personal suffering had its roots in the ostracism imposed not by the public at large but by her two hostile sons-in-law.

John and Isabella's access to their daughters and grandchildren had been cut off suddenly in 1876 by John Calvin Day and Henry Eugene Burton. Both men seem to have resented Isabella, whom they regarded as domineering and meddlesome, and the Hookers' radical views.[74] Isabella tried to maintain a calm exterior, but her inner turmoil and suffering found an outlet in her diary, in which she gave utterance to millennial visions of herself as a new messiah, a spiritual intermediary between the heavenly family and its earthly counterpart below. Like a modern Moses, she would lead God's children from the desert of materialistic illusions to the promised land of spiritual faith and good government. It is clear in retrospect that this was essentially a compensatory vision: if Isabella was not to be permitted to enjoy the common privileges entitled to a mother and grandmother, she would concentrate her energies and emotions on a single goal, that of becoming the spiritual mother of her country. Those friends and relatives who had treated her unfairly would eventually recognize their mistake and beg her forgiveness, in this world or in the next.[75] Combined with the spiritualist belief in the persistence of individual identity on "the other side," this concept of a divinely ordained martyrdom provided Isabella with the only framework within which she could hope to make sense of and endure these years of anguish and deprivation, which she experienced as suffocation and drowning.[76]

While such extraordinary intimations of impending greatness certainly appear eccentric if not downright ludicrous when exposed to the harsh light of the late twentieth century, it should be remembered that Isabella's confidential diaries were intensely private documents, never intended for public consumption. Only too aware of the highly questionable nature of her visions and communications, Isabella often begged for evidence that would either validate these spiritual messages or prove them to be utterly false, once and for all.[77] Her highly personalized version of spiritualism combined standard phenomena such as séances, the laying on of hands, spirit rappings, and Indian "helpers" with more idiosyncratic matriarchal and millennial strains. It thus represented an extension and complication of her earlier feminist thought, which had been interwoven with the popular neo-Darwinian belief in the spiritual evolution of the race. When she was not feeling utterly exhausted and totally powerless, Isabella came to envision herself as the instrument and agent of this divine evolutionary plan. Guided by the example and the mediatory offices of her own mother, she would preach the cult of "the mother," the very type of the refined and self-sacrificing human spirit, on a grander scale than ever before.

The documents of the 1870s and the 1880s in which these visions are recorded betray a not unfamiliar pattern: Isabella vacillates between moments of certainty and exaltation and prolonged periods of intense depression, confusion, and incipient invalidism. At her points of lowest ebb, when she appears to be on the verge of collapse into total paralysis of the will, Isabella's spiritualism seems to take on its most conventional form. Accounts of rappings on the roof from her mother, conversations with departed friends and relatives, and more or less trivial messages regarding how to dress, arrange furniture, and invest money (along with acknowledgements of John's skeptical reactions to these phenomena) alternate, seemingly without rhyme or reason, with sombre and at times quite penetrating meditations upon family matters, political issues, and woman's destiny.[78] The one characteristic common to all of these "varieties of religious experience" seems to be Isabella's compulsion to seek a higher authority for her every word and deed, however exalted *or* mundane it might be.

The question of individual responsibility, a theme taken quite seriously by Isabella in her writings on woman's rights, seems to have caught up with her.[79] Suffocating with emotions and ideas that she fears she has no right to express, she tends to experience herself as controlled by a "spirit helper" or possessed by the will of a recently deceased friend or relative who is eager to advise her (and who conveniently proves to be less squeamish about what he or she says). The most detailed and dramatic record of such an instance appears in Isabella's 1878 journal. In a remarkable entry that runs for seven pages, Isabella recorded what began as a rather unimportant disagreement between herself and her husband over a photograph she was fond of mailing out to her admirers across the country. John's objection to this photograph (he declares that it makes her look like "one of these dancing girls") triggers a serious argument over his lack of confidence in her judgment. He insists that he has had to lie in order to defend her to their son-in-law and she responds to this verbal blow with such anger that she feels compelled to attribute her words to her sharp tongued half sister ("it was hardly I, it was sister C.[atharine]").

"Catharine" then charges that John has ridden Isabella as Balaam rode the ass, pointedly noting that "it was the ass who saw the angel, & not Balaam." As the entry continues, Isabella rebels against Catharine's "dictation," reminding herself how "pure" and "lovable" John is and reasonably acknowledging that all reformers, including woman re-

20 MONDAY [263–102] And If we look at the lives of all men
reformers, from Abraham down to present time,
they had marked peculiarities to say the least – who
history – individualities they were, which history
calls faith, genius, magnetism, eloquence & so on –
and women reformers cannot escape the first
misjudgments of the world if they would win the
later verdict – your wife does not care to escape
them for far other & nobler reasons, but there
should weigh with you & should at least compel
you to let me alone & not molest me with
me your unreasonable criticism – (she would

21 TUESDAY [264–101] have me quite unreasonable where I
should have used a harsher term,) And now
dear friend pray try to believe according to the
influences of your higher nature, which as Mrs
H. has said is eminently spiritual – & yield not
to your lower which is masculine & so
unspiritual, at least to a degree. I have
found this out, for one thing since I came over
here – it seems to be true that sex is of the
earth – a help to development, but not in fact the
ways one might fancy that one being of the masculine gender – I am glad for my part that

22 WEDNESDAY [265–100] ☾ you have held on to this evidence of masculinity – which over here we call
obstinacy – combativeness – mulishness –
Here Mrs H. was interrupted by callers, but already
she was becoming unmanageable under my hand
– my chirography don't suit her – she can't
endure its illegibility – the consciousness coming upon
her my control grew weaker & weaker & nearly
ceased about the time the ladies came in –
but I am not easily discouraged & have induced
her to resume, sitting at your table brother John
you know & am here myself by this time
I hope – when the masculine atmosphere
helps a little perhaps. The trouble is however

formers like herself, have "marked peculiarities to say the least" that condemn them to be misjudged by the world. Suddenly, Isabella's characteristic handwriting begins to alter drastically and the narrative shifts from the first to the third person. John is admonished that "your wife does not care to escape them [these misjudgments] for far other & nobler reasons, but these should weigh with you & should at least compel you to let her alone & not molest her with your unreasonable criticism, (she would have me write *unreasonable* where I should have used a harsher term.)" An individual whose handwriting is smaller and more angular dominates the remainder of the page, urging John not to yield to his more masculine nature, here called "obstinacy," but to follow the inclinations of his higher and more spiritual nature. The speaker concludes this defense of Isabella and goes on to identify himself as "Sam[uel] Bowles."

By accepting "dictation" first from sister Catharine and then from "brother" Bowles, a close mutual friend of the Hookers who had edited *The Springfield Republican* and staunchly supported woman suffrage until his death, Isabella was able to deflect responsibility for her negative feelings towards her normally supportive husband. Transforming herself once again into a mediator, she functioned not only as a "passive" intermediary between her husband and the spirits of these two individuals (both of whom had died earlier that year) but also as a modifier of their outspoken and somewhat harsh "messages." Isabella's need for such spiritual reinforcements must be interpreted in the context of her frequent complaints about John's loss of confidence in her as a result of her role in the Beecher-Tilton scandal. As she had previously disclosed: "he [John] leans on me to the extent of my capacity to bear — pities me because I am bound to such a 'worthless husband' [a reference to John's fears of hereditary insanity in his family] — insists that I am fitted for positions of universal scope, yet will not trust me to write a note — or hire a horse, & still has a vague conviction that many of our troubles about Woodhull & Henry might have been avoided if I had only followed his counsel when present, & not dared to think my own thoughts or speak my own words, while he was absent." Earlier in this diary, Isabella had also recorded their intense reaction to the plot of Hawthorne's *The Scarlet Letter*, which she considered to be an exact parallel to the Beecher-Tilton scandal, "even to the unbelieving ones who were not convinced even by the minister's own confession."[80] Clearly, the scandal and its aftermath were at the root of the Hookers' worst marital disputes as well as Isabella's compensatory spiritualist visions.

Yet theirs was a union that was capable of weathering and triumphing over a variety of public and private difficulties. After the untimely death of their eldest daughter, Mary, in 1886, they joined in frequent attempts to contact her spirit. The results must have proved convincing to John, for by 1888 he was lecturing on spiritualism with Isabella in Connecticut and Boston.[81] In 1891, with past tensions within the Nook Farm community long forgotten or forgiven, the Hookers celebrated their fiftieth wedding anniversary in grand style. Many local and national dignitaries attended the festivities, including Susan B. Anthony. By the time John Hooker died in 1901 at the age of eighty-five, the pair could look back on almost sixty years of mutual respect and devotion.

It would be wrong to give the impression that Isabella's suffrage-related activities came to an abrupt halt as a result of the scandal and her subsequent involvement with spiritualism. She continued to lobby on both the state and national level, although she often lamented the fact that financial difficulties and poor health held her back from full-time work in Washington. As early as 1877, she had brooded about her inability to devote herself more completely to suffrage work on a national scale; but she gloried in the Connecticut State Legislature's passage of John Hooker's bill, which granted taxpaying women the right to vote. As she described the episode in a letter to their friend, Samuel Bowles, the Senate passed a special resolution that enabled her to appear before it in the bill's behalf. "Face to face & eye to eye with every man of them," she gave what John later termed a "magnificent" speech. "Now friend —," she wrote to Bowles, "how do you account for it, that this privilege, which has never before been extended to any 'white male,' should have been thus thrust upon me, the friend of Mrs. Woodhull & all other sinners?"[82]

In 1889, she would describe a similar incident to her daughter, Alice. In a hearing before the Connecticut Legislature concerning Constitutional amendments, she had spoken so forcefully in favor of striking the word "male" out of the Constitution that one legislator publicly claimed that "Mrs. Hooker was fit to be President of the U.S." (although he insisted that she was *not* typical of her sex). In the same letter, Isabella also disclosed that she was helping to form clubs in several Connecticut towns. These clubs would encourage women to study political science in order to prepare themselves "to manage town affairs as they should be managed." Experience had convinced Isabella that women must be compelled "to bear their share of burden & responsibility." Citing the case of a Litchfield teacher who had been raped twice in the same afternoon — "being nearly choked to death" by a young man from a "respectable family" — she was moved to exclaim, "so much for our protectors!!"[83]

In 1890, the year in which the two wings of the suffrage movement finally reunited, Isabella was back in Washington, where she shared the platform with Elizabeth Cady Stanton and her daughter, Harriet Stanton Blatch.[84] Isabella seems to have cherished the hope that Alice, her sole surviving daughter, would join in the campaign along with Blatch and other young suffragists such as Kate Trimble from Kentucky, one of several "adopted" daughters who referred to Isabella with affection and admiration as "Mother." When Alice proved to be more interested in Christian Science, Isabella revealed that she, too, had once been attracted to Mrs. Eddy's brand of spiritual healing, but that she "had to give her up as illogical inconsistent & egotistical & when I came to know her history all these things were explained." According to Isabella, Mary Baker Eddy's error lay in the fact that she "repudiated her spirit helpers from the other side" and maintained a "dogmatic" attitude. Perhaps sensing that Christian Science represented a competing form of mariolatry, Isabella urged Alice to consult her own "Confession of Faith," a response to the important question, "How does your belief in Spiritualism affect your religious belief?"[85]

In 1893, Isabella capped her career as a reformer and a conscientious citizen by serving on the Board of Lady Managers for the Columbian Exposition in Chicago. Always eager to identify with and assist the underdog, she became interested in the plight of the Southern delegates to the Exposition, teaching them parliamentary procedure and helping them to counter the maneuvers of the Board's high-handed chairman, Mrs. Potter Palmer, and her lieutenants. Although she retained the presidency of the Connecticut Woman Suffrage Association until 1905, Isabella's final years were increasingly devoted to her grandchildren and her communications with the spirit world, which must have seemed increasingly near to her after John's death in 1901. Then, on January 5, 1907, Isabella died of a cerebral hemorrhage, presumably confident that she would soon be reunited with her mother, her daughter, Mary, and her "lover husband" and that her entire family would be harmoniously reconstituted in "the Great Beyond."

* * *

From earliest childhood, Isabella Beecher Hooker had been conscious of a sense of power within her, but there had been "years & years of my life when it was all crushed out of me by opposition of my nearest & dearest & best till I have given up all hope of being useful in *my day & generation* . . . ." Nevertheless, she had "never resigned the hope that some time & somewhere I should be allowed to work for righteousness according to my impulses & the clear vision of great possibilities."[86] At a crucial moment in her life, internal dissension within the ranks of the woman suffrage movement provided her with a unique opportunity to harness this sense of personal power and channel it in a way that would serve the public good. Although the suffragists' avowed goal, the ballot, would not be achieved in Isabella's lifetime, the alliance between the suffrage movement and "The Last of the Beechers" proved to be a successful one. Isabella placed her keen mind and her "clear vision of great possibilities" at the service of her fellow reformers; and they, in return, participated in her development from "an unfinished woman" into an articulate theoretician, an eloquent public speaker, and a Constitutional debater of the first rank.

Footnotes

N.B. Unless otherwise noted, all items cited are letters owned by The Stowe-Day Foundation.

1. Isabella Beecher Hooker, "The Last of the Beechers: Memories on My Eighty-Third Birthday," *The Connecticut Magazine,* Vol. IX (May, 1905), p. 298. Several other appreciative articles on Mrs. Hooker appear in this issue.
2. Isabella Beecher Hooker to Rachel Burton, 1859 January 25. **Fiche 15/C11-D3.**
3. "The Last of the Beechers," p. 289.
4. Isabella Beecher Hooker to John Hooker, 1839 October 21. **Fiche 2/B12-C1.** Transcript of letter on **Fiche 1/A4-7.**
5. Isabella Beecher Hooker to John Hooker, 1839 July 21. **Fiche 2/A8-11.** See, also, Isabella Beecher Hooker to John Hooker, 1840 December 18. **Fiche 3/B5-8.** Transcript of letter on **Fiche 1/B13-C1.**
6. Isabella Beecher Hooker to John Hooker, 1839 August 30. **Fiche 2/A14-B3.**
7. "The Last of the Beechers," p. 291.
8. "The Last of the Beechers," p. 289.
9. "The Last of the Beechers," p. 291. In this article she quotes from her husband's book, John Hooker, *Some Reminiscences of a Long Life* (Hartford: Belknap & Warfield, 1899). Her Nook Farm neighbors included the Calvin E. Stowes, the Samuel L. Clemenses, the Charles Dudley Warners, the George Warners, and the Francis Gillettes. For a detailed treatment of this literary and social community, see Kenneth R. Andrews, *Nook Farm: Mark Twain's Hartford Circle* (Cambridge: Harvard University Press, 1950).
10. Isabella Beecher Hooker to John Hooker, 1842 December 30. **Fiche 4/E7-10.**
11. *Some Reminiscences of a Long Life,* pp. 37-41.
12. Marie Caskey, *Chariot of Fire: Religion and the Beecher Family* (New Haven: Yale University Press, 1978), p. 112. For a detailed discussion of the range of Beecher family response to John Hooker's antislavery activities, see pp. 109-112.
13. Isabella Beecher Hooker to John Hooker, 1841 July 19; 1844 August 8; and 1847 February 21. **Fiche 4/C7-10, Fiche 5/D11-13,** and **Fiche 8/A3-6.**
14. Isabella Beecher Hooker to John Hooker, 1847 February 21 and 1849 January 11. **Fiche 8/A3-6** and **Fiche 8/C8-11.**
15. Isabella Beecher Hooker to John Hooker, 1852 June 26. **Fiche 10/D7-E2.**

16. Isabella Beecher Hooker to John Hooker, 1853 October 16. Emphasis added. **Fiche 12/B8-C1.**

17. Isabella Beecher Hooker to Rachel Burton, 1859 January 25. First two emphases added. **Fiche 15/C11-D3.**

18. This letter has not been located and may no longer exist. However, Higginson describes its contents in a letter he wrote to Isabella Beecher Hooker on January 15, 1898. **Fiche 133/D6-7.**

19. Thomas Wentworth Higginson to Isabella Beecher Hooker, 1859 February 19. **Fiche 133/C9-12.**

20. Quoted in Anne Farnam, "Woman Suffrage as an Alternative to the Beecher Ministry: The Conversion of Isabella Beecher Hooker," *Portraits of a Nineteenth Century Family: A Symposium on the Beecher Family*, ed. by Earl A. French and Diana Royce (Hartford: The Stowe-Day Foundation, 1976), p. 81.

21. Manuscript, Isabella Beecher Hooker, Shall Women Vote? A Matrimonial Dialogue — Scene — New York, Feb. 18, 1860, 1860 February 18. **Fiche 93/C9-D7.** This dialogue has been published as "Shall Women Vote? A Matrimonial Dialogue" in *On Common Ground: A Selection of Hartford Writers*, ed. by Alice DeLana and Cynthia Reik (Hartford: The Stowe-Day Foundation, 1975), pp. 71-78.

22. Isabella Beecher Hooker to John Hooker, 1860 January 24. **Fiche 16/C12-D1.**

23. Thomas Wentworth Higginson to Isabella Beecher Hooker, 1860 March 4. **Fiche 133/C13-D2.**

24. Isabella Beecher Hooker to John Hooker, 1860 April 12. Emphasis added. **Fiche 16/D6-11.** In a subsequent letter to Catharine Beecher, Isabella refers to her monthly period as her "hard times" and discloses the fact that Mrs. Gleason is treating her for a menstrual disorder. See Isabella Beecher Hooker to Catharine Beecher, 1860 April 17. **Fiche 16/E6-8.**

25. Isabella Beecher Hooker to John Hooker, 1860 April 28. **Fiche 17/B12-C1.**

26. Isabella Beecher Hooker to John Hooker, 1860 June 24. **Fiche 21/C3-6.**

27. See Ann Douglas Wood, "'The Fashionable Diseases': Women's Complaints and Their Treatment in Nineteenth-Century America," *Clio's Consciousness Raised*, ed. by Mary Hartman and Lois W. Banner (New York: Harper Colophon Books, 1974), pp. 1-22. Wood makes use of Catharine Beecher's controversial figures concerning the prevalence of female diseases, published in her 1855 book, *Letters to the People on Health and Happiness* (Harper & Brothers, Publishers, 1855).

28. Isabella Beecher Hooker to John Hooker, 1860 June 19. **Fiche 20/D11-E12.**

29. On this point, see Carroll Smith-Rosenberg, "The Hysterical Woman: Sex Roles and Role Conflict in 19th-Century America," *Social Research*, Vol. 39, No. 4 (Winter, 1972), pp. 652-658.

30. Isabella Beecher Hooker to John Hooker, 1860 July 15. **Fiche 23/A6-B1.**

31. For an excellent analysis of this antebellum infighting, see Aileen Kraditor, *Means and Ends in American Abolitionism* (New York: Vintage Books, 1967), especially pp. 39-77.

32. Eleanor Flexner, *Century of Struggle: The Women's Rights Movement in the United States* (Cambridge: The Belknap Press of Harvard University Press, 1967), pp. 80-81. This period is also covered in Elizabeth Cady Stanton, Susan B. Anthony, and Matilda Joslyn Gage, *The History of Woman Suffrage* (New York: Fowler & Welles, 1881), Vol. I.

33. Isabella Beecher Hooker to Henry Ward Beecher, 1861 December 22 & 23. **Fiche 25/B5-C2.**

34. Alice S. Rossi, ed., *John Stuart Mill and Harriet Taylor Mill: Essays on Sex Equality* (Chicago: University of Chicago Press, 1970), pp. 43, 100. In her introductory essay, Rossi effectively discredits the popular misconception that John rather than Harriet wrote this article and provides a revisionist (and convincing) interpretation of both the nature of their controversial personal relationship and the unique terms of their literary collaboration. On this last point, see especially pp. 41-43.

35. Isabella Beecher Hooker, *A Mother's Letters to a Daughter on Woman Suffrage* (Hartford: Press of Case, Lockwood & Brainard, 1870), p. 19.

36. Two letters written during this visit are extremely informative. See Isabella Beecher Hooker to John Hooker, 1862 November 26 & 27 and 1862 December 2. **Fiche 26/B10-C3** and **Fiche 26/D4-11.** The former provides a moving account of a Thanksgiving dinner in an army barracks for 1000 freedmen, while the latter includes a vivid description of President Lincoln's personal appearance and speaking manner.

37. Isabella's 1864 letters (**Fiche 28** and **Fiche 29**) describing Hilton Head, South Carolina, provide a contemporaneous account of this unique community, which Willie Lee Rose has analyzed in her admirable study, *Rehearsal for Reconstruction: The Port Royal Experiment* (New York: Oxford University Press, 1976).

38. *A Mother's Letters to a Daughter on Woman Suffrage*, pp. 4, 11-12, 22-23.

39. Ida Husted Harper, *The Life and Work of Susan B. Anthony* (Indianapolis: The Bowen-Merrill Company, 1898), Vol. I, pp. 293-294. Anthony later maintained that she always spoke *before* Train, advocating Negro *and* woman suffrage. Only then, according to her account, did he insist "that it would be one of the grossest outrages to give suffrage to the black man and not to the white woman," p. 292. For a sample of Train's inimitable rhetoric, see the advertisement that he enclosed with his letter to Elizabeth Cady Stanton of 1870 May 22. **Fiche 141/D13-E1.**

40. Ellen Carol DuBois, A New Life: The Development of an American Woman Suffrage Movement, 1860-1869, Diss. Northwestern University 1975, p. xi. Cornell University Press has recently published DuBois's dissertation under the title *Feminism and Suffrage: The Emergence of an Independent Women's Movement in America, 1848-1869.*

41. Personal factors were also at issue. Anthony seems to have felt abandoned by Lucy Stone and Antoinette Blackwell's decision to marry; and she did not hesitate to let them know it, nor to warn them that each new baby would decrease their potential usefulness to the movement. See *The Life and Work of Susan B. Anthony*, Vol. I, pp. 128-129, 170-171, 177-178. Stone and Blackwell naturally resented Anthony's tactless remarks, especially since they contained some element of truth.

42. "The Last of the Beechers," pp. 294-295.

43. Isabella Beecher Hooker to Caroline Severance, 1869 August 27 & 29. **Fiche 41/D10-E12** and **Fiche 42/A2-9.**

44. Susan B. Anthony to Isabella Beecher Hooker, 1869 August 9 & 10. **Fiche 114/B10-C1.** Susan B. Anthony to Paulina Wright Davis, 1869 July or August. **Fiche 114/B2-5.**

45. Susan B. Anthony to Isabella Beecher Hooker, 1869 December 17. **Fiche 114/D9-E4.** Stanton was one of those who advised against this move. See Theodore Stanton and Harriet Stanton Blatch's biography of their mother, *Elizabeth Cady Stanton* (New York: Harper and Brothers, 1922), Vol. 2, pp. 123-124.

46. John Hooker prepared and presented the resolutions for this convention. For a brief account of the convention, see *The History of Woman Suffrage,* Vol. 3, pp. 321-324. It is worth noting that the original president of this organization was a man, the Reverend Nathaniel J. Burton, and that Harriet Beecher Stowe was listed as one of its vice presidents. For Stanton's humorous reaction to Isabella's preoccupation with propriety, see Elizabeth Cady Stanton to Isabella Beecher Hooker, 1869 September 23. **Fiche 137/C4-9.**

47. Caroline Severance to Isabella Beecher Hooker, 1869 c. August 17. **Fiche 135/C5-14.**

48. Henry Brown Blackwell to Isabella Beecher Hooker, 1869 December 1. **Fiche 120/C11-14.** Also, Isabella Beecher Hooker to Mary Rice Livermore, 1869 November 15. Three copies of this letter exist, each with slight variations of text. **Fiche 42/B12-C6, Fiche 42/C7-12,** and **Fiche 42/C13-D6.**

49. Isabella Beecher Hooker to Henry Brown Blackwell, 1869 December 1; Susan B. Anthony to Isabella Beecher Hooker, 1871 March 5; and Isabella Beecher Hooker to Susan Howard, 1870 January 2. **Fiche 42/D7-10, Fiche 116/A2-10,** and **Fiche 43/A2-B5.**

50. Elizabeth Cady Stanton to Isabella Beecher Hooker, 1871 January 3. **Fiche 138/A13-B2.**

51. DuBois, p. xiv.

52. Isabella Beecher Hooker to Alice Hooker Day, 1868 November 8. **Fiche 40/C4-9.** In "Woman Suffrage as an Alternative to the Beecher Ministry," Anne Farnam also emphasizes the importance of the life cycle stage. See *Portraits of a Nineteenth Century Family*, p. 86.

53. Isabella Beecher Hooker to John Stuart Mill, 1869 August 9. **Fiche 41/D4-9.** Also, John Stuart Mill to Isabella Beecher Hooker, 1869 September 13, John Stuart Mill Collection, Yale University Library. Mill's response, which could not be included in the microfiche edition because of limitations imposed on the scope of the project, can be found in Yale's collection of his papers. Both sides of this exchange were published by Isabella in *Womanhood: Its Sanctities and Fidelities* (Boston: Lee and Shepard Publishers, 1873), pp. 28-37.

54. When Isabella speaks of "woman," she is not referring to women as they already are but to an ideal, the type towards which women are (or should be) evolving.

55. According to Kraditor, this analogy provided turn-of-the-century women such as Florence Kelley and Jane Addams with a justification of and a blueprint for their entry into politics, settlement work, and other reform-related activities. See Aileen Kraditor, *The Ideas of the Woman Suffrage Movement: 1890-1920* (Garden City: Anchor Books, 1965), especially pp. 51-55. In her third chapter Kraditor contends that the 1890s saw a shift in pro-suffrage arguments "from justice to expediency." Isabella's papers and the suffrage correspondence in this project

suggest not only that this shift may have occurred much earlier but also that both types of argument could be endorsed simultaneously by an individual or group.

56. Woodhull was fond of "firsts." She became the first woman to run for president of the United States when she accepted the Equal Rights Party nomination in 1872, and she was the first to publish Karl Marx's *Communist Manifesto* in America. Her memorial to the Judiciary Committee has been reprinted in the document section of Ann F. and Andrew M. Scott, *One Half the People: The Fight for Woman Suffrage* (New York: J. B. Lippincott Co., 1975), pp. 75-80.

57. Isabella later included this speech in *The Constitutional Rights of the Women of the United States* (Hartford: The Case, Lockwood, & Brainard Co., 1900), pp. 27-30. Her early nativist views eventually resurfaced. In regard to Olympia Brown's intention to use her own study of census figures as a new justification for woman suffrage, see Isabella Beecher Hooker to Alice Hooker Day, 1889 February 5 & 6. **Fiche 63/C4-D1.**

58. After weeks of testimony, McFarland was not only acquitted but also granted custody of the couple's child. I am grateful to Professor Mara Mayor of The University of Connecticut, Hartford, for sharing with me an unpublished paper on the trial in which she links it to the Beecher-Tilton scandal. For Stanton's interpretation of the significance of the incident, see her letter to Isabella Beecher Hooker of 1870 May 29. **Fiche 137/D3-E10.** There she compares the issues raised by the McFarland trial to the growing controversy in England over the Contagious Diseases Acts.

59. Isabella Beecher Hooker to Susan B. Anthony, 1871 March 11 & 14. **Fiche 44/D7-E14.** See Harriet Beecher Stowe, *Lady Byron Vindicated* (Boston: Fields, Osgood, & Co., 1870). In a letter to Isabella Beecher Hooker dated 1869 September 1, Stanton offered Mrs. Stowe the sympathy of someone who knew all too well what unjustified public abuse was like. **Fiche 137/B4-7.** Stanton also supported Stowe's position in an editorial in *The Revolution*. Quite a large portion of the suffrage-related correspondence in this project pertains to the local and national reactions to Isabella's relationship with Woodhull. See, for example, the 1871 letters of Phebe Hanaford and Sara B. Stearns, in which they plead with Isabella to save herself by breaking once and for all with Woodhull. **Fiche 133/A3-B1.** Other suffragists such as Anthony, Stanton, Edward M. Davis, and Belva Lockwood respected Isabella's decision to support Woodhull. See Edward M. Davis to Isabella Beecher Hooker, 1871 April 8 and 1871 June 12. **Fiche 129/B9-12** and **Fiche 129/B13-C1.** Also, Belva Lockwood to Isabella Beecher Hooker, 1871 June 17. **Fiche 134/B10-13.** For additional light on the nature of the charges against Woodhull, see Whitelaw Reid's letter to Isabella's neighbor, Charles Dudley Warner, 1871 October 13. **Fiche 135/A2-5.**

60. *The Nation,* Vol. 9 (1869), p. 387. Such statements should undercut the stereotypical view of John Hooker, fostered by Marie Caskey and others, as a passive and increasingly henpecked man badgered by his domineering wife into giving reluctant support to suffrage and spiritualism, two movements whose lack of propriety supposedly offended him.

61. Isabella Beecher Hooker to Anna C. Savery, 1871 November 12 & 18; to Olympia Brown, 1872 February 14; and to Elizabeth Cady Stanton, 1872 May 12. **Fiche 46/C3-12, Fiche 47/B2-9,** and **Fiche 47/D9-E1.** The correspondence between Hooker and Stanton suggests that they became extremely close during the period between the spring of 1871 and the end of 1872, possibly as a result of their mutual defense of Victoria Woodhull. One letter from Stanton to Hooker even refers to Isabella as "beloved," quite an unusual term of endearment for Stanton. Isabella seems to have brought this period of deep intimacy to an abrupt halt in late fall of 1872 by violating a confidence. For Stanton's tantalizing but somewhat obscure reproach to Isabella, see Elizabeth Cady Stanton to Isabella Beecher Hooker, 1872 November 19. **Fiche 139/E2-5.**

62. For a stark and moving personal response from a farmer's wife in Norfolk, Connecticut, to Isabella's statewide campaign, see Mrs. S. H. Graves to Isabella Beecher Hooker, 1871 October 24. **Fiche 132/D7-10.**

63. The standard accounts of the scandal are somewhat flip in tone and markedly slanted. See Emanie Sach's biography of Woodhull, *"The Terrible Siren"* (New York: Harper & Brothers Publishers, 1928) and Paxton Hibben, *Henry Ward Beecher: An American Portrait* (New York: George H. Doran Co., 1927).

64. Elizabeth Cady Stanton to Isabella Beecher Hooker, 1873 November 3. **Fiche 140/A8-B2.**

65. Isabella Beecher Hooker to Olympia Brown, 1873 November 8; to Alice Hooker Day, c. 1874; and to Ned Hooker, 1874 July 21. **Fiche 49/B8-11, Fiche 49/C6-9,** and **Fiche 50/C12-D5.**

66. The most mysterious and unusual of these letters is one from a Mrs. M. J. Judson to Isabella Beecher Hooker dated 1875 May 4. **Fiche 133/E5-9.** The tone and text of this letter imply that

Mrs. Judson regarded herself as one of the "fallen women" for whom Isabella had publicly expressed tolerance.

67. *Womanhood: Its Sanctities and Fidelities*, pp. 18, 43. See Isabella Beecher Hooker to Mary Porter Chamberlin, 1874 October 2; 1874 October 15; and 1874 November 5. **Fiche 50/E4-5, Fiche 50/E6-13,** and **Fiche 51/A2-9.** In these letters Isabella explicitly links her role in the scandal with the mounting assault on the double standard.

68. Diary, 1876, Isabella Beecher Hooker, pp. 2, 85, The Connecticut Historical Society. **Fiche 100/D5** and **Fiche 101/E12.** See, also, Isabella Beecher Hooker to Alice Hooker Day, 1889 August 22, in which she reminisces about this event. **Fiche 66/B14-C7.**

69. See, for example, Isabella Beecher Hooker to Ned Hooker, 1875 October 26 and 1875 December 7 & 9. **Fiche 52/A2-5** and **Fiche 52/A7-B4.**

70. For a discussion of spiritualist phenomena that were studied by and became familiar to both Isabella and John Hooker, see his long chapter on the subject in *Some Reminiscences of a Long Life*, pp. 247-265.

71. R. Laurence Moore, *In Search of White Crows: Spiritualism, Parapsychology, and American Culture* (New York: Oxford University Press, 1977) and Sydney Ahlstrom, *A Religious History of the American People* (New Haven: Yale University Press, 1972), pp. 489-490.

72. Regarding Wallace, see, for example, Isabella Beecher Hooker to Alice Hooker Day, 1889 July 1. **Fiche 65/D2-13.** While Moore and others claim that spiritualism suffered a severe decline from the 1870s on, by the late 1880s Isabella would be finding that "nearly all the women I meet are more or less interested in some form of spiritual healing. It is simply amazing how the domain of the spirit is extending itself...." Isabella Beecher Hooker to Alice Hooker Day, 1888 April 10. **Fiche 60/A2-9.**

73. Moore, pp. 83, 95.

74. Henry Eugene Burton seems to have sympathized quite strongly with Henry Ward Beecher. Yale University's collection of Beecher's papers includes typescripts of three letters that Henry Ward wrote to Isabella counseling her to remain silent. Each of these letters was copied by Burton, and it is quite likely that his hostility towards Isabella can be explained, at least in part, by the scandal. See, also, Isabella Beecher Hooker's extract, taken from a copy of John Hooker's 1878 letter to John Calvin Day, in which Hooker defends his wife's role in the scandal. Memo, Isabella Beecher Hooker, 1884 February 10. **Fiche 106/E11-13.**

75. See, for example, Diary, 1876, Isabella Beecher Hooker, pp. 6, 41, 53, 86, The Connecticut Historical Society. **Fiche 100/D9, Fiche 101/B8, Fiche 101/C8,** and **Fiche 101/E13.** Also, Diary, 1878, Isabella Beecher Hooker, pp. 106, 114. **Fiche 106/C10** and **Fiche 106/D5.** On the subject of expected apologies, see Diary, 1876, Isabella Beecher Hooker, pp. 133-134, 140, The Connecticut Historical Society. **Fiche 102/D5-6** and **Fiche 102/D12.**

76. Diary, 1876, Isabella Beecher Hooker, p. 17, The Connecticut Historical Society. **Fiche 100/E6.**

77. Diary, 1876, Isabella Beecher Hooker, pp. 87-88, The Connecticut Historical Society. **Fiche 101/E14** and **Fiche 102/A2.**

78. For examples of the former, see Diary, 1876, Isabella Beecher Hooker, pp. 73, 74, 80-81, The Connecticut Historical Society. **Fiche 101/D14, Fiche 101/E1,** and **Fiche 101/E8-9.**

79. For example, see Diary, 1876, Isabella Beecher Hooker, pp. 201-202, The Connecticut Historical Society. **Fiche 103/D5-6.**

80. "Notes August 15, 1878 - December 1, 1878," Diary, 1878, Isabella Beecher Hooker, pp. 89-95, 67, 26. **Fiche 106/B7-13, Fiche 105/E9,** and **Fiche 105/B10.**

81. See, for example, Isabella Beecher Hooker to Alice Hooker Day, 1888 November 28. **Fiche 61/D14-E6.**

82. Isabella Beecher Hooker to Samuel Bowles, 1877 March 26, Samuel Bowles Papers, Yale University Library. **Fiche 86(a)/A2-13.**

83. Isabella Beecher Hooker to Alice Hooker Day, 1889 May 17. **Fiche 64/E2-12.** This letter also refers to the anti-suffrage role played by the liquor interests in Connecticut.

84. Isabella Beecher Hooker to Alice Hooker Day, 1890 February 28. **Fiche 69/A2-13.** For information regarding earlier overtures made to Susan B. Anthony, see Isabella Beecher Hooker to Alice Hooker Day, 1888 April 10. **Fiche 60/A2-9.**

85. Isabella Beecher Hooker to Alice Hooker Day, 1893 November 28. **Fiche 79/C12-D13.** This essay was first published in 1885. On the topic of Christian Science, see Isabella Beecher Hooker to Alice Hooker Day, 1893 December 30 and 1894 January 4. **Fiche 80/A2-5** and **Fiche 80/A10-B4.**

86. Isabella Beecher Hooker to Alice Hooker Day, 1889 March 5. **Fiche 63/D12-E13.**

BIBLIOGRAPHICAL NOTE

Three key factors have to be taken into account in evaluating the secondary sources on Isabella Beecher Hooker: the availability of primary sources, changing assumptions regarding "normal" female attitudes and behavior, and the relatively recent and long overdue emergence of American social history in general and women's history in particular as a legitimate field of scholarship. The earliest scholarly treatment of Mrs. Hooker's life and work, Kenneth Andrews's chapter on Isabella in his 1950 work, *Nook Farm: Mark Twain's Hartford Circle* (Cambridge: Harvard University Press), characterizes her as eccentric, hysterical, and neurotic. While Andrews had access to only one of Isabella's diaries and an extremely small portion of her letters, his highly unflattering portrait seems to have been significantly influenced by his reliance upon the papers of Mark Twain's close friend and neighbor, the Reverend Joseph Twitchell, who disliked Isabella intensely.

As Andrews's chapter also makes clear, Mrs. Hooker's involvement in spiritualism and her relationship with Victoria Woodhull have proved as disconcerting to posterity as they did to most of her family and friends; and, in this respect, Andrews is hardly alone. In an otherwise quite able biographical entry on Isabella Beecher Hooker in *Notable American Women* (Cambridge: Harvard University Press, 1971), Alice Felt Tyler displays some discomfort and obvious condescension when dealing with Isabella's role in the Beecher-Tilton scandal, her commitment to "the Spiritualist cult," and her millennial visions. Although Tyler relies primarily on secondary sources (including Andrews) and had access only to scattered Isabella Beecher Hooker letters belonging to the Schlesinger and Sophia Smith collections, she does present the researcher with a more balanced version of Mrs. Hooker's career.

Elsie Anne Farnam's unpublished master's thesis, Isabella Beecher Hooker as a Reformer: The Vote for Women or a Quest for Personal Power? (Storrs: The University of Connecticut, 1970), is the earliest full-length treatment of Isabella's career and the first study to draw upon The Stowe-Day Foundation's collection of Hooker manuscripts. While this thesis presents its subject as an essentially manipulative and domineering woman, Farnam shows greater sensitivity in her subsequent article, "Woman Suffrage as an Alternative to the Beecher Ministry: The Conversion of Isabella Beecher Hooker," which appears in *Portraits of a Nineteenth Century Family*, ed. by Earl A. French and Diana Royce (Hartford: The Stowe-Day Foundation, 1976). (See, also, Farnam's earlier article, "Isabella Beecher Hooker as a Woman Suffragist: A Centennial Frame of Reference," *Connecticut Review*, Vol. 5, No. 1 [October 1971].)

Marie Caskey's chapter on Isabella in *Chariot of Fire: Religion and the Beecher Family* (New Haven: Yale University Press, 1978) also draws largely (though not exclusively) upon the Foundation's collection of Hooker family papers. Despite an admirable command of the Beecher and Hooker manuscript material, Caskey seems unwilling to take spiritualism seriously as a variety of religious experience, nor does she explore the implications of Farnam's contention that Isabella's involvement in the suffrage movement can be seen as a religious equivalent or "alternative to the Beecher ministry."

It should be stressed that a significant portion of the suffrage-related correspondence that appears in this project did not become available to researchers until 1974, when it was donated anonymously to The Stowe-Day Foundation. Given the existence of this new material and the current level of interest in women's history, the time seems ripe for a reappraisal of Isabella Beecher Hooker's complex character and her unique role in the woman suffrage movement and allied reforms. It is hoped that the publication of her papers in microform, together with this printed guide, will serve as a catalyst for this reevaluation.

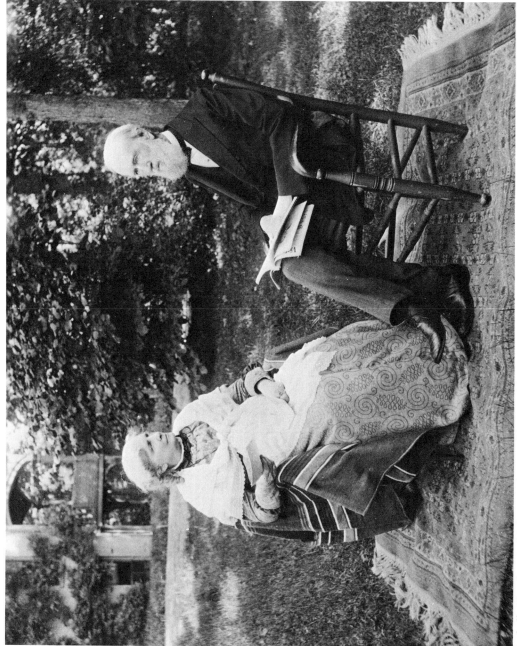

Isabella Beecher and John Hooker, Golden Wedding Anniversary, 1891

SCOPE OF THE PROJECT

It should be stated at the outset that the Isabella Beecher Hooker Project is not a definitive edition of the papers of Isabella Beecher Hooker. The National Historical Publications and Records Commission awarded The Stowe-Day Foundation a grant to produce a microform edition of its collection of Mrs. Hooker's manuscripts and the correspondence of 30 of her national and local co-workers in the woman suffrage movement. Although a nationwide search for correspondence written by and to Mrs. Hooker was not provided for, we were able to locate and film a relatively small number of Isabella Beecher Hooker letters and one diary at other institutions. These items were brought to our attention early on in the project and belong to collections that had already been fully catalogued.[1]

To the best of our knowledge, the present project does include the majority of Mrs. Hooker's extant manuscripts. It is hoped one of the by-products of this project will be that scholars and librarians at other institutions will be stimulated to communicate with the Foundation regarding the location and nature of any additional Hooker material.

In addition to owning letters and documents by and photographs of Mrs. Hooker, The Stowe-Day Foundation houses a large body of manuscript material written by or relating to Isabella Beecher Hooker's husband, children, parents, and siblings. (See Identifications of Correspondents for relevant names and dates.) This material documents the range of the intimate and at times conflict laden relationships between Mrs. Hooker and her large family, including their various responses to her ideas and activities in behalf of woman suffrage and other related reforms. John Hooker's papers are especially important in this respect, for he not only supported his wife's involvement in the woman's rights movement but also drafted bills and wrote articles and essays in which he applied his keen legal mind to the defense of both woman's rights and individual suffrage activists.

Ideally, all of these family papers should be included to complete the story of Isabella Beecher Hooker's life and work. Yet the volume of material on the Hookers and the Beechers, a consequence of the combined size of the two families as well as the frequency with which they corresponded with one another, precluded the possibility of incorporating these manuscripts into the microfiche edition. For the same reason, a thorough search for suffrage-related correspondence proved to be impracticable. Researchers who are eager to learn more about either the domestic life of the Hookers and the Beechers or their contributions to a wide variety of reform movements (as well as many other aspects of nineteenth-century American culture) will want to read the manuscript material presented here in microform in conjunction with the growing list of secondary material on the various members of the two families.[2] Scholars may also wish to consult the unpublished material at The Stowe-Day Foundation and other libraries.

Although project guidelines excluded published works by Isabella Beecher Hooker, we decided to film the title pages of works written by Mrs. Hooker that are in the possession of The Stowe-Day Foundation. However, it should be stressed that the Foundation's collection does not include copies of all her publications.

Working within the limitation that only Mrs. Hooker's manuscripts and suffrage-related correspondence by nonfamily members would be filmed, we proceeded to locate all Isabella Beecher Hooker manuscripts owned by the Foundation, including joint letters (letters written by her in conjunction with one or more family members or friends). We searched not only the collection that bears Mrs. Hooker's name but also the Katharine S. Day Collection, the Gillette Collection, the William Gillette Collection, the Joseph K. Hooker Collection, the Helen D. Perkins Collection, the Mary K. Talcott Collection, and the White Collection. Each of these name collections had been catalogued by the Foundation staff prior to the beginning of the project,[3] and we were able to identify approximately 1,240 items, including bound volumes and photographs.

However, in the case of suffrage-related correspondents,[4] our task became more difficult. We were faced with the possibility that correspondence with a significant suffrage-related content written by a relatively obscure individual (or by a well-known person not usually associated with the controversy over woman suffrage) would slip through our fingers if we limited ourselves only to letters written by those individuals previously identified by the Foundation staff as national or local suffragists. We were thus faced with the task of searching the above mentioned name collections in order to locate all suffrage-related correspondence written by nonfamily members. The search proved fruitful, for we were able to identify more than 100 individuals who wrote suffrage-related correspondence. This represents a significant increase over the 30 activists identified in the original proposal, which focused primarily on the correspondence of well-known figures, such as Susan B. Anthony (103 items), Olympia Brown (61 items), and Elizabeth Cady Stanton (52 items). We have thus been able to provide the researcher with a less strictly defined but a much richer and more varied sample of correspondence written by men and women who were allies, sympathizers, or opponents in the nineteenth-century struggle to achieve woman suffrage.

In order to document further the range of Isabella Beecher Hooker's commitment to suffrage and related reforms, we decided to film circulars and broadsides, which covered a wide variety of woman's rights issues, found in the Isabella Beecher Hooker Collection. However, we excluded a large selection of newspaper clippings, many of them annotated and suffrage-related, because of limitations of time and space. With these additions, then, the completed project totals just over 1,700 items.

Footnotes

1. The Project Director wishes to express her gratitude to Ellen DuBois, Associate Professor of History, State University of New York at Buffalo, for helping us to locate Isabella Beecher Hooker letters in the Woodhull-Martin papers at Southern Illinois University at Carbondale.
2. While the secondary material on the Hookers is quite modest, the published sources on the Beecher family are almost as voluminous as the manuscript material and much more accessible. In addition to the multiple studies of individual family members (most notably Lyman and Henry Ward Beecher, Harriet Beecher Stowe, and, more recently, Kathryn Kish Sklar's biography of Catharine Beecher), see Marie Caskey's new study of the theology of the entire family, *Chariot of Fire* (New Haven: Yale University Press, 1978).
3. The term "name collection" refers to a group of manuscripts that belonged to or were donated by the individual whose name the collection bears. After filming had begun, several additional Isabella Beecher Hooker letters were discovered by the Foundation staff in the course of cataloguing the Warner and Foote Collections.
4. The determination of what constitutes suffrage-related items involved editorial discretion. A significant portion of this correspondence was neither written by nor addressed to Isabella Beecher Hooker, although much of it was part of the Isabella Beecher Hooker Collection.

EDITING AND FILMING PROCEDURES

A. Editing Procedures

Although Isabella Beecher Hooker's papers were catalogued prior to the beginning of the project, several different individuals had worked on the various name collections. It soon became apparent that there were inconsistencies of procedure as well as a small body of undated items. We therefore felt that it was necessary to insure consistency by reviewing the identification of all items (including those from other repositories), cross-checking all dates against postmarks (when available) and with the perpetual calendar, and regularizing the use of cataloguing symbols (see table below).

When information identifying the sender or the recipient of a letter did not appear on the item itself but could be ascertained on the basis of content, handwriting, or an accompanying envelope, we provided this information on the target in brackets. The same is true for the date of each item in the project. Dates were bracketed in pencil on the items themselves when they did not appear at the head of the letter, were not entered in the hand of the author, or were corrected by us. For the purpose of this project, then, the use of brackets alone does *not* indicate uncertainty of attribution. When we were not reasonably certain about either the identity of a correspondent or the accuracy of a date, we indicated this fact by bracketing the information and inserting a question mark within the brackets.

Textual Devices and Descriptive Symbols

ALS Autographed letter, signed (For Isabella Beecher Hooker, the signature "Mother" constitutes an ALS.)

ALI Autographed letter, initialed

AL Autographed letter, unsigned (Author's name appears in brackets on target.)

LS Letter, signed (Written in a hand other than the signature bearer's; differs from an ALS (cy) in that we are presupposing that the signature bearer had directed another person to write the letter.)

ACS Autographed card, signed

ACI Autographed card, initialed

AC Autographed card, unsigned

ANS Autographed note, signed

ANI Autographed note, initialed

AN Autographed note, unsigned (Notes have been so designated on the basis of their length or the fact that they were added at a later date to a letter written by another individual. Not to be confused with joint letters, letters coauthored by two or more individuals.)

TLS Typed letter, signed

TLI Typed letter, initialed

TL Typed letter, unsigned

DS Document, signed (Generally a legal item or a signed piece of noncorrespondence.)

D Document, unsigned (Also used here to designate fragments or items of a miscellaneous nature.)

MSS Manuscript, signed (Handwritten text, generally of a literary nature.)

MS Manuscript, unsigned

L   Form letter

p   page

pp   pages

ENV envelope

ENC enclosure

(cy) copy

c.   circa

n.p. no place (Place unknown.)

n.y. no year

n.d. no date

B. Division of the Project into Four Series

To facilitate the layout and filming of the various types of manuscripts encompassed within the project, we divided the materials into four sections or series.

Series I Correspondence from all collections, including joint letters, written by Isabella Beecher Hooker from 1837-1860, arranged chronologically. **Fiche 2-24** [**Fiche 1** contains transcripts of early Isabella Beecher Hooker letters that proved difficult to read in microform.]

Series II Correspondence from all collections, including joint letters, written by Isabella Beecher Hooker from 1861-1906, arranged chronologically. **Fiche 25-86 (a)** [Undated items and errata for Series I and II appear on **Fiche 86** and **86(a)**.]

The division between Series I and II is intended to correspond roughly to the beginning of Isabella Beecher Hooker's active involvement in the woman's rights movement. Although even her earliest extant letters indicate an incipient interest in the woman question, 1861 marks a turning point of sorts.

Series III Documents from all collections written by Isabella Beecher Hooker from 1834-1906, arranged chronologically. **Fiche 87-113** This series includes diaries, autograph albums, memoranda books, scrapbooks, literary manuscripts, miscellaneous documents, and envelopes addressed or annotated by Isabella Beecher Hooker as well as the title pages of published works written by Isabella Beecher Hooker. [Photographs of Isabella Beecher Hooker owned by The Stowe-Day Foundation also appear chronologically on **Fiche 113,** where they are followed by errata for Series III.]

Series IV Suffrage-related letters written by correspondents other than Isabella Beecher Hooker, filmed alphabetically by sender from ALLEN, GEORGE R. through WRIGHT, MARTHA COFFIN and arranged chronologically for each individual correspondent. **Fiche 114-142;** followed by suffrage-related circulars and broadsides, also filmed in chronological sequence. **Fiche 143** and **144**

An alphabetical rather than a strictly chronological arrangement was employed in Series IV because Isabella Beecher Hooker is not always the recipient of this suffrage-related correspondence. In many cases, these letters had been passed on to Isabella Beecher Hooker or various other members of the woman suffrage movement after they were read by the intended recipient. On occasion, the recipient herself or a subsequent reader added comments, a note, or even an entirely new letter to the original document. In such cases we have tried to determine priority in time and have filmed the letter under the name of the original sender. Additional notes or letters are designated as such on the appropriate target as well as in the index, where they are listed along with the fiche number of the original letter.

C. Use of Chronologies

Series I and II begin with chronologies that outline important events in Isabella Beecher Hooker's life during the period covered by the letters that follow them. These chronologies are by no means exhaustive. They are intended to provide the researcher with a set of coordinates within which to situate the events and ideas described in and embodied by the letters. We have refilmed these chronologies at the beginning of Series III along with a chronological list of those publications written by Isabella Beecher Hooker that are owned by The Stowe-Day Foundation. (The title pages have also been filmed as part of Series III in order to alert the researcher to the existence of this printed material and to provide a sense of its chronological relation to Isabella Beecher Hooker's unpublished documents.)

For several reasons no attempt was made to provide a chronology for Series IV, the section of the project that contains suffrage-related letters written by correspondents other than Isabella Beecher Hooker. In the first place, the labeling of events as important varies greatly according to which wing of the woman suffrage movement is being consulted. We attempted to avoid the built-in bias involved when the six-volume *History of Woman Suffrage,* coauthored by members of the more radical New York wing, is relied upon.

Secondly, not all of the items included in this series constitute suffrage correspondence in the strict sense of the word, that is — not all of these letters deal directly or exclusively with the struggle to win the vote for women. Some items refer to the Beecher-Tilton scandal, the Contagious Diseases Acts, the day-to-day hardships of relatively anonymous women who appealed to Isabella Beecher Hooker for advice, and other matters that fall under the wider rubric of woman's rights. We have therefore preferred to designate this entire body of material as "suffrage-related." We urge researchers who desire detailed background information to consult the growing number of secondary sources on the woman suffrage movement in the United States, one of the most respected of which is Eleanor Flexner's *Century of Struggle* (Cambridge: Belknap Press, Harvard University, 1959).

D. Format of the Microfiche and Use of Targets

There are 145 fiche cards in the project, numbering 1-144 and including **Fiche 86(a).** Each fiche consists of five rows down (A through E) and fourteen columns across (1-14) for a total of 70 frames. On each card, one or more of these frames has been reserved for target information. The term "target" here refers to a list of all those documents that appear on a given fiche card. With the exception of **Fiche 1** (which begins with a resolution chart) and **Fiche 2, 25,** and **87** (each of which begins with the chronologies for Series I, II, and III respectively), targets always appear in the first frame or frames of each fiche card (position A1 or A1-3).

Each target entry contains the following information: the name of the sender and recipient (or author, in the case of documents and published material), the date on which the item was written (or published), a description of the item in terms of its type (i.e., an ALS or a DS), the number of pages and the existence of an envelope or an enclosure (where applicable), the place where the item was written (when known), and The Stowe-Day Foundation name collection to which it belongs, if *other than the Isabella Beecher Hooker Collection*. In the case of items obtained from other libraries, the name of both the institution and the collection have been provided.

Target entries for diaries and other bound manuscript volumes follow a slightly different format. The inclusive dates of the entire volume appear along with the title on the first line of the target entry. When an item spans two or more fiche cards, the second line of the target entry indicates the inclusive dates of the portion of the volume that actually appears on the particular fiche. Similarly, the number of pages indicated on the third line of the target entry refers only to the actual number of pages that appear on the individual fiche card. When this number does not correspond to the total number of pages in the volume, this information has been provided in an editorial comment following the target entry, along with a description of any special features.

Editorial comments have also been inserted to indicate the condition of a stained, torn, or otherwise damaged item. Special targets precede or accompany individual items when necessary, as in the case of photographs, miscellaneous items, and errata. A sample target entry for a letter and a document written by Isabella Beecher Hooker appear below:

LETTER

IBH to HONORABLE ADELBERT AMES

1871 April 15

LS 4 pp HARTFORD [CT] D7-10

Sophia Smith Coll.

Smith College

Y Ames (Box 12)

DOCUMENT

QUOTATIONS COPIED AND
SIGNED BY IBH

1879 JANUARY

DS [ENV + 3 ITEMS] n.p. E6-7

In order to save time and space, we have employed the two-letter abbreviations developed by the United States Postal Service for state names. We have also substituted the following abbreviations for the full names of individuals and The Stowe-Day Foundation collections that appear most frequently in the targets:

SBA	Susan B. Anthony
OB	Olympia Brown
IBH	Isabella Beecher Hooker
JH	John Hooker
ECS	Elizabeth Cady Stanton
VCW	Victoria Claflin Woodhull
KSD Coll.	Katharine S. Day Collection
JKH Coll.	Joseph K. Hooker Collection

Note: IBH Collection is assumed if no other name collection is specified on the target entry.

E. Explanation of Alphanumeric Characters Used in Targets and Index

The alphanumeric character that appears to the right of the state abbreviation in each target entry indicates the frame or inclusive frames in which the item appears. In the sample target entry found above, for example, D7-10 indicates that the letter from IBH to Adelbert Ames begins on frame D7 and ends with frame D10. (See the diagram below.) These alphanumeric characters have also been used in the index, where they appear in conjunction with the appropriate fiche card number. Thus this letter, which can be found on **Fiche 45,** frames D7-10, is listed in the index in the following manner:

Hooker, Isabella Beecher
    to AMES, ADELBERT
    1871 April 15   45/D7-10

THE ISABELLA BEECHER HOOKER PROJECT
IBH Correspondence: 1871 Mar 15 - 1871 Aug 11
© 1979 The Stowe-Day Foundation   Series II: Card 45

	1	2	3	4	5	6	7	8	9	10	11	12	13	14
A														
B														
C														
D														
E														

F. Filming Procedures and Suggested Viewing Equipment

This project was filmed by Yale Photographic Services at a 24x reduction ratio. All letters from other repositories are photocopies. The diary owned by The Connecticut Historical Society and all manuscripts owned by The Stowe-Day Foundation have been filmed from the original, with the exception of extremely faint items (or pages of items) and oversized items.

After filming for Series I and II was completed, we determined that nine early IBH letters were extremely difficult to read in microform because of cross-hatching (lines that have been written perpendicular to and overlapping the main body of the text), faintness of ink, the smallness of IBH's handwriting, or a combination of these. Transcripts of these items were therefore typed and filmed on **Fiche 1** (an explanation of symbols employed by the transcriber appears on **Fiche 1,** frame A2.) We attempted to anticipate this problem in Series IV by providing typed transcripts of those letters that we considered most likely to prove difficult or impossible to read in microform. These transcripts were filmed immediately following the original letter.

When oversized originals could not be accommodated by a slight readjustment of the reduction ratio, one of two procedures was followed: a photocopy of the item was made and then cut and pasted to 8½" × 11" size, or the item was slightly reduced in size by means of photoreduction.

In order to limit the number of frames devoted to target information, legal size paper was used when target entries proved to be too lengthy to fit on two 8½" × 11" sheets. A microfiche reader with an 11" × 11" or an 11"× 14" screen will therefore minimize the necessity for scanning these larger fiche images. Because some letters bear cross-hatching, we also recommend the use of a microfiche reader equipped with image-rotation capacity for maximum viewing ease.

All page numbers that appear in brackets on documents were added by the project staff in order to insure that items were filmed in a right reading position and in their proper page order. Enclosures have been numbered consecutively and filmed immediately following the item with which they were found. Page numbers that do not appear in brackets were entered by the correspondent, recipient, or author.

When an envelope was found with a letter, it was filmed just prior to or in the same frame as the first page of the letter that it accompanied. (Miscellaneous envelopes addressed by IBH or annotated in her hand were filmed together near the end of Series III.)

Bound volumes containing pressed flowers, photographs, newspaper clippings, and/or other enclosures have been filmed as found. When necessary, editorial notes were added to indicate any peculiarities in IBH's manner of making entries and to provide the researcher with a better sense of the physical format of the item.

LIST OF ERRATA IN THE MICROFICHE

I. Because of late discovery, acquisition after layout, or errors in layout, the following items appear in special errata sections for each series.

Series I and II

Fiche	Item	Date
86/C11-D5	IBH to Harriet Scoville	1860 Feb 13
86/D6-13	IBH to Josephine W. Griffing	[1870?] Nov 26
86/D14-E3	[IBH] to Alice (Hooker) Day	1871 Aug 6
86/E4	IBH to Leonard Bacon	1873 Mar 26
86/E5-6	IBH to JH	[1874 Mar 23]
86/E7-8	IBH to Samuel Bowles	1876 Jan 5
86(a)/A2-13	IBH to Samuel Bowles	1877 Mar 26
86(a)/A14-B1	IBH to [Samuel Bowles]	1877 Mar 26
86(a)/B2	IBH to [U.S. Congress]	1878 "Wed Feb 13"
86(a)/B3-4	IBH to Harriet [Hawley]	1886 Feb 13
86(a)/B5-14	[IBH] and [JH] to Alice (Hooker) Day	1889 Aug 4 & 6
86(a)/C1-4	[IBH] to Alice (Hooker) Day	1889 Aug 29
86(a)/C5-8	[IBH] to [Alice (Hooker) Day]	[1898?] Sep 21
86(a)/C9-12	[IBH] to George H. Warner	[1900 May 30]

Series III

Fiche	Item	Date
113/C8-D1	MS	[1874-78]
113/D2-12	Notes Re. Currency	[1876 Jun ?]
113/D13-14	Notes on Family	[Before 1890]

II. The following items were filmed out of chronological sequence.

Series II

Fiche	Item	Date
63/D12-E13	IBH and JH to Alice (Hooker) Day	1889 Mar 5
74/A13-B12	IBH to Alice (Hooker) Day	*1891 Apr 18
73/D13-E6	IBH to Alice (Hooker) Day	1891 May 21
76/B4-5	IBH to Alice (Hooker) Day	1891 Dec 2
75/B3-4	IBH to Alice (Hooker) Day	1891 Dec 21

III. The following items contain various editorial errors.
(All the below items were written in the hand of Alice (Hooker) Day, not that of IBH.)

112/C13-D2	Poem	
112/D3-5	Poem	
112/B3-9	Description of Birds	

(The actual letter was incorrectly labeled "1871 May 21.")

48/D10-13	IBH to Alice (Hooker) Day	1873 May 21

(This letter was filmed twice.)

82/B6-9	IBH to Alice (Hooker) Day	1898 Jun 29
82/B10-13	IBH to Alice (Hooker) Day	1898 Jun 29

(This letter was incorrectly dated 1898 Jul 18 and assigned **Fiche 82/B10-13** on the target.)

82/B14-C3	JH and IBH to Alice (Hooker) Day	1898 Jul 16

(This letter was not filmed.)

82/B14-C3	IBH to Alice (Hooker) Day	1898 Jul 20

(The target errors for the below items are herein corrected.)

38/D3-10	IBH to Alice (Hooker) Day	1860 Jul 1
22/A3-9	IBH to JH	1868 May 13
Target for 80, Item 13	JH and IBH to Alice (Hooker) Day	1894 May 26

Susan B. Anthony at her desk in Rochester, New York; among the photographs is one of Isabella Beecher Hooker

Sophia Smith Collection, Smith College

IDENTIFICATION OF CORRESPONDENTS

These identifications provide brief background information on the correspondents included in The Isabella Beecher Hooker Project. They highlight, where applicable, the affiliations with and contributions to the woman suffrage movement of each correspondent.

The relationships among the Hooker and Beecher families and the members of Isabella Beecher Hooker's Hartford circle are complicated and confusing, involving, as they do, frequent intermarriages. Therefore, the relatives and/or neighbors of Mrs. Hooker are identified as follows: last name, first name or initial(s), maiden name in parentheses, husband's name; for example, STOWE, HARRIET (BEECHER), MRS. CALVIN ELLIS. Designating the maiden name and providing the husband's first name are designed to aid the researcher in sorting out these relationships. Moreover, this format facilitates the identification of women who figure in the project as correspondents both before and after marriage. The format also is intended to distinguish between persons with similar names, for example, DAY, ALICE (HOOKER), MRS. JOHN CALVIN and her daughter, JACKSON, ALICE (DAY), MRS. PERCY, both of whom appear in correspondence as ALICE DAY.

Because this format was arrived at after filming had been completed, the names appearing on the targets are not always exactly the same as those found in the identifications. The names used in the index, however, have been made consistent with this procedure.

Researchers able to provide additional information about any of the correspondents, including birth and death dates, are asked to write to The Isabella Beecher Hooker Project, The Stowe-Day Foundation, 77 Forest Street, Hartford CT 06105.

Alphabetical List of Correspondents
Fully capitalized names indicate correspondents.

1. ALLEN, GEORGE R.
   Secretary, Central National Committee, Equal Rights Party.
2. ALLEN, ROBERT (1837-1895)
   Close friend of the Hooker family. Isabella Beecher Hooker referred to Allen as her "adopted son."
3. AMES, ADELBERT (1835-1933)
   Union general; senator, Mississippi; governor, Mississippi; son-in-law of BENJAMIN BUTLER. Isabella Beecher Hooker wrote Ames regarding franking privileges.
4. ANTHONY, MARY S. (1827-1907)
   Younger sister of SUSAN B. ANTHONY. In 1848 Anthony attended the Seneca Falls Convention, at which she met ELIZABETH CADY STANTON. According to her sister's biographer, Ida Husted Harper, Anthony helped convince her sister, then a temperance worker, of the importance of woman's rights. She subsequently bolstered Susan B. Anthony's pioneering suffrage work by providing financial aid and encouragement.
5. ANTHONY, SUSAN B. (1820-1906)
   One of the most active and visible members of the woman suffrage movement for over fifty years. Together with her close friend and associate, ELIZABETH CADY STANTON, Anthony symbolized woman's rights in the popular mind for several generations. In 1868 PAULINA WRIGHT DAVIS introduced Isabella Beecher Hooker to Anthony and Stanton at the Newport Convention, after which Isabel-

la's prejudices were dispelled and a close working relationship among the three women was established. Anthony's strongest contribution to the suffrage movement resulted from her organizational and administrative abilities. She traveled throughout the United States lecturing and campaigning for the suffrage cause and pioneered the tactic of petitioning.

6. ATWOOD, MRS.
Unidentified acquaintance of Isabella Beecher Hooker; resident of Hartford, Connecticut.

7. AVERY, ALIDA C.
President, Colorado State Suffrage Association; physician. Avery was instrumental in bringing prominent Eastern activists to the West to help with suffrage campaigns.

8. AVERY, RACHEL FOSTER (1858-1919)
Corresponding secretary, National American Woman Suffrage Association; friend, traveling companion, and protégée of SUSAN B. ANTHONY. A daughter of JULIA MANUEL FOSTER and a member of a wealthy family, Avery frequently contributed funds to the woman suffrage movement. After marrying Cyrus Miller Avery in 1888, she continued as an active suffragist, organizing many conventions for the cause.

9. BACON, LEONARD (1802-1881)
Congregational minister; professor, Yale Divinity School; editor, *The Independent*; antislavery advocate; friend of LYMAN BEECHER.

10. BARBER, JOHN
Secretary, New Haven Woman Suffrage Association.

11. BEECHER, CATHARINE E. (1800-1878)
Half sister of Isabella Beecher Hooker; daughter of LYMAN BEECHER and Roxana (Foote) Beecher; known as "Cate." A pioneer in both higher education for women and domestic science, Beecher founded several schools, including the Hartford Female Seminary and the Western Female Institute (both of which Isabella attended). She wrote several popular books, including *A Treatise on Domestic Economy* (1841) and *The Domestic Receipt Book* (1846). Unlike Isabella, Beecher was opposed to woman suffrage and published her arguments in *Woman Suffrage and Woman's Profession* (1871).

12. BEECHER, ESTHER M. (1779-1855)
Aunt of Isabella Beecher Hooker; stepsister of LYMAN BEECHER. Beecher lived with her stepbrother's family during Isabella's childhood. Later she was a member of the Hartford household of her niece, MARY (BEECHER) PERKINS, at the same time as Isabella, who resided with the Perkins family while attending Hartford Female Seminary.

13. BEECHER, FRANCES (JOHNSON), MRS. JAMES (1832-1903)
Sister-in-law of Isabella Beecher Hooker; known as "Franke" or "Frankie." Beecher married James Beecher after the death of his first wife, Annie Beecher. She later married Frederick Beecher Perkins, son of MARY (BEECHER) PERKINS, following his divorce from Mary (Wescott) Perkins, thus becoming the stepmother of Charlotte (Perkins) Gilman, the social theorist.

14. BEECHER, GEORGE (1807-1843)
Half brother of Isabella Beecher Hooker; son of LYMAN BEECHER and Roxana (Foote) Beecher; Presbyterian minister. Although the death of Beecher from a gunshot wound may have been a suicide, the Beecher family always believed it to have been accidental.

15. BEECHER, HENRY WARD (1813-1887)

Half brother of Isabella Beecher Hooker; son of LYMAN BEECHER and Roxana (Foote) Beecher; Congregational minister; pastor, Plymouth Church, Brooklyn, New York. A supporter of many reforms, including woman suffrage, Beecher at one point served as president of the American Woman Suffrage Association. He later denounced Isabella for refusing to support publicly his claims of innocence in connection with the Beecher-Tilton scandal.

16. BEECHER, KATHARINE (EDES), MRS. WILLIAM (-1870)

Sister-in-law of Isabella Beecher Hooker; known as "Kate."

17. BEECHER, LYDIA (BEALS) JACKSON, MRS. LYMAN (1789-1869)

Stepmother of Isabella Beecher Hooker; third wife of LYMAN BEECHER.

18. BEECHER, LYMAN (1775-1863)

Father of Isabella Beecher Hooker; Presbyterian minister; reformer; educator. Beecher both reflected and influenced many of the major religious and cultural developments of mid-nineteenth-century America. He presided over a number of religious revivals in the several parishes he served in East Hampton, New York; Litchfield, Connecticut; Boston, Massachusetts; and Cincinnati, Ohio. During his tenure as the first president of Lane Theological Seminary in Cincinnati, he became embroiled in the controversy over slavery and advocated colonization rather than abolitionism. Among the reforms he lent his voice to were the temperance and anti-dueling causes. A strong and energetic personality, Beecher supervised the entry of all seven of his sons into the ministry and saw three of his daughters achieve national prominence.

19. BEECHER, MARY FRANCES (BEECHER), MRS. HENRY WARD (1873-1954)

Niece of Isabella Beecher Hooker; one of twin daughters adopted by James Beecher and FRANCES (JOHNSON) BEECHER. Beecher's husband may have been a distant relative, but he should not be confused with Isabella's half brother, HENRY WARD BEECHER.

20. BEECHER, THOMAS KINNICUT (1824-1900)

Brother of Isabella Beecher Hooker; son of LYMAN BEECHER and Harriet (Porter) Beecher; Congregational minister. Under the ministerial direction of Beecher, the Independent Congregational Church of Elmira, New York, developed into one of the first community oriented churches in America. In addition to the facilities for religious observances, the church provided a gymnasium, a library, and special meeting rooms. With his second wife, Julia, Beecher frequently visited Isabella while she was a patient at the nearby Elmira Water Cure.

21. BELMONT, AUGUST (1816-1890)

Banker; diplomat. Isabella Beecher Hooker wrote to Belmont concerning the Democratic Party and its potential support of woman suffrage.

22. BINGHAM, JOHN ARMOR (1815-1900)

Congressman, Ohio. Bingham participated in the framing of the Fourteenth Amendment.

23. BLACKWELL, ANTOINETTE BROWN (1825-1921)

First ordained woman minister in the United States. Originally a Congregationalist and later a Unitarian, Blackwell was active in the Boston wing of the woman suffrage movement. When she married Samuel Blackwell, brother of Dr. Elizabeth Blackwell and HENRY BROWN BLACKWELL, she became the sister-in-law of LUCY STONE, her Oberlin College roommate and co-worker in the suffrage cause.

24. BLACKWELL, HENRY BROWN (1825-1909)

Abolitionist; woman suffragist. Affiliated with the conservative Boston wing of the suffrage movement, Blackwell tried to induce Isabella Beecher Hooker to ally herself with this faction. In 1855 he married LUCY STONE and together they edited *The Woman's Journal*. Throughout their married life they agitated for woman suffrage on a state by state basis. The couple's daughter, Alice Stone Blackwell, carried on her parents' suffrage work. She became editor of *The Woman's Journal* and was instrumental in the eventual reunification of the two branches of the movement.

25. BLADEN, MRS. E. S.
Unidentified woman suffrage worker; acquaintance of Isabella Beecher Hooker; residence unknown.

26. BLAKE, LILLIE DEVEREUX (1833-1913)
President, New York State Suffrage Association; president, New York City Woman Suffrage League. The popular author of *Rockford, Fettered for Life,* and numerous other books and magazine articles, Blake lectured frequently on woman's rights. She was involved in many social reform movements, such as providing women doctors in mental institutions and supplying chairs for saleswomen in stores.

27. BONNER, ROBERT (1824-1899)
Editor, *New York Ledger*. The *Ledger* was noted for the large sums paid to famous authors, such as HENRY WARD BEECHER for his novel, *Norwood*.

28. BOWLES, SAMUEL (1826-1878)
Founder, publisher, and editor, *The Springfield Republican;* suffrage supporter; friend of Isabella Beecher Hooker and JOHN HOOKER. According to her 1878 diary, Isabella believed herself to be in communication with the spirit of Bowles shortly after his death.

29. BRISTOL, AUGUSTA COOPER
Lecturer and worker for woman suffrage; resident of Vineland, New Jersey.

30. BROWN, BENJAMIN GRATZ (1826-1885)
Senator, Missouri; governor, Missouri. In 1872 the Liberal Republican Party nominated Brown for vice president.

31. BROWN, MARTHA McCLELLAN (1838-1916)
Active worker in temperance and reform movements. Brown hoped to unite the woman suffrage and temperance causes.

32. BROWN, MARY O.
Unidentified worker in suffrage movement. SUSAN B. ANTHONY described Brown as "a dear good woman in the wilds of Washington Territory."

33. BROWN, OLYMPIA (1835-1926)
Universalist minister; pastor of a Universalist church in Bridgeport, Connecticut. Though closely allied with the National Woman Suffrage Association, Brown remained on good terms with both factions of the movement. She carried on an amiable correspondence with Isabella Beecher Hooker, who often addressed her as "Brownie" in correspondence. After marrying John Henry Willis in 1873, Brown continued to use her maiden name. In 1878 she moved with her family to Racine, Wisconsin, where her most extensive suffrage work was done.

34. BURR, FRANCES ELLEN (1831-1923)
Neighbor of Isabella Beecher Hooker at Nook Farm; sister of Alfred Burr, publisher, *The Hartford Times*. Burr shared Isabella's interests in woman suffrage and spiritualism.

35. BURRITT, ELIHU (1810-1879)
Reformer; publisher and editor; resident of Connecticut. In a letter to Isabella Beecher Hooker, Burritt expressed uncertainty about woman suffrage.

Olympia Brown

The Schlesinger Library, Radcliffe College

Benjamin F. Butler   *Sophia Smith Collection, Smith College*

Edward M. Davis   *Sophia Smith Collection, Smith College*

36. BURTON, AGNES (MOSS), MRS. RICHARD
Friend of Isabella Beecher Hooker; residence unknown.

37. BURTON, HENRY EUGENE (1840-1904)
Son-in-law of Isabella Beecher Hooker; attorney; known as "Eugene." Burton had a strained relationship with Isabella throughout his married life. Following the death of his wife, MARY (HOOKER) BURTON, in 1886, the relationship worsened.

38. BURTON, MARY (HOOKER), MRS. HENRY EUGENE (1845-1886)
Daughter of Isabella Beecher Hooker. Burton died of tuberculosis following a long estrangement from her husband. After Burton's death Isabella sought communication with the spirit of her daughter.

39. BURTON, RACHEL (CHASE), MRS. NATHANIEL J. (1826-1904)
Neighbor and friend of Isabella Beecher Hooker in Hartford; sister-in-law of HENRY EUGENE BURTON.

40. BUTLER, BENJAMIN F. (1818-1893)
Union general; commander at capture of New Orleans, 1862; congressman, Massachusetts; governor, Massachusetts; father-in-law of ADELBERT AMES. Butler coauthored the House Judiciary minority report supporting woman suffrage on January 30, 1871. Ida Husted Harper termed this report "perhaps the strongest and most exhaustive argument ever written on Woman's Right to vote under the Constitution."

41. BUTLER, JOSEPHINE (1828-1906)
English abolitionist; reformer. Butler campaigned extensively against Britain's Contagious Diseases Acts, which provided for the legalization of prostitution and subjected women suspected of being prostitutes to compulsory medical examination.

42. CAMERON, KATE
Unidentified acquaintance of PAULINA WRIGHT DAVIS; residence unknown.

43. CARRINGTON, "FRIEND"
Unidentified correspondent of Isabella Beecher Hooker; presumably worker in suffrage movement.

44. CHAMBERLIN, MARY (PORTER), MRS. FRANKLIN (-1908)
Neighbor of Isabella Beecher Hooker at Nook Farm. Chamberlin wrote Isabella regarding the Beecher-Tilton scandal while Isabella was in Europe.

45. CHASE, MARGUERITE B.
"Short hand writer" in Washington, D.C. Chase wrote Isabella Beecher Hooker seeking aid in finding employment.

46. CHENEY, EDNAH DOW (1824-1904)
Writer; reformer; suffragist. Cheney pioneered in a number of fields, including medical and art education for women. She was active in the women's club movement and supported the New England Freedmen's Aid Society.

47. CHENEY, MARY B. (1840-1917)
Acquaintance of Isabella Beecher Hooker; wife of silk mill owner, Frank W. Cheney; resident of South Manchester, Connecticut.

48. CHILDS, GEORGE WILLIAM (1829-1894)
Philanthropist; founder, *American Publishers' Circular and Literary Gazette;* owner, *The Public Ledger;* member, Childs and Peterson; member, J. B. Lippincott & Co.; author, *Recollections of General Grant* and *Recollections of George W. Childs.*

49. CHITTENDEN, LUCY B.
Acquaintance of Isabella Beecher Hooker and JOHN HOOKER; resident of Brooklyn, New York.

50. CLARK, CHARLES H. (1848-1926)
Editor, *The Hartford Courant;* acquaintance of Isabella Beecher Hooker and JOHN HOOKER. Clark was opposed to woman suffrage.

51. CLEMENS, OLIVIA (LANGDON), MRS. SAMUEL (1845-1904)
Wife of Mark Twain; a roommate of Isabella Beecher Hooker at the Elmira Water Cure. Clemens became a close friend of Isabella's daughter, ALICE (HOOKER) DAY. From 1871-1874 she and her husband rented the Hooker house at Nook Farm, after which they built their own house, an elaborate Victorian mansion, in the same neighborhood.

52. CLEMENS, SAMUEL (1835-1910)
Mark Twain; author and humorist; neighbor of Isabella Beecher Hooker at Nook Farm. Like several other neighbors at Nook Farm, Clemens criticized Isabella for her role in the Beecher-Tilton scandal, although relations between the Clemens and Hooker families improved once again with time. Clemens partially shared Isabella's fascination with spiritualism. On the subject of woman suffrage he commented, "I should like to see the time when women shall help to make the laws. I should like to see that whiplash, the ballot, in the hands of women." (Speech at the annual meeting of the Hebrew Technical School for Girls, Temple Emmanuel, January 20, 1901. Quoted in *Mark Twain's Speeches.*)

53. COLBY, MRS.
Acquaintance of OLYMPIA BROWN; worker in suffrage movement; residence unknown.

54. COLEMAN, O. O.
Unidentified worker in suffrage movement; resident of Middletown, Connecticut. Coleman was involved in petitioning faculty and students, probably of Wesleyan University.

55. COMSTOCK, HANNAH M.
Friend of Isabella Beecher Hooker. Comstock was active in the suffrage movement in the New Haven, Connecticut, area.

56. COOKE, HELEN M.
Secretary, New York City Woman Suffrage Association.

57. CROCKER, MRS. FRANK S.
Unidentified resident of Washington, D.C. Crocker wrote to Isabella Beecher Hooker regarding the relationship between the woman's labor and woman suffrage movements.

58. DALGHREN, SARAH MADELINE VINTON (1825-1898)
Active anti-suffrage campaigner. Dalghren wrote from Washington, D.C.

59. DAVIS, EDWARD M.
President, Philadelphia Citizens' Suffrage Association; son-in-law of LUCRETIA COFFIN MOTT; close friend of SUSAN B. ANTHONY.

60. DAVIS, PAULINA WRIGHT (1813-1876)
Suffrage leader; abolitionist; publisher, *UNA;* contributor to and financial backer of *The Revolution.* Wright introduced Isabella Beecher Hooker to SUSAN B. ANTHONY and ELIZABETH CADY STANTON.

61. DAY, ALICE (HOOKER), MRS. JOHN CALVIN (1847-1928)
Daughter of Isabella Beecher Hooker. After their marriage in 1869 Alice and John Calvin Day resided in Hartford. John Day alienated his parents-in-law and discouraged his wife and daughters from associating with Isabella. The Days spent several years in Europe, during which time Isabella and her daughter corresponded extensively.

Paulina Wright Davis

62. DAY, KATHARINE SEYMOUR (1870-1964)
Granddaughter of Isabella Beecher Hooker. Day, the founder and benefactor of The Stowe-Day Foundation, made many significant contributions to historic preservation in Connecticut. She traveled extensively, studied painting in Paris, and earned a master's degree from Trinity College, Hartford, at the age of sixty-six.

63. DIXON, ARCHIBALD (1802-1876)
Senator, Kentucky; lawyer. Isabella Beecher Hooker wrote to Dixon urging him to speak for the suffrage resolution at the convention in Baltimore in 1872.

64. DODGE, MARY ABIGAIL (1833-1896)
Editor, *Our Young Folks;* author (pseudonym, Gail Hamilton); teacher, Hartford Public High School, 1851-1858. Dodge opposed woman suffrage.

65. ELLIS, A. A.
Unidentified worker in suffrage movement; resident of Hartford, Connecticut.

66. ELMER, HELEN F.
Worker in suffrage movement. Elmer discouraged OLYMPIA BROWN from coming to Kentucky.

67. EMERSON, GEORGE H.
Clergyman; editor, unidentified paper.

68. FAXON, MR.
Military officer. Isabella Beecher Hooker wrote Faxon regarding the career of ROBERT ALLEN.

69. FIELD, MARY E.
Worker in suffrage movement in New York City.

70. FLETCHER, ALICE C.
Secretary, Hartford branch of Sorosis, a national literary society; friend of HARRIET (FOOTE) HAWLEY; agent for Woman's National Indian Association.

71. FOOTE, CHARLOTTE A. (WILCOX), MRS. ANDREW WARD (1836-   )
Mother of LILLY GILLETTE FOOTE.

72. FOOTE, LILLY GILLETTE (1860-1932)
Cousin of ELISABETH (GILLETTE) WARNER. Foote resided at Nook Farm while serving as governess to the children of SAMUEL and OLIVIA (LANGDON) CLEMENS.

73. FOSTER, JULIA
Secretary, Philadelphia Citizens' Suffrage Association; close friend of SUSAN B. ANTHONY; daughter of JULIA MANUEL FOSTER; sister of RACHEL FOSTER AVERY.

74. FOSTER, JULIA MANUEL
Mother of RACHEL FOSTER AVERY and JULIA FOSTER. Foster, the wealthy widow of the founder of *The Pittsburgh Dispatch,* often played hostess to SUSAN B. ANTHONY in Philadelphia.

75. FOWLER, MARIA A.
Unidentified correspondent. Fowler wrote to Isabella Beecher Hooker requesting a letter of celebration in honor of the birthday of OLYMPIA BROWN.

76. FULLER, SARAH E.
Corresponding secretary, Hartford branch of Sorosis, a national literary society.

77. GAGE, MATILDA JOSLYN (1826-1898)
President, National Woman Suffrage Association; president, secretary, New York State Suffrage Association. Gage was one of the most active lieutenants of SUSAN B. ANTHONY and ELIZABETH CADY STANTON in the suffrage movement and coauthored *History of the Woman Suffrage Movement.*

Matilda Joslyn Gage   *The Schlesinger Library, Radcliffe College*

Phebe Coffin Hanaford   *The Schlesinger Library,*
Radcliffe College

78. GALLAGHER, WILLIAM D. (1808-1894)
Journalist; associated with several newspapers, including *The Union*.

79. GARRISON, WILLIAM LLOYD, SR. (1805-1879)
Abolitionist; reformer; journalist. Garrison tried to bring Isabella Beecher Hooker into the conservative American Woman Suffrage Association. He was one of the few male abolitionists to support the right of women to speak at the World Anti-Slavery Convention held in England in 1840. Although Garrison remained a consistent supporter of woman's rights issues, like many abolitionists, he was willing to postpone the enfranchisement of women until after the black man received the vote.

80. GARRISON, WILLIAM LLOYD, JR. (1838-1909)
Active suffrage supporter; reformer; editor.

81. GIDDINGS, AMELIA
Worker in suffrage movement in Washington Territory.

82. GILLETTE, ELISABETH (HOOKER), MRS. FRANCIS (1813-1893)
Sister-in-law of Isabella Beecher Hooker; mother of WILLIAM GILLETTE. The Gillettes and the Hookers founded the Nook Farm community in Hartford, Connecticut.

83. GILLETTE, HELEN (NICKLES), MRS. WILLIAM (1860-1888)
Actress. Six years after her marriage, Gillette died of appendicitis.

84. GILLETTE, WILLIAM (1853-1937)
Actor; playwright; nephew of JOHN HOOKER. Gillette was born and raised on Nook Farm. He became most famous for his role as Sherlock Holmes.

85. GRANT, JULIA DENT (1826-1902)
Wife of ULYSSES S. GRANT. Isabella Beecher Hooker wrote urging Grant to influence her husband to support woman's rights.

86. GRANT, ULYSSES S. (1822-1885)
Eighteenth president of the United States. Isabella Beecher Hooker wrote urging Grant to support woman suffrage.

87. GRAVES, MRS. S. H.
Wife of Norfolk, Connecticut, farmer. Graves wrote to Isabella Beecher Hooker confiding her dissatisfaction with married life and seeking guidance.

88. GREELEY, HORACE (1811-1872)
Editor, *The New York Tribune*; abolitionist; political leader. A onetime ally of the suffragists, Greeley was alienated by SUSAN B. ANTHONY and ELIZABETH CADY STANTON and subsequently refused to support the movement in his influential newspaper.

89. GRIFFING, JOSEPHINE W. (1814-1872)
Secretary, National Woman Suffrage Association; founder and president, American Equal Rights Association. Griffing was among the most active abolitionists in the West. After the Civil War she was instrumental in founding and administering the Freedman's Bureau. She also campaigned extensively for woman suffrage.

90. HALL, MARY (1843-1927)
First woman lawyer in Hartford, Connecticut; friend of JOHN HOOKER.

91. HANAFORD, PHEBE COFFIN (1829-1921)
Universalist minister; lecturer; author; cousin of LUCRETIA COFFIN MOTT. Hanaford was affiliated with the American Woman Suffrage Association and lent her support to various woman's rights organizations.

92. HARBERT, ELIZABETH BOYNTON (1845-1925)
President, Illinois Suffrage Association; editor, *Woman's Kingdom*; acquaintance of Isabella Beecher Hooker.

93. HART, EDWARD L. (1813-1873)
Husband of NANCY (HOOKER) HART; resident of Farmington, Connecticut.

94. HART, NANCY (HOOKER), MRS. EDWARD L. (1813-1880)
Cousin of JOHN HOOKER; resident of Farmington, Connecticut.

95. HAWLEY, HARRIET (FOOTE), MRS. JOSEPH ROSWELL (1831-1886)
Niece of Roxana (Foote) Beecher; cousin by marriage of Isabella Beecher Hooker. Hawley was a roommate of Isabella Beecher Hooker at the Elmira Water Cure. Later she became involved in the United States Sanitary Commission during the Civil War.

96. HAWLEY, JOSEPH ROSWELL (1826-1905)
Editor, *The Hartford Courant*; Union general; governor, Connecticut; neighbor of Isabella Beecher Hooker in Hartford. Hawley opposed woman suffrage.

97. HAZLETT, M. ADELLE
Unidentified worker in suffrage movement; residence unknown.

98. HEATH, S. ANNA
Friend of Isabella Beecher Hooker in Boston. Interested in woman's rights and spiritualism, Heath encouraged Isabella to give a series of lectures in Boston.

99. HICKORY, MRS. M. C.
Supporter of woman suffrage in Litchfield, Connecticut.

100. HIGGINSON, THOMAS WENTWORTH (1823-1911)
Reformer; activist in many causes; affiliated with the Boston wing; author, *Woman and the Alphabet*. When Isabella Beecher Hooker sent Higginson her first article, Shall Women Vote? A Matrimonial Dialogue — Scene — New York, Feb. 18, 1860, he responded with encouragement and criticism.

101. HINCKLEY, FREDERICK (1845-1917)
Chairman, Executive Committee, Connecticut Woman Suffrage Association; Unitarian minister.

102. HOLLOWAY, LAURA C.
Unidentified acquaintance of Isabella Beecher Hooker. Affiliated with *The Brooklyn Daily Eagle*, Holloway wrote to Isabella regarding a flare-up of the Beecher-Tilton scandal.

103. HOOKER, EDWARD BEECHER (1855-1927)
Son of Isabella Beecher Hooker; homeopathic physician; close confidant of his mother; known as "Eddie" and later as "Ned."

104. HOOKER, ELISABETH (DAGGETT), MRS. EDWARD (1786-1869)
Mother-in-law of Isabella Beecher Hooker. Isabella and JOHN HOOKER lived with his parents for the first ten years of their married life. Later Hooker lived near them at Nook Farm.

105. HOOKER, JOHN (1816-1901)
Husband of Isabella Beecher Hooker; reporter, Supreme Court, Connecticut; lawyer. Throughout their sixty-year marriage Hooker supported and encouraged his wife's career. An ardent abolitionist, he authored several bills and articles in support of woman suffrage. In 1899 Hooker published his recollections and opinions on several issues, including woman suffrage and spiritualism, in *Some Reminiscences of a Long Life*.

106. HOOKER, MARTHA (KILBOURNE), MRS. EDWARD BEECHER (1853-1930)
Daughter-in-law of Isabella Beecher Hooker; known as "Mattie."

107. HOWARD, SUSAN RAYMOND (1812-1887)
Friend of Isabella Beecher Hooker; resident of Brooklyn, New York. Howard wrote to Isabella confiding her concerns about persons and issues involved in the struggle for woman's rights.

108. HOWE, JULIA WARD (1819-1910)
Founder, New England Woman Suffrage Association; author, "Battle Hymn of the Republic." Howe was affiliated with the conservative Boston wing of the suffrage movement. Her advocacy of woman suffrage lent respectability to the cause.

109. HOWLAND, MARIE
Suffragist; unsuccessful author from Hammonton, New Jersey.

110. HUBBARD, JULIA A.
Unidentified acquaintance of Isabella Beecher Hooker. Hubbard wrote from Madison, Connecticut, confiding her views on woman's rights.

111. HUGO, VICTOR MARIE (1802-1885)
Author, *Les Misérables*. While in Paris, Isabella Beecher Hooker wrote Hugo complimenting his article in the *Continental Herald* that had favored the establishment of a "Society for the Amelioration of the Position of Women" and seeking an interview.

112. JACKSON, ALICE (DAY), MRS. PERCY (1872-1926)
Granddaughter of Isabella Beecher Hooker; known as "Allie."

113. JARVIS, MISS
Unidentified young acquaintance of Isabella Beecher Hooker. Isabella urged Jarvis to work for the advancement of women.

114. JUDSON, MRS. M. J.
Unidentified resident of Hartford, Connecticut. Judson wrote to Isabella Beecher Hooker seeking to establish acquaintance.

115. KOONS, MRS. I. S.
Worker in suffrage movement; resident of Storrs, Connecticut.

116 KRIFFIN, G. C.
Unidentified male acquaintance of Isabella Beecher Hooker; supporter of woman suffrage; resident of Paris, Kentucky.

117. LANGDON, OLIVIA (LEWIS), MRS. JERVIS (1810-1890)
Friend of Isabella Beecher Hooker; mother of OLIVIA (LANGDON) CLEMENS. Langdon frequently entertained Isabella and her daughters at her Elmira, New York, home.

118. LINCOLN, ABRAHAM (1809-1865)
Sixteenth president of the United States. Isabella Beecher Hooker wrote Lincoln in 1861 on behalf of fugitive slaves.

119. LIVERMORE, DANIEL PARKER (1818-1899)
Universalist minister; suffrage supporter; husband of MARY RICE LIVERMORE.

120. LIVERMORE, MARY RICE (1820-1905)
President, American Woman Suffrage Association; president, Massachusetts Woman Suffrage Association; president, Woman's Christian Temperance Union; editor, *The Woman's Journal*; popular author and lecturer. During the Civil War, Livermore was involved in the United States Sanitary Commission.

121. LLEWELLEN, W. H.
Secretary to JOSEPHINE BUTLER in British movement for repeal of the Contagious Diseases Acts.

122. LOCKWOOD, BELVA (1830-1917)
First woman lawyer to appear before the United States Supreme Court. Lockwood was active in the temperance, peace, and woman suffrage movements.

123. LUCAS, MARGARET B.
Acquaintance of PAULINA WRIGHT DAVIS; resident of London, England. Lucas was involved in the repeal of the Contagious Diseases Acts.

124. MANNING, EMILY S.
Unidentified correspondent of OLYMPIA BROWN in Norwich, Connecticut.

*Belva A. Lockwood - Washington D.C.
Atty at-law.*

463, 465, Penna. Ave.,
WASHINGTON, D. C.

Belva Lockwood

Sophia Smith Collection, Smith College

Manning was involved in the woman suffrage movement.

125. McMANUS, ELLA BURR (1848-1906)
Lifelong friend of Isabella Beecher Hooker; daughter of Alfred Burr, owner and editor, *The Hartford Times;* author, "Homelife of Isabella Beecher Hooker," *Connecticut Magazine,* Vol. 9, No. 2, April 1905, the manuscript of which is included in this project. Burr was not a correspondent.

126. MERRITT, ISABEL (HOOKER), MRS. WALTER G. (1881-1963)
Granddaughter of Isabella Beecher Hooker.

127. MILL, JOHN STUART (1806-1873)
Philosopher; economist; ethical theorist; author, with wife, Harriet Taylor Mill, *The Subjection of Women.* Isabella Beecher Hooker's *Womanhood: Its Sanctities and Fidelities* quotes an exchange of letters between her and Mill.

128. MITCHELL, JOHN HIPPLE (1835-1905)
Senator, Oregon; supporter of woman suffrage.

129. MOTT, LUCRETIA COFFIN (1793-1880)
Pioneer suffragist; Hicksite Quaker. With ELIZABETH CADY STANTON, Mott organized the first Woman's Rights Convention in Seneca Falls, New York, in 1848. The convention was an outgrowth of their experience at the World Anti-Slavery Convention in London, England, at which women were not allowed to speak. She was named president of the American Equal Rights Association in 1866. At the time of the split in the woman suffrage movement she attempted to prevent the division. Mott continued to be active in the suffrage movement throughout her life, often inspiring younger women in the movement.

130. NEWMAN, FRANCIS W. (1805-1897)
British reformer. Isabella Beecher Hooker sent Newman a copy of her *Womanhood: Its Sanctities and Fidelities.* He responded, taking issue with some of her views.

131. NICOLL, CORNELIA COMSTOCK
Acquaintance of Isabella Beecher Hooker in New Haven, Connecticut; supporter of woman suffrage.

132. PARKER, JULIA E. (SMITH)
See SMITH, JULIA E.

133. PATTON, ABIGAIL HUTCHINSON (1829-1892)
Singer; member of the Hutchinson Quartet, noted for its songs in favor of various reforms; known as "Abby."

134. PERKINS, EMILY
Acquaintance of Isabella Beecher Hooker and JOHN HOOKER in London, England.

135. PERKINS, FRANCES (JOHNSON) BEECHER, MRS. FREDERICK
See BEECHER, FRANCES (JOHNSON), MRS. JAMES.

136. PERKINS, MARY (BEECHER), MRS. THOMAS CLAP (1805-1900)
Half sister of Isabella Beecher Hooker; daughter of LYMAN BEECHER and Roxana (Foote) Beecher. Isabella lived with Perkins while attending the Hartford Female Seminary. Later they were neighbors at Nook Farm.

137. PERRY, CAROLINE GROSVENOR
Acquaintance of Isabella Beecher Hooker; principal of Grosvenor Grange, a private boarding school; resident of Pomfret, Connecticut. Perry corresponded with Isabella about woman's rights and the Beecher-Tilton scandal.

138. PHILLEO, ELIZABETH P.
Acquaintance of Isabella Beecher Hooker in Suffield, Connecticut; wife of Calvin W. Philleo, stepson of Prudence Crandall Philleo, who amid severe local harassment maintained a school for young black women in Canterbury, Connecticut,

from 1832-1833. Philleo wrote to Isabella regarding the work of the suffrage movement and the United States Sanitary Commission.

139. PHILLIPS, CURTIS
Unidentified recipient or recipients of a circular letter sent by Isabella Beecher Hooker regarding the 1870 Washington Convention. The letter was addressed to "Curtis Phillips & others."

140. PILLSBURY, PARKER (1809-1898)
Abolitionist; coeditor, *The Revolution*; editor, *Herald of Freedom and National Anti-Slavery Standard*.

141. PRICHARD, SARA J. (1830-1909)
Acquaintance of Isabella Beecher Hooker from Waterbury, Connecticut; author, *Hugh's Fire on the Mountain, Rose Marbury*, and other books. Prichard expressed interest in the woman's rights and temperance movements.

142. REID, WHITELAW (1837-1912)
Successor to Horace Greeley as editor, *The New York Tribune*; diplomat; journalist; author.

143. ROGERS, SADIE M.
Unidentified worker in suffrage movement in Cedar Creek, New Jersey.

144. RUSSELL, FANNY ELDRIDGE
Unidentified contributor to *The Revolution* from Silver Lake, McCleod County, Minnesota.

145. SANDS, JOHN L.
Chairman, Central National Committee, Equal Rights Party.

146. SARGENT, ELLEN CLARK
Treasurer, National Woman Suffrage Association; wife of Aaron Augustus Sargent, senator and diplomat. Sargent corresponded with Isabella Beecher Hooker on suffrage matters over a period of years.

147. SAVERY, ANNA C.
Western acquaintance of Isabella Beecher Hooker. Savery was affiliated with an unidentified newspaper for which Isabella described her impression of VICTORIA WOODHULL.

148. SAYLES, LITA BARNEY
Suffragist; resident of Killingly, Connecticut.

149. SCOVILLE, HARRIET (BEECHER), MRS. SAMUEL (1838-1911)
Niece of Isabella Beecher Hooker; daughter of HENRY WARD BEECHER.

150. SEVERANCE, CAROLINE (1820-1914)
Abolitionist; reformer; pioneer in woman's club movement; close friend of Isabella Beecher Hooker. After traveling with Isabella in the South during the Civil War, Severance helped to introduce her to the politics of the woman suffrage movement. Their correspondence deals largely with the split in the movement; ultimately they allied themselves with opposing wings.

151. SHELDON, ABBY B.
Worker in the suffrage movement in New Haven, Connecticut.

152. SHELDON, J. E.
Suffragist in New Haven, Connecticut; possibly husband of ABBY B. SHELDON.

153. SHIPMAN, WILLIAM D. (1818-1898)
Judge in New York City; acquaintance of Isabella Beecher Hooker. Isabella wrote Shipman inquiring about his views on woman suffrage.

154. SLAYTON, HENRY L.
Proprietor and manager, Slayton's Lecture Bureau of Chicago. Slayton handled the lectures of SUSAN B. ANTHONY in 1878.

Elizabeth Cady Stanton with son   *Seneca Falls Historical Society, Seneca Falls, New York*

155. SMITH, JULIA E. (1792-1886)
Abolitionist; suffragist; resident of Glastonbury, Connecticut. With her sister, Abby, Smith protested the taxation of women denied the right to vote, by refusing to pay taxes in 1873. Both sisters later became active workers in the suffrage movement.

156. SMITH, MRS. L. M.
Unidentified suffragist from Hanover, New London County, Connecticut. Smith was interested in petitioning the women in her district.

157. SPENCER, SARAH J. ANDREWS (1837-1909)
Chairman, Resident Congressional Committee, National Woman Suffrage Association. With her husband Spencer founded Spencerian Business College in Washington, D.C. She was actively involved in petitioning and fund raising for the National Woman Suffrage Association, particularly in support of the Sixteenth Amendment.

158. STANTON, EDWIN McMASTERS (1814-1869)
Secretary of war during the Civil War. Stanton aided Isabella Beecher Hooker during her journey in the South.

159. STANTON, ELIZABETH CADY (1815-1902)
Pioneer and theoretician of the woman suffrage movement. With LUCRETIA COFFIN MOTT, Stanton organized the first Woman's Rights Convention in 1848 in Seneca Falls, near her home. Her friendship with SUSAN B. ANTHONY proved a source of emotional support for both women for over fifty years and contributed to the development of their complementary talents and skills. Anthony usually assumed the tasks of research and practical organization, while Stanton was especially effective as a writer and speaker. Her "radical" ideas concerning dress, sex, divorce, and religion often embarrassed her more conservative colleagues.

160. STANTON, MARGARET (1852-1938)
Daughter of ELIZABETH CADY STANTON; married Frank Lawrence in 1878.

161. STEARNS, SARAH BURGER (1836-   )
Worker in suffrage movement in Rochester, Minnesota; close friend of SUSAN B. ANTHONY. Stearns wrote to JOSEPHINE GRIFFING expressing concern about the role of VICTORIA WOODHULL in the woman suffrage movement.

162. STEBBINS, CATHARINE A. F.
Suffragist affiliated with the National Woman Suffrage Association; residence unknown. Stebbins corresponded with Isabella Beecher Hooker while Isabella was on her European trip.

163. STEELE, FANNY
Unidentified correspondent of NANCY (HOOKER) HART, cousin of Isabella Beecher Hooker. Steele wrote Hart commenting upon Isabella's role in the Beecher-Tilton scandal and the suffrage movement.

164. STONE, LUCY (1818-1893)
Founder, New England Woman Suffrage Association; founder, American Woman Suffrage Association. With her husband, HENRY BROWN BLACKWELL, Stone edited *The Woman's Journal*, the organ of the Boston wing of the suffrage movement. Her insistence upon retaining her maiden name after marriage caused some consternation among other participants in the suffrage movement, including Isabella Beecher Hooker, who feared this "radical" behavior might damage the cause.

165. STOW, MRS. J. W.
Unidentified suffragist from New York City. Stow hoped that Isabella Beecher Hooker would support the newly formed Social Science Association in New York.

166. STOWE, HARRIET (BEECHER), MRS. CALVIN ELLIS (1811-1896)
Author, *Uncle Tom's Cabin;* half sister of Isabella Beecher Hooker; daughter of LYMAN BEECHER and Roxana (Foote) Beecher. In numerous writings Stowe commented upon the role and influence of women, particularly as mothers, but she never publicly espoused the cause of woman suffrage or woman's rights.

167. STRONG, HELEN P.
Unidentified resident of Matawan, New Jersey. Strong wrote to Isabella Beecher Hooker seeking information on the history of the woman's rights movement.

168. SUMNER, CHARLES (1811-1874)
Senator, Massachusetts; antislavery leader in Congress; supporter of woman suffrage.

169. TALCOTT, MARY KINGSBURY (1847-1917)
Cousin and friend of KATHARINE SEYMOUR DAY; daughter of MARY (SEYMOUR) TALCOTT.

170. TALCOTT, MARY (SEYMOUR), MRS. RUSSELL (1820-1883)
Cousin of KATHARINE SEYMOUR DAY. Talcott boarded briefly with the Hooker family during the 1870s.

171. TILTON, THEODORE (1835-1907)
Editor, *The Independent;* journalist; author of a biography of VICTORIA WOODHULL; supporter of woman suffrage. Tilton, a member of the Plymouth Church in Brooklyn, New York, was an admirer and protege of its pastor, HENRY WARD BEECHER. He later sued Beecher for alienation of affections in connection with Beecher's alleged affair with Elizabeth Tilton, his wife.

172. TINGLEY, ANNIE H.
Worker for woman suffrage in Willimantic, Connecticut.

173. TRAIN, GEORGE FRANCIS (1829-1904)
Shipping and railroad merchant; financier of *The Revolution.* Train's involvement with the suffrage movement proved a source of tension between the New York and Boston wings of the movement.

174. TRIMBLE, KATE (c. 1859-   )
Wealthy young woman who wrote to Isabella Beecher Hooker to express her concerns about the prejudices against woman's rights in her home state of Kentucky. Eventually a close relationship developed between the two women, and Trimble came to address Isabella as "dear Mother."

175. TRIMBLE, MARY F.
Mother of KATE TRIMBLE. Trimble encouraged her daughter's interest in woman suffrage and expressed gratitude to Isabella Beecher Hooker for her interest in KATE TRIMBLE.

176. UNDERWOOD, MR.
Unidentified acquaintance of Isabella Beecher Hooker; residence unknown.

177. VAN VORRHIS, JOHN (1826-1905)
Lawyer for SUSAN B. ANTHONY during her trial for illegal voting in Rochester, New York. Van Voorhis corresponded with JOHN HOOKER regarding the Anthony case.

178. VIBBERT, GEORGE H.
Unidentified suffragist. Vibbert, along with LUCY STONE, JULIA WARD HOWE, CAROLINE SEVERANCE, and THOMAS WENTWORTH HIGGINSON, signed a circular regarding the initial formation of the American Woman Suffrage Association.

179. VINTON, ALEXANDER HAMILTON (1807-1881)
Episcopalian priest; cousin of SARAH MADELINE VINTON DALGHREN.

Theodore Tilton

180. WAISBROCKER, LOIS
Supporter of suffrage movement from Riverside, California. Waisbrocker, who met Isabella Beecher Hooker at the home of PAULINA WRIGHT DAVIS, was interested in uniting woman's rights with the concerns of labor.

181. WAITE, CATHARINE VAN VALKENBERG (1829-1913)
Founder, Illinois Woman Suffrage Association; lawyer; legal journalist. Affiliated with the National Woman Suffrage Association, Waite was a close friend of ELIZABETH CADY STANTON and SUSAN B. ANTHONY. She served as hostess to Isabella Beecher Hooker on visits to Washington, D.C.

182. WALKER, MISS C. C.
Unidentified resident of Frankford, Pennsylvania. Walker wrote SUSAN B. ANTHONY for an autograph.

183. WALKER, FRANCIS A. (1840-1897)
President, Massachusetts Institute of Technology; economist; acquaintance of Isabella Beecher Hooker.

184. WALLER, THOMAS MACDONALD (1840-1924)
Judge. Waller wrote to Isabella Beecher Hooker concerning her nomination as a Centennial Commissioner from Connecticut.

185. WARNER, CHARLES DUDLEY (1829-1900)
Editor, *The Hartford Courant;* coauthor, with Mark Twain (SAMUEL CLEMENS), *The Gilded Age;* author, *My Summer in a Garden* and other books; neighbor of Isabella Beecher Hooker at Nook Farm. Warner corresponded with WHITELAW REID, editor of *The New York Tribune*, regarding Isabella's criticisms of Reid's treatment of VICTORIA WOODHULL.

186. WARNER, ELISABETH (GILLETTE), MRS. GEORGE H. (1838-1915)
Niece of JOHN HOOKER; sister-in-law of CHARLES DUDLEY WARNER; neighbor of Isabella Beecher Hooker at Nook Farm; known as "Lilly."

187. WARNER, GEORGE H. (1833-1919)
Brother of CHARLES DUDLEY WARNER; neighbor of Isabella Beecher Hooker at Nook Farm; agent, American Emigrant Company. The American Emigrant Company encouraged Europeans, and particularly Scandinavians, to settle in the United States. JOHN HOOKER invested heavily in the company and lost a substantial amount of money.

188. WARNER, SUSAN (LEE), MRS. CHARLES DUDLEY (c. 1838-1921)
Neighbor of Isabella Beecher Hooker at Nook Farm.

189. WELLES, MARY CROWELL
Recipient of a circular letter about woman suffrage written by Isabella Beecher Hooker and sent to women of the Connecticut Children's Aid Society.

190. WHEELER, F. G.
Unidentified acquaintance of Isabella Beecher Hooker in New York; supporter of woman's rights.

191. WHITMORE, HARRIET GOULDER (1847-1915)
Acquaintance of Isabella Beecher Hooker in Hartford, Connecticut.

192. WILDMAN, J. K.
Acquaintance of LUCRETIA COFFIN MOTT in Philadelphia, Pennsylvania. Wildman wrote a letter to *The Philadelphia Standard* regarding the Cleveland convention.

193. WOOD, EMMA A.
Treasurer, Woman's Club, Washington, D.C.; secretary to Board of Trustees, Girls' Reform School. Wood wrote to Isabella Beecher Hooker seeking aid in obtaining subscribers to *The Alpha,* a monthly newspaper proposed by the Moral Education Society of Boston.

194. **WOODHULL, VICTORIA CLAFLIN (1838-1927)**
Suffragist; spiritualist; faith healer; advocate of free love and more liberal divorce laws. Among the most sensational figures in nineteenth-century American history — she was one of the first woman stockbrokers; she was the first woman to seek the presidency, prompting the reference, "the prostitute who ran for president" — Woodhull was thought to possess compelling personal charm and enormous effectiveness as a public speaker. Her attractive personality won her the good opinion of many of the more respectable women in the suffrage movement, despite the mystery and gossip surrounding her background. Woodhull eventually left the country and settled in England, where she married Sir John Biddolph Martin. As Mrs. Martin she repudiated many of her radical opinions on social issues.

195. **WOOLSEY, JANE STUART (1830-1891)**
Civil War nurse; acquaintance of one of Isabella Beecher Hooker's brothers, probably THOMAS KINNICUT BEECHER. With her sisters, Abby and Georgenna, Woolsey made significant contributions to war relief work. She was later the resident directress of Presbyterian Hospital in New York City. Isabella attempted to interest her in the suffrage movement.

196. **WRIGHT, MARTHA COFFIN (1806-1875)**
Sister of LUCRETIA COFFIN MOTT; mother-in-law of WILLIAM LLOYD GARRISON, JR. Affiliated with the National Woman Suffrage Association, Wright was frequently called upon for advice by ELIZABETH CADY STANTON and SUSAN B. ANTHONY. Along with her sister she helped to organize the first Woman's Rights Convention in Seneca Falls, New York.

Martha Coffin Wright

Sophia Smith Collection, Smith College

USING THE INDEX

This index contains an entry for each individual who figures as a sender and/or a recipient in the project. There is also an entry for each photograph and each suffrage-related circular and broadside in the microfiche. The index is designed to enable the researcher to locate all the items written by and to a particular correspondent by means of the alphanumeric character used in the targets.

The index is organized alphabetically by correspondent, with the exception of photographs and suffrage-related circulars and broadsides, which appear under "P" and "S" respectively. The first part of each entry contains a list of all letters in the project *written by* that individual. This list is arranged alphabetically by recipient, with each item appearing in chronological order. An identifying alphanumeric fiche number is assigned to each item in an entry.

The second section of each entry lists all letters *received by* that particular correspondent. These letters are grouped alphabetically according to sender. Where applicable, a third section lists chronogically all documents that were written by that correspondent.

For Isabella Beecher Hooker, there are four groupings: letters written by her, letters written to her, documents (noncorrespondence) written by her, and suffrage-related letters written by other correspondents in which her name is mentioned. In the documents section, titles appearing in italics were supplied by Isabella Beecher Hooker; other titles have been assigned by the project staff.

An asterisk before an item indicates a joint letter (one written by two or more correspondents) or a letter that includes notes by subsequent correspondents. (For this reason, several family members and friends who have not been defined as suffrage-related correspondents appear in the index as senders.) In all such cases, the alphanumeric characters designate the entire item, not just the portion written by or addressed to the correspondent named in the entry.

The brackets and question marks used in the targets have been eliminated from the index and fiche titles in order to save space and facilitate readability. In the case of letters written over a time span of two or more days, the date cited is the day on which the item was begun.

Key to Abbreviations Used in the Index and Fiche Titles

a.	after	misc.	miscellaneous
A.A.	autograph album	n.d.	no date
A.W.S.A.	American Woman Suffrage Association	N.W.S.A.	National Woman Suffrage Association
b.	before	n.y.	no year
bet.	between	o.e.	or earlier
c.	circa	o.l.	or later
CN.	constitution	PN.	petition
CR.	circular	w/	with

Allen, George R.
to Anthony, Susan B.

Allen, George R.
  to ANTHONY, SUSAN B.
    *1872   May 16 135/A14-B4
  to HOOKER, ISABELLA BEECHER
    *1872   May 16 135/A14-B4
  to STANTON, ELIZABETH CADY
    *1872   May 16 135/A14-B4
  from HOOKER, ISABELLA BEECHER
    *1872   46/D14-E3
    1872   May 24 47/E2-5

Allen, Robert
  from BEECHER, CATHARINE E.
    *1870 Jan 4 43/B6-11
  from HOOKER, ISABELLA BEECHER
    1867   32/D13-14
    1867 Feb 16 34/B4-7
    1867 Mar 10 34/D7-14
    1867 Mar 18 34/E5-12
    1867 May 16 35/D4-7
    1867 Jun 24 35/D8-E1
    1867 Jun 29 35/E2-9
    1867 Sep 12 36/C4-11
    1867 Oct 23 37/A2-13
    1867 Nov 17 37/A14-B13
    1867 Nov 29 37/B14-C7
    1868 Jan 1 37/D5-E6
    1868 Feb 4 38/A2-13
    1868 Apr 1 38/A14-C1
    1868 Apr 14 38/C2-7
    1868 May 19 38/D11-14
    1868 May 29 39/A2-13
    1868 Jun 8 39/A14-B2
    1868 Jul 28 39/D3-E4
    1868 Aug 18 40/A2-9
    1868 Nov 6 40/A10-C3
    1868 Nov 9 40/C8-11
    1868 Nov 28 40/D2-7
    1869 Feb 22 41/A2-7
    1869 Oct 10 42/B4-11
    *1870 Jan 4 43/B6-11
    1870 May 9 43/C2-5
    1870 May 15 43/C6-D3
    1870 Oct 11 43/D8-13

Ames, Adelbert
  from HOOKER, ISABELLA BEECHER
    1871 Apr 15 45/D7-10
    1872 Jan 7 46/E8-11

Anonymous
  to HOOKER, ISABELLA BEECHER
    *1872 Apr 2 114/A6-9
  to WOODHULL, VICTORIA CLAFLIN
    1871 Apr 18 114/A2-5
  from ANTHONY, SUSAN B.
    *a. 1871 May 8 135/A6-9
  from DAVIS, PAULINA WRIGHT
    1869 Jul or
          Aug 129/E9-10
  from HOOKER, ISABELLA BEECHER
    1860 Apr 25 17/B6-7

Anthony, Susan B.
to Hooker, Isabella Beecher

    1871   44/C12-14
    1871 Mar 24 45/C5
    1871 Apr 14 45/D4-6
    1871 Dec-
    1872 Jan 46/C13-D2
    1875 Apr 7 51/C11-13
    1890 Nov 4 72/B12-13
    1901 Apr 25 83/E8-10
    1903 Apr 2 85/A10
  from STANTON, ELIZABETH CADY
    1870-
    1871   137/C10-13

Anthony, Mary S.
  to ANTHONY, SUSAN B.
    *1873 Sep 10-
          Dec 15 118/D3-8
  to DAVIS, PAULINA WRIGHT
    *1871 Sep 20 130/D3-6
  from DAVIS, PAULINA WRIGHT
    *1871 Sep 16 130/D3-6

Anthony, Susan B.
  to ANONYMOUS
    *a. 1871 May 8 135/A6-9
  to BROWN, OLYMPIA
    1871 May 24 116/C10-13
    *1872 Jan 25 47/A2-B1
    1872 Sep 117/C6-11
    1872 Oct 9 117/D10-13
    *1873 Jan 7 117/E7-11
    1873 Sep 29 118/C4-7
    1875 Nov 3 119/B1-4
  to DAVIS, PAULINA WRIGHT
    1869 Jul or
          Aug 114/B2-5
  to GIDDINGS, AMELIA
    *1872 May 23 132/D3-6
  to HALL, MARY
    1904 Oct 28 120/B7
  to HOOKER, ISABELLA BEECHER
    1869 Jun 11 114/A10-B1
    1869 Jul 29 114/B6-9
    1869 Aug 9 114/B10-C1
    1869 Sep or
          Oct 114/C2-5
    1869 Oct 15 114/C6-8
    1869 Nov 3 114/C9-12
    1869 Nov 8 114/C13-D4
    1869 Dec 114/D5-8
    1869 Dec 17 114/D9-E4
    1869 Dec 29 114/E5-8
    1870 Jan 10 114/E9-12
    1870 Jan 12 115/A2-9
    1870 Jan 27 115/A10-11
    1870 Jan 30 115/A12-B6
    1870 Feb 8 115/B7-8
    1870 Mar 21 115/B9-C3
    1870 c. May 115/C4-5
    1870 May 2 115/C6-7
    1870 Dec 2 115/C8-D1
    *1871   115/D2-5

1871	Jan	5	115/D6-8
1871	Jan	21	115/D9-12
1871	Jan	29	115/D13-E3
1871	Feb	6	115/E4-9
1871	Mar	5	116/A2-10
1871	Mar	11	116/A11-B3
1871	Mar	21	116/B4-7
1871	Apr	22	116/B12-C5
1871	Apr	30	116/C6-9
1871	Jun		116/C14-D4
1871	Jun	6	116/D5-10
1871	Jun	11	116/D11-14
1871	Jun	12	116/E1-2
1872	Jan	29	116/E7-10
1872	Feb	6	116/E11-12
1872	May	19	117/A2-5
*1872	a. May 23		132/D3-6
1872	Jun	19	117/A10-13
1872	Jun	24	117/A14-B7
1872	Jul	20	117/B8-10
1872	Jul	24	117/B11-12
1872	Aug	5	117/B13-C2
1872	Aug	7	117/C3-5
1872	Sep	6	117/C12-D1
1872	Sep	10	117/D2-9
1872	Oct	9	117/D14-E3
1872	Oct	10	117/E4-6
*1873	Jan	7	117/E7-11
1873	Apr	21	118/A2-6
1873	May	12	118/A7-8
1873	Jul	11	118/A9-12
1873	Aug	5	118/A13-B2
1873	Aug	11	118/B3-6
1873	Sep	7	118/B7-10
1873	Sep	11	118/B11-14
1873	Sep	12	118/C1-3
1873	Sep	29	118/C4-7
*1873	Oct	4	121/C3-6
1873	Oct	13	118/C8-11
1873	c. Oct 15		118/C12-13
1873	Nov		118/C14-D1
1873	Dec	13	118/D2
*1873	Dec	15	118/D3-8
1874	Feb	17	118/D9-E2
1874	Feb	21	118/E5-8
1875	Jan	20	118/E9-14
1875	Sep	29	119/A2-7
1875	Oct	12	119/A8-10
1875	Oct	21	119/A11-14
1876	Aug	3	119/B5-6
1876	Sep	4	119/B7-14
1876	Dec	6	119/C1-4
1877	Jan	20	119/C5-11
1877	Sep	1	119/C14-D3
1877	Nov	11	119/D6-E1
1878	Jun	18	119/E2-5
1878	Oct		119/E6-9
1879	Oct	7	119/E10-13
1878	Oct	11	120/A3-4
1878	Oct	15	120/A5-8
1878	Nov	15	120/A9-10
1878	Dec	12	120/A11-14

1880	Dec	6	120/B1-4
1900	Mar	23	120/B5-6

to HOOKER, JOHN

1873	Aug	11	118/B3-6
1874	Feb	19	118/E3-4

to LIVERMORE, DANIEL PARKER

1870	Jan	25	134/A7-8

to STANTON, ELIZABETH CADY

1871	Apr	2	116/B8-11
1871	Sep	10	116/E3-6
*1871	a. Sep 16		130/D3-6
1872	May	29	117/A6-9
1877	Sep		119/C12-13
1877	Oct	5	119/D4-5
*1892	Nov	27	140/D11-E4

to WRIGHT, MARTHA COFFIN

1871	Mar	21	116/B4-7

from ALLEN, GEORGE R.

*1872	May	16	135/A14-B4

from ANTHONY, MARY S.

*1873	Sep 10-		
	Dec	15	118/D3-8

from AVERY, ALIDA C.

1877	Sep	20	120/B8-10

from BLACKWELL, ANTOINETTE BROWN

*1873	Sep 10-		
	Dec	15	118/D3-8

from BLACKWELL, HENRY BROWN

*1873	Sep 10-		
	Dec	15	118/D3-8

from BROWN, MARY O.

*1873	Oct	4	121/C3-6

from HOOKER, ISABELLA BEECHER

1869			40/E6-10
1871	Mar	11	44/D7-E14
*1872	Jan	21	47/A2-B1
1872	May	26	47/E4-5
1872	Jul	18	48/B12-C3
1875	Feb	18	51/B2-7

from LIVERMORE, DANIEL PARKER

1870	Jan	20	134/A7-8

from ROGERS, SADIE M.

*1871	May	8	135/A6-9

from RUSSELL, FANNY ELDREDGE

1870	Jan	24	135/A10-13

from SANDS, JOHN L.

*1872	May	16	135/A14-B4

from STANTON, ELIZABETH CADY

1871	May	27	138/C2-3

from WALKER, MISS C. C.

*1871			115/D2-5

Atwood, Mrs.
from HOOKER, ISABELLA BEECHER

1880 or			
1886	Jun	11	54/E10

Avery, Alida C.
to ANTHONY, SUSAN B.

1877	Sep	20	120/B8-10

Avery, Rachel Foster
   to HOOKER, ISABELLA BEECHER
      1879   Apr   6   120/B11-C4

Bacon, Leonard
   from HOOKER, ISABELLA BEECHER
      1873   Mar 26   86/E4

Barber, John
   to HOOKER, ISABELLA BEECHER
      1876   Aug 31   120/C5-7
      1879   Nov 10   120/C8
      1880   Mar 24   120/C9-10
   from HOOKER, ISABELLA BEECHER
      1876   c. Aug 31 53/B8-9

Beecher, Catharine E.
   to ALLEN, ROBERT
      *1870   Jan   4   43/B6-11
   to BEECHER, ESTHER M.
      *1840   Jan   7   2/D4-7
   to HOOKER, JOHN
      *1839   Oct 21   2/B12-C1
      *transcript   1/A4-7

   from HOOKER, ISABELLA BEECHER
      1860   Apr 17   16/E9-14
      c. 1869   40/D8-E1

Beecher, Esther M.
   from BEECHER, CATHARINE E.
      *1840   Jan   7   2/D4-7
   from HOOKER, ISABELLA BEECHER
      *1840   Jan   7   2/D4-7
      1842   Feb 26   4/D1-4
      1842   Aug 8   4/D10-13
      1846   Aug 22 +
      1847   Jun 22   6/E1-9

Beecher, Frances (Johnson), Mrs. James
   from HOOKER, ISABELLA BEECHER
      1891   Jul   74/D5-6
      1893   Aug 24   79/C2-3
      *1899   Jan 22   82/E1-4
   from HOOKER, JOHN
      *1899   Jan 22   82/E1-4

Beecher, George
   to BEECHER, LYDIA (BEALS) JACKSON,
   MRS. LYMAN
      *1837   Jul   3   2/A4-7
   to BEECHER, LYMAN
      *1837   Jul   3   2/A4-7

Beecher, Henry Ward
   from HOOKER, ISABELLA BEECHER
      1860   May   17/C2-5
      1861   Dec 22   25/B5-C2
      1863   Apr 20   27/C3-D4

Beecher, Katharine (Edes), Mrs. William
   from HOOKER, ISABELLA BEECHER
      1839   Dec 30   2/C14-D3
      transcript   1/B7-9

Beecher, Lydia (Beals) Jackson, Mrs. Lyman
   from BEECHER, GEORGE
      *1837   Jul   3   2/A4-7
   from HOOKER, ISABELLA BEECHER
      *1837   Jul   3   2/A4-7
      1846   May 10   6/D7-8
      1860s   16/A11-14
   from STOWE, HARRIET (BEECHER),
   MRS. CALVIN ELLIS
      *1837   Jul   3   2/A4-7

Beecher, Lyman
   from BEECHER, GEORGE
      *1837   Jul   3   2/A4-7
   from HOOKER, ISABELLA BEECHER
      *1837   Jul   3   2/A4-7
      1846   May 10   6/D7-8
   from STOWE, HARRIET (BEECHER),
   MRS. CALVIN ELLIS
      *1837   Jul   3   2/A4-7

Beecher, Mary Frances (Beecher), Mrs. Henry Ward
   from HOOKER, ISABELLA BEECHER
      1898-
      1899   Nov 26   82/B4-5
      1902   Feb 10   84/B9-11

Beecher, Thomas Kinnicut
   from HOOKER, ISABELLA BEECHER
      1863   Apr   1   27/B9-C2

Belmont, August
   from HOOKER, ISABELLA BEECHER
      1872   Apr 13   47/D2-4

Bingham, John Armor
   from HOOKER, ISABELLA BEECHER
      1871   Jan   44/D1-4

Blackwell, Antoinette Brown
   to ANTHONY, SUSAN B.
      *1873   Sep 10-
              Dec 15   118/D3-8

Blackwell, Henry Brown
   to ANTHONY, SUSAN B.
      *1873   Sep 10-
              Dec 15   188/D3-8
   to BROWN, OLYMPIA
      1870   Mar 19   120/E7-10
   to BURR, FRANCES ELLEN
      1876   Jul 15   121/B5-9
   to HOOKER, ISABELLA BEECHER
      1869   Dec   1   120/C11-14
      1869   Dec 16   120/D1-10
      1870   Mar 16   120/E3-6
      1870   Mar 28   120/E11 -
                           121/A5
      1872   Jul 19   121/A11-14

Blackwell, Henry Brown
to Hooker, John

    to HOOKER, JOHN
        1869   Dec 19   120/D11-12
        1870   Mar 16   120/D13-E2
        1870   Mar 30   121/A6
        1871   Jan 28   121/A7-10
    to STANTON, ELIZABETH CADY
        1872   Jul 27   121/B1-2
    *1872   Aug 6   121/B3-4
    from HOOKER, ISABELLA BEECHER
        1869   Dec 1   42/D7-10
        1872   Jul 14   48/A10-B11
        1873   a. Nov 22   49/B12-13
        1897   Aug 25   82/A2-3
    from WRIGHT, MARTHA COFFIN
        1870   Jan 2   142/D14-E4

Bladen, Mrs. E. S.
    from DAVIS, EDWARD
        1871   Dec 7   129/C2-3

Blake, Lillie Devereux
    to HOOKER, ISABELLA BEECHER
        1892   Dec 13   121/B10-12

Bonner, Robert
    from HOOKER, ISABELLA BEECHER
        b. 1899   82/D14

Bowles, Samuel
    from HOOKER, ISABELLA BEECHER
        1876   Jan 5   86/E7-8
        1877   Mar 26   86(a)/A2-13
        1877   Mar 26 86(a)/A14-B1

Bristol, Augusta Cooper
    to HOOKER, ISABELLA BEECHER
        b. 1879 Feb 21   121/B13-14
        1879   Feb 21   121/C1-2

Brown, Benjamin Gratz
    from HOOKER, ISABELLA BEECHER
        1872   Mar 8   47/C5-8
        1872   Apr 8   47/C9-11

Brown, Mary O.
    to ANTHONY, SUSAN B.
        *1873   Oct 4   121/C3-6

Brown, Martha McClellan
    to HOOKER, ISABELLA BEECHER
        1896   Oct 26   121/C7-9

Brown, Olympia
    to COMSTOCK, HANNAH M.
        1878   Jun 18 126/B13-C5
    to DAVIS, PAULINA WRIGHT
        *1870   Dec 8   122/B4-11
    to HOOKER, ISABELLA BEECHER
        1870   Mar 9   121/C10-11
        1870   Apr 6   121/C12-14
        1870   May 28   121/D1-6
        1870   Jul 20   121/D7-12

Brown, Olympia
from Anthony, Susan B.

    1870   Jul 25   121/D13-E14
    1870   Jul 27   122/A3-6
    1870   Aug 15   122/A7-10
    1870   Aug 29   122/A11-13
    1870   Oct 5   122/A14-B3
    *1870   Dec 8   122/B12-C1
    1870   Dec 22   122/C2-11
    1871   Mar 23   122/C12-D1
    1871   Sep 25   122/D2-4
    1871   Sep 26   122/D5-12
    1871   Oct 20   122/D13-E1
    1871   Oct 26   122/E2-5
    1871   c. Oct 26   122/E6-7
    1871   Dec 6   123/A2-11
    1871   Dec 9 123/A12-B10
    1872   Jan 2   123/B11-C2
    1872   Jan 12   123/C3-6
    1872   Jan 26   123/C7-10
    1872   Feb 3   123/C11-D4
    1872   Feb 7   123/D5-12
    1872   Feb 9   123/D13-E5
    1872   Sep 25   123/E6-9
    1872   Oct 10   123/E10-12
    1873   Feb 24   124/A2-5
    1873   Mar 28   124/A8-11
    1873   Apr 24   124/A12-B1
    1873   May 9   124/B2-9
    1873   Dec 31   124/D10-12
    *1874   a. Jan 3   131/A13-B2
    1874   Jan 6   124/D13-E8
    1874   Jan a. 6   124/E9-12
    1874   Jan a. 6   125/A2-10
    1874   Mar 13   125/A11-B8
    1874   Mar 30   125/B9-13
    1874   Apr 9   125/B14-C7
    1875-
    1876   Jun 26   125/C8-13
    1875   Dec 27 125/C14-D10
    1876   Jan 3   125/D11-14
    1876   Jan 21   125/E1-4
    1876   Jan 28   125/E5-6
    1876   Feb 2   125/E7-10
    1876   Mar 1   125/E11-12
    1876   May 31   125/E13-14
    1877   Feb 1   126/A3-10
    1877   Mar 17   126/A11-12
    1877   Apr 12   126/A13-B2
    1877   Oct 19   126/B3
    b. 1878   126/B4-5
    b. 1878   126/B6-9
    1878   Mar 16   126/B10-12
    1878   Sep 15   126/C6-7
    1878   Oct 15   126/C8
    to HOOKER, JOHN
        1873   Mar 18   124/A6-7
        1873   Sep 22   124/B10-C7
        1873   Sep 22   124/C8-D9
    from ANTHONY, SUSAN B.
        1871   May 24   116/C10-13
        *1872   Jan 25   47/A2-B1
        1872   Sep   117/C6-11
        1872   Oct 9   117/D10-13

Brown, Olympia
from Anthony, Susan B.

*1873	Jan	7	117/E7-11
1873	Sep	29	118/C4-7
1875	Nov	3	119/B1-4

from BLACKWELL, HENRY BROWN
1870	Mar	19	120/E7-10

from ELMER, HELEN F.
*1874	Jan	3	131/A13-B2

from HOOKER, ISABELLA BEECHER
1871	Aug	5	45/E5-8
1872	Feb	14	47/B2-9
1873	Nov	8	49/B8-11
1873	Dec	30	49/B14-C5
1874	Jan	6	49/C14-D3
1874	Aug	28	50/D6-E3
1881	Jul	28	55/B11-C2
1889	Feb	18	63/D10-11
1891	b. Aug 5		74/E1
*1892	Apr	26	77/B4-7
1901	Apr	25	83/E8-10

from MANNING, EMILY S.
1871	Dec	6	134/C7-9

from STANTON, ELIZABETH CADY
*1873	Jan	7	117/E7-11
*1892	Apr	26	77/B4-7

from TINGLEY, ANNIE H.
1871	Dec	4	141/D11-12

Burr, Frances Ellen
to HOOKER, ISABELLA BEECHER
1874	Jan		126/C9-10
1874	Nov	1	126/C11-14
1878	Jul	17	126/D1-2

from BLACKWELL, HENRY BROWN
1876	Jul	15	121/B5-9

Burritt, Elihu
to HOOKER, ISABELLA BEECHER
1871	Oct	4	126/D3-5

Burton, Agnes (Moss), Mrs. Richard
from HOOKER, ISABELLA BEECHER
1904	Sep	6	85/C12-13

Burton, Henry Eugene
to DAY, ALICE (HOOKER),
MRS. JOHN CALVIN
*1863	Aug	31	27/D13-14

Burton, Mary (Hooker), Mrs. Henry Eugene
to DAY, ALICE (HOOKER),
MRS. JOHN CALVIN
*1862	Apr-		
	May		25/D4-7
*1867	Feb	28	34/C10-D2

to HOOKER, EDWARD BEECHER
*1859	Aug	9	16/A7-10
*1876	Jan	16	52/C3-14

to HOOKER, ELIZABETH (DAGGETT),
MRS. EDWARD
*1847	Apr	29	8/B12-C1

to HOOKER, JOHN
*1859	Aug	7	16/A3-6

Burton, Mary (Hooker), Mrs. Henry Eugene
from Hooker, John

from HOOKER, ISABELLA BEECHER
1856	Jun	12	12/D9-12
1856	Jun	16	12/D13-14
1856	Jun	19	12/E3-5
1857	Apr		13/A3-6
1857	Apr	17	13/B13-C1
1859	Apr	23	15/D8-11
1859	May	1	15/E10-12
1860s			16/B1-2
1860s			16/B3
1860s			16/B4-6
1860	Apr	12	16/D6-11
1860	Apr	17	16/E6-8
1860	Apr	18	17/A3-5
1860	Apr	19	17/A6-9
1860	Apr	25	17/B8-11
1860	May	8	17/D14-E3
1860	May	12	17/E10-13
1860	May	15	18/A7-14
1860	May	19	18/C1-4
1860	May	23	18/E3-6
1860	May	27	19/A3-8
1860	Jun	1	19/B5-8
1860	Jun	11	20/A3-6
1860	Jun	12	20/A7-12
1860	Jun	13	20/A13-B2
1860	Jun	15	20/B11-C4
1860	Jun	18	20/D3-10
1860	Jun	20	21/A3-6
1860	Jun	23	21/B5-12
1860	Jun	25	21/C7-10
1860	Jun	30	21/E5-11
1860	Jul	4	22/B8-11
1860	Jul	5	22/B12-C1
1860	Jul	8	22/D2-5
1860	Jul	11	22/D10-13
1860	Jul	13	23/A2-5
1860	Jul	17	23/B2-9
1860	Jul	24	23/D11-14
1860	Aug	1	24/A6-11
1860	Aug	15	24/E9-12
1862	Nov	19	25/E7-14
1864	Mar	4	28/C2-9
1864	Mar	6	28/C10-13
1864	Mar	7	28/C14-D3
1864	Mar	8	28/D4-E5
1867	Feb	13	34/A2-13
1867	Jul	4	36/A10-B3
1867	Sep	15	36/C12-D5
1867	Sep	18	36/D6-9
1868	Jul	19	39/C3-6
c.1870			42/E3-4
1870	Oct	6	43/D4-7
1873	Jul	17	48/E11-14
1877	Jul	26	53/C10-D3
1881	Apr	1	55/B7-10
1882	Apr	8	55/C7-10
*1883	Aug	7	55/E1-4

from HOOKER, JOHN
*1883	Aug	7	55/E1-4

Burton, Rachel (Chase), Mrs. Nathaniel J.
    from HOOKER, ISABELLA BEECHER
        1859   Jan 25   15/C11-D3

Butler, Benjamin F.
    to HOOKER, ISABELLA BEECHER
        1871   Apr 14   126/D6
        1871   Apr 30   126/D7
        1877   Jan 25   126/D8-9
        1884   Sep 22   126/D10

Butler, Josephine
    to HOOKER, ISABELLA BEECHER
        1874   May 22   126/D11-14

Cameron, Kate
    to HOOKER, ISABELLA BEECHER
        *1875   Mar 16   131/A3-5

Carrington, "Friend"
    from HOOKER, ISABELLA BEECHER
        1872   46/D11-13

Chamberlin, Mary (Porter), Mrs. Franklin
    from HOOKER, ISABELLA BEECHER
        1874   Oct   2   50/E4-5
        1874   Oct 15   50/E6-13
        1874   Nov   5   51/A2-9

Chase, Marguerite B.
    to HOOKER, ISABELLA BEECHER
        1878   May 15   126/E1-2

Cheney, Edna Dow
    from HOOKER, ISABELLA BEECHER
        1884-
        1887   Feb 27   55/E5-8
        1889   Mar 23   64/B2-5

Cheney, Mary B.
    to HOOKER, ISABELLA BEECHER
        1889   Jun   6   126/E3-10

Childs, George William
    from HOOKER, ISABELLA BEECHER
        *1880   a. Jan 27   54/E2-5

Chittenden, Lucy B.
    to HOOKER, JOHN
        1880   Mar 25   126/E11-13
        1880   Apr   5   127/A3-6
    from HOOKER, ISABELLA BEECHER
        1881   Mar 18   55/B3-6

Clark, Charles H.
    to HOOKER, JOHN
        1889   May 31   127/A7-9

Clemens, Olivia (Langdon), Mrs. Samuel
    from HOOKER, ISABELLA BEECHER
        1883   b. May 3   55/D3-4

Clemens, Samuel
    from HOOKER, ISABELLA BEECHER
        1883   May   3   55/D5-6
        1905   Aug 25   85/E6-11

Colby, Mrs.
    from HOOKER, ISABELLA BEECHER
        1903   Jun 23   85/A11-14

Coleman, O. O.
    to HOOKER, ISABELLA BEECHER
        1874   Apr 25   127/A10-12

Comstock, Hannah M.
    to GALLAGHER, WILLIAM D.
        1873   b. Nov 11   127/C6-13
    to HOOKER, ISABELLA BEECHER
        1871   Nov 20   127/A13-B4
        1872   Dec 31+
        1873   Jan   6   127/B5-9
        1873   Jan 23   127/B10-11
        1873   Jun 12   127/B12-C1
        1873   Jun 19   127/C2-5
        1873   Nov 11   127/C14-D3
        1874   Feb 25   127/D4-7
        1874   Apr 17   127/D8-11
        1874   Apr 26   127/D12-14
        1874   Jun 25   127/E1-6
        1874   Aug   6   127/E7-10
        1874   Sep 15   127/E11-14
        1874   Dec 10   128/A3-6
        1875   Feb   5   128/A13
        1875   Nov 23   128/A14-B3
        1876   Apr   1   128/B4
        1876   Jun   8   128/B5-6
        1876   Jun 16   128/B7-10
        1877   Apr 19   128/B11-12
        1877   Sep 22   128/B13-Cs
        1877   Oct 21   128/C3-7
        1877   Nov   2   128/C8-11
        1877   Dec 16   128/C12-D1
        1878   Jul 10   128/D2-4
        1878   Jul 25   128/D5-9
        1878   Oct   3   128/D10-11
        1878   Oct   8   128/D12-13
        1878   Oct 16   128/D14-E2
        1879   Jan 27   128/E3-5
        1879   Oct 17   128/E6-9
    from BROWN, OLYMPIA
        1878   Jun 18   126/B13-C5

    DOCUMENTS:
        1874   Dec 28
            Essay re Woman
            and Bible   128/A7-12

Cooke, Helen M.
    to HOOKER, ISABELLA BEECHER
        1877   May   4   128/E10-12
        1877   May   5   128/E13
        1878   May   5   129/A3-5
    to HOOKER, JOHN
        1877   May   5   128/E13

Crocker, Mrs. Frank S.
to Hooker, Isabella Beecher

Crocker, Mrs. Frank S.
to HOOKER, ISABELLA BEECHER
1877   May 31   129/A6-B2

Dalghren, Sarah Madeline Vinton
to VINTON, A.H.
1870   Apr 11   129/B3-6

Davis, Edward M.
to BLADEN, MRS. E. S.
1871   Dec 7   129/C2-3
to HOOKER, ISABELLA BEECHER
1870   Apr 17   129/B7
1871   Mar 31   129/B8
1871   Apr 8   129/B9-12
1871   Jun 12   129/B13-C1
1874   Mar 14   129/C5
1874   Mar 26   129/C6-7
1875   Dec 9   129/C8-9
1876   Apr 2   129/C10-11
1876   Apr 3   129/C12-13
1876   Apr 9   129/C14-D1
1876   May 2   129/D2
1876   May 12   129/D3-4
1876   Oct 24   129/D5-6
1877   Dec 7   129/D7
1878   Feb 27   129/D8-9
1878   Feb 27   129/D10-11
1878   Mar 26   129/D12-13
1878   Apr 4   129/D14-E1
to STANTON, ELIZABETH CADY
1872   Aug 31   129/C4
from HOOKER, ISABELLA BEECHER
1878   Mar 31   53/E1-14

Davis, Paulina Wright
to ANONYMOUS
1869   Jul or
            Aug   129/E9-10
to ANTHONY, MARY S.
*1871   Sep 16   130/D3-6
to HOOKER, ISABELLA BEECHER
c. 1869   129/E3-8
1869   Aug 17   129/E11-14
1869   Sep 27   130/A3-6
1869   Dec   130/A7-10
1869   Dec 4   130/A11-14
1869   Dec 23   130/B1-4
1870 or
1871   Mar 12   130/B5-8
1870   May 23   130/B9-12
1870   Jul 10   130/B13-C4
1870   Nov 29   130/C5-D1
*1870   a. Dec 8   122/B4-11
1871   Jan 1   130/D2
1874   Mar 1   130/E10-13
*1875   Mar 16   131/A3-5
1875   Oct 26   131/A6-8
to STANTON, ELIZABETH CADY
1872   Jul 13   130/D7-12
1872   Aug 5   130/D13-E2
to WOODHULL, VICTORIA CLAFLIN

Day, Alice (Hooker), Mrs. John Calvin
from Hooker, Isabella Beecher

1874   Feb b. 27   130/E3-9
from ANTHONY, MARY S.
*1871   Sep 20   130/D3-6
from ANTHONY, SUSAN B.
1869   Jul or
            Aug   114/B2-5
from BROWN, OLYMPIA
*1870   Dec 8   122/B4-11
from HIGGINSON, THOMAS WENTWORTH
*1869   Aug 5   141/C3-4
from HOOKER, ISABELLA BEECHER
1870   Oct 12   43/D14-E3
1871   May 8   45/D11-14
from HOWE, JULIA WARD
*1869   Aug 5   141/C3-4
from LUCAS, MARGARET B.
1873   May 28   134/B14-C6
from SEVERANCE, CAROLINE
*1869   Aug 5   141/C3-4
from STANTON, ELIZABETH CADY
1869   Jul or
            Aug   137/A2-B3
from STONE, LUCY
*1869   Aug 5   141/C3-4
from VIBBERT, GEORGE
*1869   Aug 5   141/C3-4

Day, Alice (Hooker), Mrs. John Calvin
from BURTON, HENRY EUGENE
*1863   Aug 31   27/D13-14
from BURTON, MARY (HOOKER),
MRS. HENRY EUGENE
*1862   Apr-
            May   25/D4-7
*1867   Feb 28   34/C10-D2
from FOOTE, LILLY GILLETTE
*1890   Mar 27   69/B14-C11
from GILLETTE, HELEN (NICKLES),
MRS. WILLIAM
*1882   Aug 24   55/C11-14
*1887   Oct 25   57/A10-B3
from GILLETTE, WILLIAM
*1882   Aug 24   55/C11-14
from HOOKER, EDWARD BEECHER
*1889   Nov 28   67/C6-D3
*1891   Nov 26   75/E3 -
                        76/A5
from HOOKER, ISABELLA BEECHER
1853   Sep 3   12/B4-7
1853   Oct 25   12/C2-4
1856   Jun 12   12/D9-12
1856   Jun 16   12/D13-14
1856   Jun 19   12/E3-5
1857   12/E6-8
1857   Apr   13/A3-6
1857   Apr 17   13/B13-C1
1859   Apr 23   15/D8-11
1859   May 1   15/E10-12
1860s   16/B1-2
1860s   16/B3
1860s   16/B4-6
1860s   16/B7-8

1860	Jan	24	16/C9-11
1860	Apr	12	16/D6-11
1860	Apr	16	16/E2-5
1860	Apr	23	17/A10-13
1860	Apr	25	17/B8-11
1860	May	7	17/D10-13
1860	May	15	18/A7-14
1860	May	21	18/C13-D2
1860	May	22	18/D9-12
1860	Jun	2	19/B13-C2
1860	Jun	11	20/A3-6
1860	Jun	12	20/A7-12
1860	Jun	13	20/A13-B2
1860	Jun	15	20/B11-C4
1860	Jun	16	20/C5-8
1860	Jun	20	21/A7-10
1860	Jun	24	21/B13-C2
1860	Jun	30	21/E5-11
1860	Jul	4	22/B8-11
1860	Jul	8	22/D2-5
1860	Jul	10	22/D6-9
1860	Jul	13	23/A2-5
1860	Jul	17	23/B2-9
1860	Jul	24	23/D11-14
1860	Jul	30	24/A2-5
1861	Mar	27	25/A5-8
1861	Sep	3	25/A9-12
1862	Apr or May		25/C14-D3
*1862	Apr or May		25/D4-7
1862	Apr or May		25/D8-10
1862	Jul	30	25/D11-14
1862	Nov	22	26/A8-11
1862	Dec	1	26/C8-11
1863			26/D12-13
*1863	Aug	31	27/D13-14
1864			28/A2-4
1864	Jan	29	28/A5-9
1864	Oct		29/C3-4
1865			29/E2-5
1865	Jan	8	29/E6-9
1865	Jan	9	29/E10-13
1865	Jan	10	30/A2-4
1865	Jan	11	30/A5-6
1865	Jan	12	30/A7-10
1865	Jan	14	30/A11-14
1865	Jan	14	30/B1-4
1865	Jan	17	30/B5-6
1865	Jan	21	30/B7-8
1865	Jan	27	30/B9-12
1865	Feb	1	30/B13-C6
1865	Feb	6	30/C7-10
1865	Feb	9	30/C11-D8
1865	Feb	15	30/D9-E4
1865	Feb	21	30/E5-8
1865	Feb	24	30/E9-12
1865	Mar	2	31/A2-5
1865	Mar	6	31/A6-9
1865	Mar	21	31/A10-12
1865	Jun	13	31/D12-E1

c. 1866			32/A2
1866	Jan	18	32/A3-6
1866	Jan	27	32/A7-10
1866	Feb	15	32/A11-B1
1866	Feb	18	32/B2-5
1866	Mar	11	32/B6-10
1866	Nov	21	32/C1-4
1866	Dec	6	32/C5-11
1866	Dec	12	32/C12-D1
1866	Dec	20	32/D2-4
1866	Dec	21	32/D5-12
1867			32/E1-4
1867			32/E5-8
1867	Jan		33/A2-11
*1867	Jan	1	33/A12-B13
1867	Jan	4	33/B14-C3
1867	Jan	8	33/C4-6
1867	Jan	10	33/C7-10
1867	Jan	20	33/C11-14
1867	Jan	28	33/D1-4
1867	Feb	3	33/D5-12
1867	Feb	16	34/B8-C3
*1867	Feb	28	34/C10-D2
1867	Mar	7	34/D3-6
1867	Mar	17	34/E1-4
1867	Mar	26	35/A2-5
1867	Mar	27	35/A6-9
1867	Apr		35/A10-11
1867	Apr	2	35/A12-B1
1867	Apr	4	35/B2-5
1867	Apr	18	35/B6-13
1867	Apr	29	35/B14-C3
1867	May	2	35/C4-9
1867	May	11	35/C10-13
1867	May	16	35/C14-D3
1867	Jun	30	36/A2-9
1867	Jul	4	36/A10-B3
1867	Jul	13	36/B4-9
1867	Sep		36/B10-13
1867	Sep		36/B14-C3
1867	Sep	15	36/C12-D5
1867	Sep	18	36/D6-9
1867	Sep	22	36/D10-E7
1867	Sep	27	36/E8-11
1868			37/C11-14
1868			37/D1-4
1868	May		38/C8-11
1868	May	8	38/C12-13
1868	May	8	38/C14-D2
1868	May	13	38/D3-10
*1868	May	19	38/E1-4
1868	Jul	4	39/B3-6
1868	Jul	4	39/B7-8
1868	Jul	16	39/B13-C2
1868	Jul	21	39/C7-D2
1868	Aug	4	39/E5-7
1868	Aug	9	39/E8-11
1868	Nov	8	40/C4-7
1869	May	28	41/A8-11
1869	Jun	21	41/A12-B9
1869	Jun	22	41/B10-C7
1869	Jun	30	41/C8-11

1869	Aug	29	42/A10-B3
1870	Oct	6	43/D4-7
1870	Oct	13	43/E4-7
1870	Nov	4	44/A10-B3
1871	Aug	6	86/D14-E3
1871	Aug	16	46/A2-9
1873	May	1	48/D6-9
1873	May	21	48/D10-13
1873	Jun	20	48/E3-6
1873	Sep	1	49/A14-B7
c. 1874			49/C6-9
1874	Jan	25	49/C10-13
1874	Jan	28	49/D4-7
1874	Feb	2	49/D8-11
1874	Feb	8	49/D12-E1
1874	Mar	1	49/E2-5
1874	Mar	11	49/E6-9
1874	Mar	23	50/B2-9
1874	Apr	18	50/B10-C3
1874	May	2	50/C4-11
1875	Fall		51/E10-11
1876	Jul	3	53/A6-13
1877	Apr	17	53/B14-C9
1878	Aug	1	54/B14-C3
1879			54/C4-7
1879	Jun	25	54/D4-7
1880	Aug	23	54/E11-14
1880	Aug	25	55/A2-4
*1880	Sep	2	55/A5-8
1882			55/C3-6
1882	Apr	8	55/C7-10
*1882	Aug	24	55/C11-14
1882	Oct	18	55/D1-2
*1883	Jul	10	55/D7-10
1883	Jul	27	55/D11-14
1884	Dec	21	55/E9-10
1885	Jul	21	55/E11-14
*1885	Aug	3	56/A2-5
*1885	Aug	11	56/A6-13
*1885	Aug	14	56/A14-B3
*1885	Aug	31	56/B4-7
1886	Feb	2	56/B12-13
1886	May	25	56/B14-C11
1886	Jun	5	56/C12-D3
1886	Jun	22	56/D4-11
1887	Jul	22	56/D12-E1
*1887	Oct	16	56/E2-5
1887	Oct	16	56/E6-9
1887	Oct	17	56/E10-13
*1887	Oct	19	57/A2-9
*1887	Oct	25	57/A10-B3
1887	Nov	3	57/B4-7
1887	Nov	13	57/B8-13
*1887	Nov	14	57/B14-C7
1887	Nov	23	57/C8-D1
*1887	Nov	23	57/D2-9
*1887	Dec	1	57/D10-E3
1887	Dec	9	57/E4-11
*1887	Dec	11	58/A2-5
1887	Dec	13	58/A6-13
1887	Dec	21	58/A14-B3
1887	Dec	31	58/B4-7

Day, Alice (Hooker), Mrs. John Calvin
from Hooker, Isabella Beecher

1888	Jan	3	58/B8-11
*1888	Jan	10	58/B12-C9
1888	Jan	17	58/C10-13
1888	Jan	25	58/C14-E1
1888	Jan	27	58/E2-3
*1888	Feb	1	58/E4-12
*1888	Feb	5	59/A2-13
*1888	Feb	13	59/A14-B11
1888	Feb	21	59/B12-C5
1888	Feb	29	59/C6-9
1888	Feb	29	59/C10-D11
1888	Mar	14	59/D12-E3
1888	Mar	20	59/E4-11
1888	Apr	10	60/A2-9
1888	Apr	18	60/A10-11
*1888	Apr	22	60/A12-B11
*1888	Oct	5	60/C7-D4
1888	Oct	17	60/D11-14
*1888	Oct	22	60/E1-8
1888	Oct	30	61/A2-B3
*1888	Oct	31	61/B4-7
*1888	Nov	3	61/B8-C7
1888	Nov	14	61/C8-D5
1888	Nov	21	61/D6-13
1888	Nov	28	61/D14-E6
*1888	Dec	7	61/E7-10
1888	Dec	18	62/A2-13
*1888	Dec	25	62/A14-C3
1889	Jan	2	62/C6-D1
*1889	Jan	8	62/D2-13
*1889	Jan	15	63/A2-13
1889	Jan	18	63/A14-B5
1889	Jan	30	63/B6-9
*1889	Feb	5	63/C4-D1
1889	Feb	13	63/D2-9
*1889	Feb	20	64/A2-3
*1889	Mar	5	63/D12-E13
1889	Mar	13	64/A4-7
1889	Mar	22	64/A8-B1
1889	Mar	29	64/B6-C5
1889	Apr	5	64/C6-9
1889	Apr	12	64/C10-D1
1889	Apr	18	64/D2-5
1889	May	3	64/D6-E1
1889	May	17	64/E2-12
1889	May	27	65/A2-9
1889	Jun	2	65/A10-13
1889	Jun	9	65/A14-B11
*1889	Jun	16	65/B12-C5
1889	Jun	21	65/C6-13
1889	Jun	26	65/C14-D1
*1889	Jul	1	65/D2-13
1889	Jul	10	65/D14-E7
*1889	Jul	11	65/E8-9
1889	Jul	18	65/E10-13
*1889	Jul	26	66/A2-5
1889	Jul	28	66/A6-9
1889	Aug	4	86(a)/B5-14
*1889	Aug	4	66/B4-7
1889	Aug	13	66/B8-13
1889	Aug	22	66/B14-C7
1889	Aug	23	66/C8-11

Day, Alice (Hooker), Mrs. John Calvin
from Hooker, Isabella Beecher

1889	Aug	27	66/C12-D3
1889	Aug	29	86(a)/C1-4
*1889	Aug	30	66/D4-7
1889	Sep	3	66/D8-11
*1889	Sep	8	66/D12-E1
*1889	Sep	19	66/E2-9
1889	Oct	4	66/E10-13
*1889	Oct	6	67/A2-9
1889	Oct	15	67/A10-13
1889	Nov	4	67/A14-B7
*1889	Nov	18	67/B8-C5
*1889	Nov	28	67/C6-D3
1889	Dec	11	67/D4-11
*1889	Dec	14	67/D12-13
1889	Dec	19	67/D14-E5
*1889	Dec	22	67/E6-11
1890	Jan	7	68/A2-B3
1890	Jan	16	68/B4-11
1890	Jan	19	68/B12-C1
1890	Jan	23	68/C2-13
*1890	Jan	31	68/C14-D7
*1890	Feb	7	68/D8-E8
1890	Feb	13	68/E9-12
1890	Feb	28	69/A2-13
*1890	Mar	14	69/A14-B9
*1890	Mar	19	69/B10-13
*1890	Mar	27	69/B14-C11
1890	Apr	2	69/C12-D1
*1890	Apr	11	69/D2-11
*1890	Apr	18	69/D12-E5
1890	May	1	69/E6-13
*1890	May	9	70/A2-9
*1890	May	13	70/A10-B7
*1890	May	23	70/B8-C5
1890	May	29	70/C6-9
1890	Jun	4	70/C10-D7
1890	Jun	13	70/D8-11
*1890	Jun	13	70/D12-E7
*1890	Jun	27	70/E8-11
*1890	Jul	2	71/A2-B1
*1890	Jul	11	71/B2-5
1890	Jul	16	71/B6-13
1890	Jul	25	71/B14-C3
*1890	Jul	27	71/C4-7
*1890	Jul	31	71/C8-13
1890	Aug	8	71/D2-5
*1890	Aug	12	71/D6-7
*1890	Aug	20	71/D8-E1
*1890	Aug	31	71/E2-9
1890	Sep	2	71/E10-11
*1890	Oct	12	72/A2-13
1890	Oct	21	72/A14-B5
1890	Oct	28	72/B6-11
1890	Nov	7	72/B14-C5
*1890	Nov	9	72/C6-13
1890	Nov	16	72/C14-D3
1890	Dec	5	72/D4-E1
1890	Dec	10	72/E2-6
1890	Dec	16	72/E7-14
1890	Dec	30	73/A2-13
b. 1891			73/A14-B2
1891	Jan	7	73/B7-14

1891	Jan	14	73/C1-4
1891	Jan	27	73/C5-8
*1891	Feb	16	73/C9-12
1891	Mar	11	73/C13-D2
1891	Mar	15	73/D3-12
1891	Mar	22	73/E7-10
*1891	Apr	18	74/A13-B12
1891	May	21	73/D13-E6
1891	May	24	74/A2-12
*1891	Jun	15	74/B13-C6
1891	Jun	19	74/C7-14
1891	Jun	23	74/D1-4
1891	Jul	7	74/D7-10
1891	Jul	14	74/D11-14
1891	a. Aug 5		74/E2-3
1891	Aug	17	74/E8-11
1891	Aug	23	75/A2-5
1891	Sep	20	75/A6-7
1891	Sep	21	75/A8-13
1891	Sep	21	75/A14-B2
*1891	Sep	27	75/B5-12
*1891	Oct	5	75/B13-C3
1891	Oct	11	75/C4-8
1891	Oct	19	75/C9-D2
*1891	Nov	1	75/D3-8
*1891	Nov	14	75/D9-E2
*1891	Nov	26	75/E3 - 76/A5
*1891	Dec	6	76/A6-13
1891	Dec	11	76/A14-B3
1891	Dec	22	75/B3-4
1891	Dec	22	76/B4-5
1891	Dec	29	76/B6-13
1892	Jan	27	76/B14-C5
1892	Feb	4	76/C6-13
*1892	Feb	8	76/C14-D3
1892	Feb	17	76/D4-13
*1892	Feb	21	76/D14-E3
*1892	Mar	3	76/E4-8
1892	Mar	24	76/E9-14
1892	Apr	4	77/A2-5
1892	Apr	11	77/A6-9
1892	Apr	20	77/A10-13
1892	May	4	77/B8-11
1892	Jun	2	77/C4-12
1892	Jul	25	77/C13-D10
1892	Aug	7	77/D11-E4
1892	Sep	5	77/E5-10
1892	Sep	19	77/E11-14
1892	Sep	28	78/A2-5
1892	Oct	10	78/A6-13
1892	Oct	27	78/A14-B7
1892	Dec	2	78/C7-9
1892	Dec	9	78/C10-D3
1892	Dec	27	78/D4-11
1893	Feb	3	78/E6-9
1893	Jun	29	78/E10-13
1893	Jul	23	79/A2-5
1893	Aug	1	79/A6-9
*1893	Oct	12	79/C4-7
*1893	Nov	18	79/C8-11
1893	Nov	28	79/C12-D13

Day, Alice (Hooker), Mrs. John Calvin
from Hooker, Isabella Beecher

1893	Dec	15	79/D14-E7
1893	Dec	17	79/E8-13
1893	Dec	30	80/A2-5
*1894	Jan	4	80/A10-B4
*1894	Jan	24	80/B5-8
*1894	Feb	22	80/B9-C2
*1894	Feb	28	80/C3-6
*1894	Mar	4	80/C7-10
*1894	Mar	11	80/C11-14
*1894	Mar	21	80/D1-4
1894	Apr	15	80/D5-8
*1894	Apr	22	80/D9-12
1894	May	15	80/D13-E6
*1894	May	26	80/E7-14
1894	Jun	11	81/A2-5
1894	Jul	4	81/A6-9
1894	Jul	6	81/A10-13
1894	Jul	10	81/A14-B3
*1894	Jul	15	81/B4-7
*1894	Jul	20	81/B8-11
1894	Aug	5	81/B12-C1
1896	Dec	22	81/C6-9
1896	Dec	25	81/C10-13
*1897	Aug	7	81/D13-E6
1897	Aug	12	81/E7-10
1897	Aug	19	81/E11-14
1897	Aug	25	82/A2-3
*1897	Dec	6	82/A4-7
1897	Dec	22	82/A8-10
1897	Dec	26	82/A11-14
1898	Jun	29	82/B6-9
1898	Jul	16	82/B6-9
*1898	Jul	31	82/C4-7
1898	Aug	9	82/C8-11
*1898	Aug	23	82/C12-D1
1898	Sep	4	82/D2-3
1898	Sep	21	86(a)/C5-8
1898	Nov	30	82/D4-7
1899	Dec	18	82/E5-8
1899	Dec	18	82/E9-12
1900	Jan	8	83/A3-8
1900	Jan	20	83/A9-12
1900	Jan	26	83/B6-13
1900	Feb	1	83/B14-C3
1900	Mar	2	83/C7-10
1900	Mar	11	83/C11-14
1900	Mar	13	83/D1-3
1900	Mar	14	83/D4-6
1900	Mar	27	83/D7-10
1900	Sep	23	83/D11-13
1901	May	27	83/E11-14
1902	May	3	84/D2-5
1905	Sep	23	86/A5-7
n.d.			86/B13-C2

from HOOKER, JOHN

*1868	May	19	38/E1-4
*1880	Sep	2	55/A5-8
*1883	Jul	10	55/D7-10
*1885	Aug	3	56/A2-5
*1885	Aug	11	56/A6-13
*1885	Aug	14	56/A14-B3
*1885	Aug	31	56/B4-7

Day, Alice (Hooker), Mrs. John Calvin
from Hooker, John

*1887	Oct	16	56/E2-5
*1887	Oct	19	57/A2-9
*1887	Nov	23	57/D2-9
*1887	Dec	1	57/D10-E3
*1887	Dec	11	58/A2-5
*1888	Jan	10	58/B12-C9
*1888	Feb	5	59/A2-13
*1888	Feb	13	59/A14-B11
*1888	Apr	22	60/A12-B11
*1888	Oct	5	60/C7-D4
*1888	Oct	22	60/E1-8
*1888	Oct	31	61/B4-7
*1888	Nov	3	61/B8-C7
*1888	Dec	7	61/E7-10
*1889	Jan	15	63/A2-13
*1889	Feb	5	63/C4-D1
*1889	Mar	5	63/D12-E13
*1889	Feb	20	64/A2-3
*1889	Jun	16	65/B12-C5
*1889	Jul	1	65/D2-13
*1889	Jul	11	65/E8-9
*1889	Jul	26	66/A2-5
*1889	Aug	4	66/B4-7
*1889	Aug	4	86(a)/B5-14
*1889	Aug	30	66/D4-7
*1889	Sep	8	66/D12-E1
*1889	Sep	19	66/E2-9
*1889	Oct	6	67/A2-9
*1889	Nov	18	67/B8-C5
*1889	Nov	28	67/C6-D3
*1889	Dec	14	67/D12-13
*1889	Dec	22	67/E6-11
*1890	Jan	31	68/C14-D7
*1890	Feb	7	68/D8-E8
*1890	Mar	14	69/A14-B9
*1890	Mar	19	69/B10-13
*1890	Mar	27	69/B14-C11
*1890	May	9	70/A2-9
*1890	May	13	70/A10-B7
*1890	May	23	70/B8-C5
*1890	Jun	13	70/D12-E7
*1890	Jun	27	70/E8-11
*1890	Jul	2	71/A2-B1
*1890	Jul	11	71/B2-5
*1890	Jul	27	71/C4-7
*1890	Jul	31	71/C8-13
*1890	Aug	12	71/D6-7
*1890	Aug	20	71/D8-E1
*1890	Aug	31	71/E2-9
*1890	Oct	12	72/A2-13
*1890	Nov	9	72/C6-13
*1891	Feb	16	73/C9-12
*1891	Apr	18	74/A13-B12
*1891	Sep	27	75/B5-12
*1891	Oct	5	75/B13-C3
*1891	Nov	1	75/D3-8
*1891	Nov	14	75/D9-E2
*1891	Nov	26	75/E3 - 76/A5
*1891	Dec	6	76/A6-13
*1892	Feb	21	76/D14-E3
*1892	Mar	3	76/E4-8

Day, Alice (Hooker), Mrs. John Calvin
from Hooker, John

*1893	Oct	12	79/C4-7
*1893	Nov	18	79/C8-11
*1894	Jan	24	80/B5-8
*1894	Feb	22	80/B9-C2
*1894	Feb	28	80/C3-6
*1894	Mar	4	80/C7-10
*1894	Mar	11	80/C11-14
*1894	Mar	21	80/D1-4
*1894	Apr	22	80/D9-12
*1894	May	26	80/E7-14
*1894	Jul	15	81/B4-7
*1894	Jul	20	81/B8-11
*1897	Aug	7	81/D13-E6
*1897	Dec	6	82/A4-7
*1898	Jul	16	82/B14-C3
*1898	Jul	31	82/C4-7
*1898	Aug	23	82/C12-D1

from HOOKER, MARTHA (KILBOURNE),
MRS. EDWARD BEECHER

*1880	Sep	2	55/A5-8
*1887	Oct	25	57/A10-B3
*1887	Nov	14	57/B14-C7
*1888	Feb	1	58/E4-12
*1888	Nov	3	61/B8-C7
*1889	Jan	8	62/D2-13
*1889	Nov	28	67/C6-D3
*1891	Nov	26	75/E3 - 76/A5

from MERRITT, ISABEL (HOOKER),
MRS. WALTER G.

*1888	Feb	1	58/E4-12
*1891	Nov	26	75/E3 - 76/A5

Day, Katharine Seymour
from GILLETTE, HELEN (NICKLES),
MRS. WILLIAM

*1887	Oct	25	57/A10-B3

from HOOKER, MARTHA (KILBOURNE),
MRS. EDWARD

*1887	Oct	25	57/A10-B3

from HOOKER, ISABELLA BEECHER

1870s			42/D12
1875	Jun	8	51/D13-E1
*1887	Oct	25	57/A10-B3
*1891	Jan	2	73/B3-6
1891	Aug	13	74/E4-7
1892	Nov	14	78/B8-C6
1893	Jan	10	78/E2-5
1894 o.l.			80/A6-9
1897	Jan	27	81/C14-D3
1897	Mar	3	81/D7-12
1898- 1902			82/B1-3
1898	Dec	7	82/D8-11
1898	Dec	21	82/D12-13
1901	Feb	25	83/D14-E1
1901	Mar	7	83/E2-4
1901	Apr	8	83/E5-7
1901	Jul	2	84/A3-9
1901	Dec	5	84/A10-12
1902			84/A13-B4

Fletcher, Alice C.
from Hooker, Isabella Beecher

1902	Jan	12	84/B5-8
1902	Mar	19	84/B12-C12
1902	Apr	8	84/C13-D1
1902	Jul	30	84/D6-8
1902	Aug	1	84/D9-12
1902	Sep	14	84/D13-E1
1902	Sep	17	84/E2-4
1902	Sep	19	84/E5-7
1902	Sep	29	84/E8-9
1902	Nov	4	85/A2-7
1902	Dec	19	85/A8-9
1903	Aug	16	85/B1-6
1904	Sep	22	85/C14-D1
1905	Feb	7	85/D4-13
1905	Jul	27	85/D14-E2
1905	Aug	13	85/E3-5
1905	Aug	31	86/A2-4
1906	Jul	12	86/A8-9
1906	Jul	27	86/A10-13
1906	Aug	21	86/A14-B1
n.d.			86/B11-12
n.d.			86/C3-4

from HOOKER, JOHN

*1891	Jan	2	73/B3-6

Dixon, Archibald
from HOOKER, ISABELLA BEECHER

1872	Jun	20	47/E10-13

Dodge, Mary Abigail
to HOOKER, ISABELLA BEECHER

1872	Mar	25	131/A9-10

Ellis, A. A.
to HOOKER, ISABELLA BEECHER

1874	Apr	27	131/A11-12

Elmer, Helen F.
to BROWN, OLYMPIA

*1874	Jan	3	131/A13-B2

Emerson, George H.
from HOOKER, ISABELLA BEECHER

1870- 1873	Feb	23	42/D13-E2

Equal Rights Convention
from HOOKER, ISABELLA BEECHER

1872	May	24	47/E2-5

Faxon, Mr.
from HOOKER, ISABELLA BEECHER

1868			37/C8-10

Field, Mary E.
to HOOKER, ISABELLA BEECHER

1870	May	5	131/B3-6

Fletcher, Alice C.
from HOOKER, ISABELLA BEECHER

1871	Dec	8	46/D3-6

Foote, Charlotte A. (Wilcox), Mrs. Andrew Ward
    from HOOKER, ISABELLA BEECHER
        1888   Oct 10   60/D5-10

Foote, Lilly Gillette
    to DAY, ALICE (HOOKER),
    MRS. JOHN CALVIN
       *1890   Mar 27 69/B14-C11
    from HOOKER, ISABELLA BEECHER
        1906   Sep   5   86/B2-4

Foster, Julia
    to HOOKER, ISABELLA BEECHER
        1878   Sep 18   131/B7-8
        1879   Feb 18   131/B9

Foster, Julia Manuel
    to HOOKER, ISABELLA BEECHER
        1879   Apr   6 131/B10-11

Fowler, Maria A.
    from HOOKER, ISABELLA BEECHER
       *1893   Jan   1   78/D12-E1

Fuller, Sarah E.
    to HOOKER, ISABELLA BEECHER
        1877   May 28 131/B12-13
    to HOOKER, JOHN
        1877   May 28 131/B12-13

Gage, Matilda Joslyn
    to HOOKER, ISABELLA BEECHER
      *a. 1872 Apr   2   114/A6-9
        1872   Sep 16   131/C3-4
        1875   Nov 22   131/C5-10
        1875   Dec 11   131/C11-14
        1875   Dec 23   131/D1-11
        1876   Feb   1   131/D12-E1
        1876   Feb   4   131/E2-7
        1876   Feb 14   131/E8-13
        1876   Feb 16   132/A3-4
        1876   Mar   7   132/A5-8
        1878   Oct 15   132/A9-10
        1878   Oct 28   132/A11-12
        1878   Dec   9   132/A13-14
        1879   Feb 22   132/B1-2
        1879   Feb 27   132/B3-4
        1879   Feb 27   132/B5-6
        1879   Mar 12   132/B7-8
        1879   Mar 24   132/B9-10
        1879   Jul   3   132/B11-12
        1879   Jul 12   132/B13-14
    to STANTON, ELIZABETH CADY
        1870   Jun   4   131/B14-C2

Gallagher, William D.
    from COMSTOCK, HANNAH M.
        1873 b. Nov 11 127/C6-13

Garrison, William Lloyd, Sr.
    to HOOKER, ISABELLA BEECHER
        1869   Nov 12   132/C1-14

Garrison, William Lloyd, Jr.
    to HOOKER, ISABELLA BEECHER
        1889   Feb 17   132/D1-2
    from HOOKER, ISABELLA BEECHER
        1889   Jan 14   62/D14-E7

Giddings, Amelia
    to HOOKER, ISABELLA BEECHER
       *1872   MAY¼⅜ ⅛⅜¼/D3-6
    from ANTHONY, SUSAN B.
       ·*1872   May 23   132/D3-6

Gillette, Elisabeth (Hooker), Mrs. Francis
    from HOOKER, ISABELLA BEECHER
        1850s   9/E9-11

Gillette, Helen (Nickles), Mrs. William
    to DAY, ALICE (HOOKER),
    MRS. JOHN CALVIN
       *1882   Aug 24 55/C11-14
       *1887   Oct 25 57/A-10-B3
    to DAY, KATHARINE SEYMOUR
       *1887   Oct 25 57/A10-B3
    to JACKSON, ALICE (DAY), MRS. PERCY
       *1887   Oct 25 57/A10-B3

Gillette, William
    to DAY, ALICE (HOOKER),
    MRS. JOHN CALVIN
       *1882   Aug 24 55/C11-14

Grant, Julia Dent
    from HOOKER, ISABELLA BEECHER
        1872   46/D7-10

Grant, Ulysses S.
    from HOOKER, ISABELLA BEECHER
        1872   46/D7-10

Graves, Mrs. S. H.
    to HOOKER, ISABELLA BEECHER
        1871   Oct 24   132/D7-10

Greeley, Horace
    from HOOKER, ISABELLA BEECHER
        1872   Jun 29   48/A2-5
        1872   Jun 29   48/A6-9

Griffing, Josephine W.
    to HOOKER, ISABELLA BEECHER
        1870   Nov 27   132/D11-14
        1871   c. Oct   132/E1-6
    from HOOKER, ISABELLA BEECHER
        1870   Nov 26   86/D6-13
    from STEARNS, SARAH BURGER
        1871   Jun 12   141/A3-10
        1871   Jun 15   141/A11
        1871   Jun 20   141/A12-B1

Hall, Mary
    from ANTHONY, SUSAN B.
        1904   Oct 28   120/B7

Hooker, Edward Beecher
from Hooker, Isabella Beecher

*1876	Feb	20	52/D9-E2
1876	Apr	11	52/E3-14
1876	May	23	53/A2-5
1878	Feb	15	53/D9-12
1878	Apr	7	54/A2-13
1878	Apr	12	54/A14-B5
1878	Apr	15	54/B6-13
1879	Mar	5	54/C8-11
1879	Jul	5	54/D8-11
1880	Jan		54/D12-E1
1880	Sep	8	55/A9-12
1880	Sep	8	55/A13-B2

from HOOKER, JOHN

*1874	Jul	21	50/C12-D5
*1875	Jul	18	51/E2-5
*1875	Dec	14	52/B5-8
*1876	Jan	16	52/C3-14
*1876	Feb	20	52/D9-E2

Hooker, Elisabeth (Daggett), Mrs. Edward
from BURTON, MARY (HOOKER),
MRS. HENRY EUGENE

*1847	Apr	29	8/B12-C1

from HART, EDWARD L.

*1847	Apr	29	8/B12-C1

from HART, NANCY (HOOKER),
MRS. EDWARD L.

*1847	Apr	29	8/B12-C1

from HOOKER, ISABELLA BEECHER

*1847	Jan	22	7/B14
*1847	Apr	29	8/B12-C1
1849	Jul	4	8/E7-10
*1853	a. May 24		12/A2-B1

from HOOKER, JOHN

*1853	May	16	12/A2-B1

Hooker, Isabella Beecher
to ALLEN, GEORGE R.

*1872			46/D14-E3
1872	May	24	47/E2-5

to ALLEN, ROBERT

1867			32/D13-14
1867	Feb	16	34/B4-7
1867	Mar	10	34/D7-14
1867	Mar	18	34/E5-12
1867	May	16	35/D4-7
1867	Jun	24	35/D8-E1
1867	Jun	29	35/E2-9
1867	Sep	12	36/C4-11
1867	Oct	23	37/A2-13
1867	Nov	17	37/A14-B13
1867	Nov	29	37/B14-C7
1868	Jan	1	37/D5-E6
1868	Feb	4	38/A2-13
1868	Apr	1	38/A14-C1
1868	Apr	14	38/C2-7
1868	May	19	38/D11-14
1868	May	29	39/A2-13
1868	Jun	8	39/A14-B2
1868	Jul	28	39/D3-E4
1868	Aug	18	40/A2-9
1868	Nov	6	40/A10-C3

Hooker, Isabella Beecher
to Beecher, Lydia (Beals) Jackson, Mrs. Lyman

1868	Nov	9	40/C8-11
1868	Nov	28	40/D2-7
1869	Feb	22	41/A2-7
1869	Oct	10	42/B4-11
*1870	Jan	4	43/B6-11
1870	May	9	43/C2-5
1870	May	15	43/C6-D3
1870	Oct	11	43/D8-13

to AMES, ADELBERT

1871	Apr	15	45/D7-10
1872	Jan	7	46/E8-11

to ANONYMOUS

1860	Apr	25	17/B6-7
1871			44/C12-14
1871	Mar	24	45/C5
1871	Apr	14	45/D4-6
1871	Dec-		
1872	Jan		46/C13-D2
1875	Apr	7	51/C11-13
1890	Nov	4	72/B12-13
1901	Apr	25	83/E8-10
1903	Apr	2	85/A10

to ANTHONY, SUSAN B.

1869			40/E6-10
1871	Mar	11	44/D7-E14
*1872	Jan	21	47/A2-B1
1872	May	26	47/E4-5
1872	Jul	18	48/B12-C3
1875	Feb	18	51/B2-7

to ATWOOD, MRS.

1880 or			
1886	Jun	11	54/E10

to BACON, LEONARD

1873	Mar	26	86/E4

to BARBER, JOHN

1876	c. Aug 31		53/B8-9

to BEECHER, CATHARINE E.

1860	Apr	17	16/E9-14
c. 1869			40/D8-E1

to BEECHER, ESTHER M.

*1840	Jan	7	2/D4-7
1842	Feb	26	4/D1-4
1842	Aug	8	4/D10-13
1846	Aug 22+		
1847	Jun	22	6/E1-9

to BEECHER, FRANCES (JOHNSON),
MRS. JAMES

1891	Jul		74/D5-6
1893	Aug	24	79/C2-3
*1899	Jan	22	82/E1-4

to BEECHER, HENRY WARD

1860	May		17/C2-5
1861	Dec	22	25/B5-C2
1863	Apr	20	27/C3-D4

to BEECHER, KATHARINE (EDES),
MRS. WILLIAM

1839	Dec	30	2/C14-D3
transcript			1/B7-9

to BEECHER, LYDIA (BEALS) JACKSON,
MRS. LYMAN

*1837	Jul	3	2/A4-7

Hooker, Isabella Beecher
to Beecher, Lydia (Beals) Jackson, Mrs. Lyman

1846	May 10	6/D7-8
1860s		16/A11-14

to BEECHER, LYMAN

*1837	Jul	3	2/A4-7
1846	May	10	6/D7-8

to BEECHER, MARY FRANCES (BEECHER), MRS. HENRY WARD

1898 or			
1899	Nov	26	82/B4-5
1902	Feb	10	84/B9-11

to BEECHER, THOMAS KINNICUT

1863	Apr	1	27/B9-C2

to BELMONT, AUGUST

1872	Apr	13	47/D2-4

to BINGHAM, JOHN ARMOR

1871	Jan	44/D1-4

to BLACKWELL, HENRY BROWN

1869	Dec	1	42/D7-10
1872	Jul	14	48/A10-B11
1873	a. Nov 22		49/B12-13
1897	Aug	25	82/A2-3

to BONNER, ROBERT

b. 1899	82/D14

to BOWLES, SAMUEL

1876	Jan	5	86/E7-8
1877	Mar	26	86(a)/A2-13
1877	Mar	26	86(a)/A14-B1

to BROWN, BENJAMIN GRATZ

1872	Mar	8	47/C5-8
1872	Apr	8	47/C9-11

to BROWN, OLYMPIA

1871	Aug	5	45/E5-8
1872	Feb	14	47/B2-9
1873	Nov	8	49/B8-11
1873	Dec	30	49/B14-C5
1874	Jan	6	49/C14-D3
1874	Aug	28	50/D6-E3
1881	Jul	28	55/B11-C2
1889	Feb	18	63/D10-11
1891	b. Aug 5		74/E1
*1892	Apr	26	77/B4-7
1901	Apr	25	83/E8-10

to BURTON, AGNES (MOSS), MRS. RICHARD

1904	Sep	6	85/C12-13

to BURTON, MARY (HOOKER), MRS. HENRY EUGENE

1856	Jun	12	12/D9-12
1856	Jun	16	12/D13-14
1856	Jun	19	12/E3-5
1857	Apr		13/A3-6
1857	Apr	17	13/B13-C1
1859	Apr	23	15/D8-11
1859	May	1	15/E10-12
1860s			16/B1-2
1860s			16/B3
1860s			16/B4-6
1860	Apr	12	16/D6-11
1860	Apr	17	16/E6-8
1860	Apr	18	17/A3-5
1860	Apr	19	17/A6-9
1860	Apr	25	17/B8-11

Hooker, Isabella Beecher
to Clemens, Olivia (Langdon), Mrs. Samuel

1860	May	8	17/D14-E3
1860	May	12	17/E10-13
1860	May	15	18/A7-14
1860	May	19	18/C1-4
1860	May	23	18/E3-6
1860	May	27	19/A3-8
1860	Jun	1	19/B5-8
1860	Jun	11	20/A3-6
1860	Jun	12	20/A7-12
1860	Jun	13	20/A13-B2
1860	Jun	15	20/B11-C4
1860	Jun	18	20/D3-10
1860	Jun	20	21/A3-6
1860	Jun	23	21/B5-12
1860	Jun	25	21/C7-10
1860	Jun	30	21/E5-11
1860	Jul	4	22/B8-11
1860	Jul	5	22/B12-C1
1860	Jul	8	22/D2-5
1860	Jul	11	22/D10-13
1860	Jul	13	23/A2-5
1860	Jul	17	23/B2-9
1860	Jul	24	23/D11-14
1860	Aug	1	24/A6-11
1860	Aug	15	24/E9-12
1862	Nov	19	25/E7-14
1864	Mar	4	28/C2-9
1864	Mar	6	28/C10-13
1864	Mar	7	28/C14-D3
1864	Mar	8	28/D4-E5
1867	Feb	13	34/A2-13
1867	Jul	4	36/A10-B3
1867	Sep	15	36/C12-D5
1867	Sep	18	36/D6-9
1868	Jul	19	39/C3-6
c. 1870			42/E3-4
1870	Oct	6	43/D4-7
1873	Jul	17	48/E11-14
1877	Jul	26	53/C10-D3
1881	Apr	1	55/B7-10
1882	Apr	8	55/C7-10
*1883	Aug	7	55/E1-4

to BURTON, RACHEL (CHASE), MRS. NATHANIEL J.

1859	Jan	25	15/C11-D3

to CARRINGTON, "FRIEND"

1872	46/D11-13

to CHAMBERLIN, MARY (PORTER), MRS. FRANKLIN

1874	Oct	2	50/E4-5
1874	Oct	15	50/E6-13
1874	Nov	5	51/A2-9

to CHENEY, EDNA DOW

1884-			
1887	Feb	27	55/E5-8
1889	Mar	23	64/B2-5

to CHILDS, GEORGE WILLIAM

*1880	a. Jan 27		54/E2-5

to CHITTENDEN, LUCY B.

1881	Mar	18	55/B3-6

to CLEMENS, OLIVIA (LANGDON), MRS. SAMUEL

1883	b. May 3	55/D3-4

to CLEMENS, SAMUEL			
1883	May	3	55/D5-6
1905	Aug	25	85/E6-11

to COLBY, MRS.			
1903	Jun	23	85/A11-14

to DAVIS, EDWARD M.			
1878	Mar	31	53/E1-14

to DAVIS, PAULINA WRIGHT			
1870	Oct	12	43/D14-E3
1871	May	8	45/D11-14

to DAY, ALICE (HOOKER), MRS. JOHN CALVIN			
1853	Sep	3	12/B4-7
1853	Oct	25	12/C2-4
1856	Jun	12	12/D9-12
1856	Jun	16	12/D13-14
1856	Jun	19	12/E3-5
1857			12/E6-8
1857	Apr		13/A3-6
1857	Apr	17	13/B13-C1
1859	Apr	23	15/D8-11
1859	May	1	15/E10-12
1860s			16/B1-2
1860s			16/B3
1860s			16/B4-6
1860s			16/B7-8
1860	Jan	24	16/C9-11
1860	Apr	12	16/D6-11
1860	Apr	16	16/E2-5
1860	Apr	23	17/A10-13
1860	Apr	25	17/B8-11
1860	May	7	17/D10-13
1860	May	15	18/A7-14
1860	May	21	18/C13-D2
1860	May	22	18/D9-12
1860	Jun	2	19/B13-C2
1860	Jun	11	20/A3-6
1860	Jun	12	20/A7-12
1860	Jun	13	20/A13-B2
1860	Jun	15	20/B11-C4
1860	Jun	16	20/C5-8
1860	Jun	20	21/A7-10
1860	Jun	24	21/B13-C2
1860	Jun	30	21/E5-11
1860	Jul	4	22/B8-11
1860	Jul	8	22/D2-5
1860	Jul	10	22/D6-9
1860	Jul	13	23/A2-5
1860	Jul	17	23/B2-9
1860	Jul	24	23/D11-14
1860	Jul	30	24/A2-5
1861	Mar	27	25/A5-8
1861	Sep	3	25/A9-12
1862	Apr-May		25/C14-D3
*1862	Apr-May		25/D4-7
1862	Apr-May		25/D8-10
1862	Jul	30	25/D11-14
1862	Nov	22	26/A8-11
1862	Dec	1	26/C8-11
1863			26/D12-13
*1863	Aug	31	27/D13-14

1864			28/A2-4
1864	Jan	29	28/A5-9
1864	Oct		29/C3-4
1865			29/E2-5
1865	Jan	8	29/E6-9
1865	Jan	9	29/E10-13
1865	Jan	10	30/A2-4
1865	Jan	11	30/A5-6
1865	Jan	12	30/A7-10
1865	Jan	14	30/A11-14
1865	Jan	14	30/B1-4
1865	Jan	17	30/B5-6
1865	Jan	21	30/B7-8
1865	Jan	27	30/B9-12
1865	Feb	1	30/B13-C6
1865	Feb	6	30/C7-10
1865	Feb	9	30/C11-D8
1865	Feb	15	30/D9-E4
1865	Feb	21	30/E5-8
1865	Feb	24	30/E9-12
1865	Mar	2	31/A2-5
1865	Mar	6	31/A6-9
1865	Mar	21	31/A10-12
1865	Jun	13	31/D12-E1
c. 1866			32/A2
1866	Jan	18	32/A3-6
1866	Jan	27	32/A7-10
1866	Feb	15	32/A11-B1
1866	Feb	18	32/B2-5
1866	Mar	11	32/B6-10
1866	Nov	21	32/C1-4
1866	Dec	6	32/C5-11
1866	Dec	12	32/C12-D1
1866	Dec	20	32/D2-4
1866	Dec	21	32/D5-12
1867			32/E1-4
1867			32/E5-8
1867	Jan		33/A2-11
*1867	Jan	1	33/A12-B13
1867	Jan	4	33/B14-C3
1867	Jan	8	33/C4-6
1867	Jan	10	33/C7-10
1867	Jan	20	33/C11-14
1867	Jan	28	33/D1-4
1867	Feb	3	33/D5-12
1867	Feb	16	34/B8-C3
*1867	Feb	28	34/C10-D2
1867	Mar	7	34/D3-6
1867	Mar	17	34/E1-4
1867	Mar	26	35/A2-5
1867	Mar	27	35/A6-9
1867	Apr		35/A10-11
1867	Apr	2	35/A12-B1
1867	Apr	4	35/B2-5
1867	Apr	18	35/B6-13
1867	Apr	29	35/B14-C3
1867	May	2	35/C4-9
1867	May	11	35/C10-13
1867	May	16	35/C14-D3
1867	Jun	30	36/A2-9
1867	Jul	4	36/A10-B3
1867	Jul	13	36/B4-9

1867	Sep		36/B10-13
1867	Sep		36/B14-C3
1867	Sep	15	36/C12-D5
1867	Sep	18	36/D6-9
1867	Sep	22	36/D10-E7
1867	Sep	27	36/E8-11
1868			37/C11-14
1868			37/D1-4
1868	May		38/C8-11
1868	May	8	38/C12-13
1868	May	8	38/C14-D2
1868	May	13	38/D3-10
*1868	May	19	38/E1-4
1868	Jul	4	39/B3-6
1868	Jul	4	39/B7-8
1868	Jul	16	39/B13-C2
1868	Jul	21	39/C7-D2
1868	Aug	4	39/E5-7
1868	Aug	9	39/E8-11
1868	Nov	8	40/C4-7
1869	May	28	41/A8-11
1869	Jun	21	41/A12-B9
1869	Jun	22	41/B10-C7
1869	Jun	30	41/C8-11
1869	Aug	29	42/A10-B3
1870	Oct	6	43/D4-7
1870	Oct	13	43/E4-7
1870	Nov	4	44/A10-B3
1871	Aug	6	86/D14-E3
1871	Aug	16	46/A2-9
1873	May	1	48/D6-9
1873	May	21	48/D10-13
1873	Jun	20	48/E3-6
1873	Sep	1	49/A14-B7
c. 1874			49/C6-9
1874	Jan	25	49/C10-13
1874	Jan	28	49/D4-7
1874	Feb	2	49/D8-11
1874	Feb	8	49/D12-E1
1874	Mar	1	49/E2-5
1874	Mar	11	49/E6-9
1874	Mar	23	50/B2-9
1874	Apr	18	50/B10-C3
1874	May	2	50/C4-11
1875	Fall		51/E10-11
1876	Jul	3	53/A6-13
1877	Apr	17	53/B14-C9
1878	Aug	1	54/B14-C3
1879			54/C4-7
1879	Jun	25	54/D4-7
1880	Aug	23	54/E11-14
1880	Aug	25	55/A2-4
*1880	Sep	2	55/A5-8
1882			55/C3-6
1882	Apr	8	55/C7-10
*1882	Aug	24	55/C11-14
1882	Oct	18	55/D1-2
*1883	Jul	10	55/D7-10
1883	Jul	27	55/D11-14
1884	Dec	21	55/E9-10
1885	Jul	21	55/Ell-14
*1885	Aug	3	56/A2-5

*1885	Aug	11	56/A6-13
*1885	Aug	14	56/A14-B3
*1885	Aug	31	56/B4-7
1886	Feb	2	56/B12-13
1886	May	25	56/B14-C11
1886	Jun	5	56/C12-D3
1886	Jun	22	56/D4-11
1887	Jul	22	56/D12-E1
*1887	Oct	16	56/E2-5
1887	Oct	16	56/E6-9
1887	Oct	17	56/E10-13
*1887	Oct	19	57/A2-9
*1887	Oct	25	57/A10-B3
1887	Nov	3	57/B4-7
1887	Nov	13	57/B8-13
*1887	Nov	14	57/B14-C7
1887	Nov	23	57/C8-D1
*1887	Nov	23	57/D2-9
*1887	Dec	1	57/D10-E3
1887	Dec	9	57/E4-11
*1887	Dec	11	58/A2-5
1887	Dec	13	58/A6-13
1887	Dec	21	58/A14-B3
1887	Dec	31	58/B4-7
1888	Jan	3	58/B8-11
*1888	Jan	10	58/B12-C9
1888	Jan	17	58/C10-13
1888	Jan	25	58/C14-E1
1888	Jan	27	58/E2-3
*1888	Feb	1	58/E4-12
*1888	Feb	5	59/A2-13
*1888	Feb	13	59/A14-B11
1888	Feb	21	59/B12-C5
1888	Feb	29	59/C6-9
1888	Feb	29	59/C10-D11
1888	Mar	14	59/D12-E3
1888	Mar	20	59/E4-11
1888	Apr	10	60/A2-9
1888	Apr	18	60/A10-11
*1888	Apr	22	60/A12-B11
*1888	Oct	5	60/C7-D4
1888	Oct	17	60/D11-14
*1888	Oct	22	60/E1-8
1888	Oct	30	61/A2-B3
*1888	Oct	31	61/B4-7
*1888	Nov	3	61/B8-C7
1888	Nov	14	61/C8-D5
1888	Nov	21	61/D6-13
1888	Nov	28	61/D14-E6
*1888	Dec	7	61/E7-10
1888	Dec	18	62/A2-13
*1888	Dec	25	62/A14-C3
1889	Jan	2	62/C6-D1
*1889	Jan	8	62/D2-13
1889	Jan	15	63/A2-13
*1889	Jan	18	63/A14-B5
1889	Jan	30	63/B6-9
*1889	Feb	5	63/C4-D1
1889	Feb	13	63/D2-9
*1889	Feb	20	64/A2-3
*1889	Mar	5	63/D12-E13
1889	Mar	13	64/A4-7

1889	Mar	22	64/A8-B1
1889	Mar	29	64/B6-C5
1889	Apr	5	64/C6-9
1889	Apr	12	64/C10-D1
1889	Apr	18	64/D2-5
1889	May	3	64/D6-E1
1889	May	17	64/E2-12
1889	May	27	65/A2-9
1889	Jun	2	65/A10-13
1889	Jun	9	65/A14-B11
*1889	Jun	16	65/B12-C5
1889	Jun	21	65/C6-13
1889	Jun	26	65/C14-D1
*1889	Jul	1	65/D2-13
1889	Jul	10	65/D14-E7
*1889	Jul	11	65/E8-9
1889	Jul	18	65/E10-13
*1889	Jul	26	66/A2-5
1889	Jul	28	66/A6-9
1889	Aug	4	86(a)/B5-14
*1889	Aug	4	66/B4-7
1889	Aug	13	66/B8-13
1889	Aug	22	66/B14-C7
1889	Aug	23	66/C8-11
1889	Aug	27	66/C12-D3
1889	Aug	29	86(a)/C1-4
*1889	Aug	30	66/D4-7
1889	Sep	3	66/D8-11
*1889	Sep	8	66/D12-E1
*1889	Sep	19	66/E2-9
1889	Oct	4	66/E10-13
*1889	Oct	6	67/A2-9
1889	Oct	15	67/A10-13
1889	Nov	4	67/A14-B7
*1889	Nov	18	67/B8-C5
*1889	Nov	28	67/C6-D3
1889	Dec	11	67/D4-11
*1889	Dec	14	67/D12-13
1889	Dec	19	67/D14-E5
*1889	Dec	22	67/E6-11
1890	Jan	7	68/A2-B3
1890	Jan	16	68/B4-11
1890	Jan	19	68/B12-C1
1890	Jan	23	68/C2-13
*1890	Jan	31	68/C14-D7
*1890	Feb	7	68/D8-E8
1890	Feb	13	68/E9-12
1890	Feb	28	69/A2-13
*1890	Mar	14	69/A14-B9
*1890	Mar	19	69/B10-13
*1890	Mar	27	69/B14-C11
1890	Apr	2	69/C12-D1
*1890	Apr	11	69/D2-11
1890	Apr	18	69/D12-E5
1890	May	1	69/E6-13
*1890	May	9	70/A2-9
*1890	May	13	70/A10-B7
*1890	May	23	70/B8-C5
1890	May	29	70/C6-9
1890	Jun	4	70/C10-D7
1890	Jun	13	70/D8-11
*1890	Jun	13	70/D12-E7
*1890	Jun	27	70/E8-11
*1890	Jul	2	71/A2-B1
*1890	Jul	11	71/B2-5
1890	Jul	16	71/B6-13
1890	Jul	25	71/B14-C3
*1890	Jul	27	71/C4-7
*1890	Jul	31	71/C8-13
1890	Aug	8	71/D2-5
*1890	Aug	12	71/D6-7
*1890	Aug	20	71/D8-E1
*1890	Aug	31	71/E2-9
1890	Sep	2	71/E10-11
*1890	Oct	12	72/A2-13
1890	Oct	21	72/A14-B5
1890	Oct	28	72/B6-11
1890	Nov	7	72/B14-C5
*1890	Nov	9	72/C6-13
1890	Nov	16	72/C14-D3
1890	Dec	5	72/D4-E1
1890	Dec	10	72/E2-6
1890	Dec	16	72/E7-14
1890	Dec	30	73/A2-13
b. 1891			73/A14-B2
1891	Jan	7	73/B7-14
1891	Jan	14	73/C1-4
1891	Jan	27	73/C5-8
*1891	Feb	16	73/C9-12
1891	Mar	11	73/C13-D2
1891	Mar	15	73/D3-12
1891	Mar	22	73/E7-10
*1891	Apr	18	74/A13-B12
1891	May	21	73/D13-E6
1891	May	24	74/A2-12
1891	Jun	15	74/B13-C6
1891	Jun	19	74/C7-14
1891	Jun	23	74/D1-4
1891	Jul	7	74/D7-10
1891	Jul	14	74/D11-14
1891	a. Aug 5		74/E2-3
1891	Aug	17	74/E8-11
1891	Aug	23	75/A2-5
1891	Sep	20	75/A6-7
1891	Sep	21	75/A8-13
1891	Sep	21	75/A14-B2
*1891	Sep	27	75/B5-12
*1891	Oct	5	75/B13-C3
1891	Oct	11	75/C4-8
1891	Oct	19	75/C9-D2
*1891	Nov	1	75/D3-8
*1891	Nov	14	75/D9-E2
*1891	Nov	26	75/E3 - 76/A5
*1891	Dec	6	76/A6-13
1891	Dec	11	76/A14-B3
1891	Dec	22	75/B3-4
1891	Dec	22	76/B4-5
1891	Dec	29	76/B6-13
1892	Jan	27	76/B14-C5
1892	Feb	4	76/C6-13
*1892	Feb	8	76/C14-D3
1892	Feb	17	76/D4-13
*1892	Feb	21	76/D14-E3

*1892	Mar 3	76/E4-8
1892	Mar 24	76/E9-14
1892	Apr 4	77/A2-5
1892	Apr 11	77/A6-9
1892	Apr 20	77/A10-13
1892	May 4	77/B8-11
1892	Jun 2	77/C4-12
1892	Jul 25	77/C13-D10
1892	Aug 7	77/D11-E4
1892	Sep 5	77/E5-10
1892	Sep 19	77/E11-14
1892	Sep 28	78/A2-5
1892	Oct 10	78/A6-13
1892	Oct 27	78/A14-B7
1892	Dec 2	78/C7-9
1892	Dec 9	78/C10-D3
1892	Dec 27	78/D4-11
1893	Feb 3	78/E6-9
1893	Jun 29	78/E10-13
1893	Jul 23	79/A2-5
1893	Aug 1	79/A6-9
*1893	Oct 12	79/C4-7
*1893	Nov 18	79/C8-11
1893	Nov 28	79/C12-D13
1893	Dec 15	79/D14-E7
1893	Dec 17	79/E8-13
1893	Dec 30	80/A2-5
1894	Jan 4	80/A10-B4
*1894	Jan 24	80/B5-8
*1894	Feb 22	80/B9-C2
*1894	Feb 28	80/C3-6
*1894	Mar 4	80/C7-10
*1894	Mar 11	80/C11-14
*1894	Mar 21	80/D1-4
1894	Apr 15	80/D5-8
*1894	Apr 22	80/D9-12
1894	May 15	80/D13-E6
*1894	May 26	80/E7-14
1894	Jun 11	81/A2-5
1894	Jul 4	81/A6-9
1894	Jul 6	81/A10-13
1894	Jul 10	81/A14-B3
*1894	Jul 15	81/B4-7
*1894	Jul 20	81/B8-11
1894	Aug 5	81/B12-C1
1896	Dec 22	81/C6-9
1896	Dec 25	81/C10-13
*1897	Aug 7	81/D13-E6
1897	Aug 12	81/E7-10
1897	Aug 19	81/E11-14
1897	Aug 25	82/A2-3
*1897	Dec 6	82/A4-7
1897	Dec 22	82/A8-10
1897	Dec 26	82/A11-14
1898	Jun 29	82/B6-9
*1898	Jul 16	82/B14-C3
*1898	Jul 31	82/C4-7
1898	Aug 9	82/C8-11
*1898	Aug 23	82/C12-D1
1898	Sep 4	82/D2-3
1898	Sep 21	86(a)/C5-8
1898	Nov 30	82/D4-7

1899	Dec 18	82/E5-8
1899	Dec 18	82/E9-12
1900	Jan 8	83/A3-8
1900	Jan 20	83/A9-12
1900	Jan 26	83/B6-13
1900	Feb 1	83/B14-C3
1900	Mar 2	83/C7-10
1900	Mar 11	83/C11-14
1900	Mar 13	83/D1-3
1900	Mar 14	83/D4-6
1900	Mar 27	83/D7-10
1900	Sep 23	83/D11-13
1901	May 27	83/E11-14
1902	May 3	84/D2-5
1905	Sep 23	86/A5-7
n.d.		86/B13-C2

to DAY, KATHARINE SEYMOUR

1870s		42/D12
1875	Jun 8	51/D13-E1
*1887	Oct 25	57/A10-B3
*1891	Jan 2	73/B3-6
1891	Aug 13	74/E4-7
1892	Nov 14	78/B8-C6
1893	Jan 10	78/E2-5
1894 *o.l.*		80/A6-9
1897	Jan 27	81/C14-D3
1897	Mar 3	81/D7-12
1898-1902		82/B1-3
1898	Dec 7	82/D8-11
1898	Dec 21	82/D12-13
1901	Feb 25	83/D14-E1
1901	Mar 7	83/E2-4
1901	Apr 8	83/E5-7
1901	Jul 2	84/A3-9
1901	Dec 5	84/A10-12
1902		84/A13-B4
1902	Jan 12	84/B5-8
1902	Mar 19	84/B12-C12
1902	Apr 8	84/C13-D1
1902	Jul 30	84/D6-8
1902	Aug 1	84/D9-12
1902	Sep 14	84/D13-E1
1902	Sep 17	84/E2-4
1902	Sep 19	84/E5-7
1902	Sep 29	84/E8-9
1902	Nov 4	85/A2-7
1902	Dec 19	85/A8-9
1903	Aug 16	85/B1-6
1904	Sep 22	85/C14-D1
1905	Feb 7	85/D4-13
1905	Jul 27	85/D14-E2
1905	Aug 13	85/E3-5
1905	Aug 31	86/A2-4
1906	Jul 12	86/A8-9
1906	Jul 27	86/A10-13
1906	Aug 21	86/A14-B1
n.d.		86/B11-12
n.d.		86/C3-4

to DIXON, ARCHIBALD

1872	Jun 20	47/E10-13

to EMERSON, GEORGE H.

1870-

1873			42/D13-E2

to EQUAL RIGHTS CONVENTION

1872	May	24	47/E2-5

to FAXON, MR.

1868			37/C8-10

to FLETCHER, ALICE C.

1871	Dec	8	46/D3-6

to FOOTE, CHARLOTTE A. (WILCOX),
MRS. ANDREW WARD

1888	Oct	10	60/D5-10

to FOOTE, LILLY GILLETTE

1906	Sep	5	86/B2-4

to FOWLER, MARIA A.

*1893	Jan	1	78/D12-E1

to GARRISON, WILLIAM LLOYD, JR.

1889	Jan	14	62/D14-E7

to GILLETTE, ELISABETH (HOOKER),
MRS. FRANCIS

1850s			9/E9-11

to GRANT, JULIA DENT

1872			46/D7-10

to GRANT, ULYSSES S.

1872			46/D7-10

to GREELEY, HORACE

1872	Jun	29	48/A2-5
1872	Jun	29	48/A6-9

to GRIFFING, JOSEPHINE W.

1870	Nov	26	86/D6-13

to HARBERT, ELIZABETH BOYNTON

1878	Jan	17	53/D8

to HAWLEY, HARRIET (FOOTE),
MRS. JOSEPH ROSWELL

1886	Feb	13	86(a)/B3-4

to HAWLEY, JOSEPH ROSWELL

*1855	Jan	20	12/C10-D2
1900	Feb	18	83/C4-5

to HAZLETT, M. ADELLE

1871	Mar	28	45/C6-11

to HOOKER, EDWARD BEECHER

1857	Apr		13/A3-6
1859	Apr	23	15/D8-11
*1859	Aug	9	16/A7-10
1860s			16/B9-11
1860	May	15	18/A7-14
1860	Jun	14	20/B7-10
1864	Jan	30	28/A10-12
1867	Jul	4	36/A10-B3
1867	Sep	18	36/D6-9
1868	Jul	7	39/B9-12
1868	Nov	17	40/C12-D1
1869	Jul	24	41/C12-D3
1870	Oct	6	43/D4-7
1870	Oct	27	44/A2-9
1870	Nov	10	44/B4-7
1871	Aug	11	45/E9-12
1872	Mar	7	47/B10-C4
1872	Apr	13	47/D5-6
1872	Apr	18	47/D7-8
1872	Jun	7	47/E6-9
1873	Jun	12	48/D14-E2
1873	Jun	24	48/E7-10

1873	Jul	19	49/A2-5
1873	Jul	26	49/A6-7
1873	Jul	31	49/A8-9
1873	Aug	17	49/A10-13
*1874	Jul	21	50/C12-D5
*1875	Jul	18	51/E2-5
1875	Oct	26	52/A2-5
1875	Oct	30	52/A6
1875	Dec	7	52/A7-B4
*1875	Dec	14	52/B5-8
*1876	Jan	16	52/C3-14
1876	Jan	20	52/D1-4
1876	Jan	31	52/D5-8
*1876	Feb	20	52/D9-E2
1876	Apr	11	52/E3-14
1876	May	23	53/A2-5
1878	Feb	15	53/D9-12
1878	Apr	7	54/A2-13
1878	Apr	12	54/A14-B5
1878	Apr	15	54/B6-B13
1879	Mar	5	54/C8-11
1879	Jul	5	54/D8-11
1880	Jan		54/D12-E1
1880	Sep	8	55/A9-12
1880	Sep	8	55/A13-B2

to HOOKER, ELISABETH (DAGGETT),
MRS. EDWARD

*1847	Jan	22	7/B14
*1847	Apr	29	8/B12-C1
1849	Jul	4	8/E7-10
*1853	a. May 24		12/A2-B1

to HOOKER, JOHN

1839	Jul	21	2/A8-11
1839	Jul	27	2/A12-13
1839	Aug	30	2/A14-B3
1839	Sep	12	2/B4-7
1839	Sep	25	2/B8-11
*1839	Oct	21	2/B12-C1
*transcript			1/A4-7
1839	Nov	9	2/C2-5
transcript			1/A8-12
1839	Dec	2	2/C6-9
transcript			1/A13-B3
1839	Dec	25	2/C10-13
transcript			1/B4-6
1840	Jan	22	2/D8-11
1840	Feb	22	2/D12-E1
1840	Mar	17	2/E2-5
1840	Apr	8	2/E6-9
1840	May	5	2/E10-13
1840	May	30	3/A3-6
1840	Nov	14	3/A7-10
1840	Nov	28	3/A11-14
1840	Dec	9	3/B1-4
transcript			1/B10-12
1840	Dec	18	3/B5-8
transcript			1/B13-C1
1841	Jan	2	3/B9-12
1841	Jan	16	3/B13-C2
1841	Jan	22	3/C3-6
transcript			1/C2-4
1841	Feb	7	3/C7-10

transcript			1/C5-7
1841	Feb	11	3/C11-14
1841	Feb	22	3/D1-4
1841	Mar	1	3/D5-6
1841	Mar	9	3/D7-8
1841	Mar	16	3/D9-11
1841	Apr	21	3/D12-E1
1841	Apr	22	3/E2-5
1841	May	16	3/E6-9
1841	May	27	3/E10-11
1841	Jun	7	4/A3-6
1841	Jun	12	4/A7-10
1841	Jun	19	4/A11-14
1841	Jun	25	4/B1-4
1841	Jun	29	4/B5-7
1841	Jul	2	4/B8-11
1841	Jul	9	4/B12-13
1841	Jul	12	4/B14-C2
1841	Jul	14	4/C3-6
1841	Jul	19	4/C7-10
1841	Aug	2	4/C11-14
1842	Jun	30	4/D5-6
1842	Jul	15	4/D7-9
1842	Aug	13	4/D14-E1
1842	Dec	2	4/E2-3
1842	Dec	4	4/E4-6
1842	Dec	30	4/E7-10
1843	Jan	2	4/E11-13
1843	Jan	4	5/A3-6
1843	Mar	25	5/A7-10
1843	Apr	6	5/A11-14
1843	May	6	5/B1-3
1843	Sep	6	5/B4-7
1843	Sep	7	5/B8-10
1843	Sep	19	5/B11-14
1843	Sep	22	5/C1-4
1843	Sep	26	5/C5-8
1843	Sep	28	5/C9-12
1843	Sep	29	5/C13-D2
1843	Dec	7	5/D3-4
1844	Feb	16	5/D5-7
1844	Apr	16	5/D8-10
1844	Aug	8	5/D11-13
1844	Aug	27	5/D14-E3
1844	Nov	11	5/E4-6
1844	Nov	14	5/E7-10
1844	Dec	5	5/E11-14
1844	Dec	11	6/A3-6
1844	Dec	25	6/A7-10
1845	May	22	6/A11-14
1845	May	28	6/B1-3
1845	May	29	6/B4-7
1845	Jun	11	6/B8-9
1845	Jun	12	6/B10-13
1845	Jun	13	6/B14-C1
1845	Jul	9	6/C2-4
1845	Sep	24	6/C5-8
1845	Sep	29	6/C9-11
1845	Nov	19	6/C12-14
1846	Mar	26	6/D1-4
1846	Mar	28	6/D5-6
1846	May	11	6/D9-10
1846	Jul	8	6/D11-14
1846	Oct	9	6/E10-13
1846	Oct	11	7/A3-5
1846	Nov	5	7/A6-7
1846	Nov	10	7/A8-9
1846	Nov	17	7/A10-13
1846	Nov	18	7/A14-B2
1846	Nov	19	7/B3-6
1846	Dec	9	7/B7-9
1847	Jan	21	7/B10-13
1847	Jan	22	7/C1-2
1847	Jan	29	7/C3-4
1847	Feb	2	7/C5-6
1847	Feb	3	7/C7-9
1847	Feb	4	7/C10-12
1847	Feb	5	7/C13-D1
1847	Feb	8	7/D6-8
1847	Feb	9	7/D13-14
1847	Feb	14	7/E1-4
1847	Feb	15	7/E5-7
1847	Feb	16	7/E8-11
1847	Feb	21	8/A3-6
1847	Feb	22	8/A7-10
1847	Feb	27	8/A11-13
1847	a. Feb 27		8/A14-B2
1847	Mar	23	8/B3-5
1847	Mar	29	8/B6-9
1847	Mar	30	8/B10-11
1848	Jun	29	8/C2-4
1848	Jul	11	8/C5-6
1849			8/C7
1849	Jan	11	8/C8-11
1849	Jan	16	8/C12-D1
1849	Mar	8	8/D2-3
1849	Mar	22	8/D4-8
1849	Mar	27	8/D9-12
1849	Jun	2	8/D13-E2
1849	Jun	18	8/E3-6
1849	Aug	15	9/A3-6
1849	Sep	11	9/A7-11
1849	Sep	12	9/A12-B2
1849	Sep	14	9/B3-7
1849	Sep	16	9/B8-C2
1849	Sep	18	9/C3-9
1849	Sep	20	9/C10-13
1849	c. Oct 2		9/C14-D3
1849	Oct	3	9/D4-7
1849	Oct	14	9/D8-14
1849	Oct	16	9/E1-4
1849	Oct	18	9/E5-8
1850	Jan	23	10/A2-4
1850	Jan	31	10/A5-7
1850	Feb	6	10/A8-12
1850	Mar	26	10/A13-B1
1850	May	3	10/B2-3
1850	May	27	10/B4-7
1850	Sep	20	10/B8-10
1850	Oct	8	10/B11-12
1851	Mar	5	10/B13-C1
1851	Apr	19	10/C2-3
1852	Jun	10	10/C4-7
1852	Jun	12	10/C8-11

1852	Jun	20	10/C12-D2
1852	Jun	25	10/D3-6
1852	Jun	26	10/D7-E2
1852	Jun	30	10/E3-14
1852	Jul	4	11/A3-B4
1852	Jul	7	11/B5-C2
1852	Jul	9	11/C3-10
1852	Jul	11	11/C11-D4
1852	Jul	17	11/D5-8
1852	Jul	18	11/D9-12
1852	Sep	9	11/D13-E2
1853	May	20	11/E7-10
1853	Jul		12/B2-3
1853	Oct	16	12/B8-C1
1853	Oct	26	12/C5
1854	Aug	2	12/C6-9
*1855	Jan	20	12/C10-D2
1855	Feb		12/D3-8
1856	Jun	17	12/E1-2
1857	Mar	28	12/E9-14
1857	Apr	2	13/A7-14
1857	Apr	8	13/B1-12
1857	Apr	18	13/C2-13
1857	Apr	23	13/C14-D7
1857	May b. 6		13/D8-E1
1857	May	6	13/E2-5
1857	May	16	14/A3-B6
1857	May	19	14/B7-14
1857	May	21	14/C1-4
1857	May	29	14/C5-D2
1857	Jun	4	14/D3-12
1857	Jun	11	14/D13-E2
1857	Jun	14	14/E3-10
1857	Jun	18	14/E11-13
*1857	Jun	28	15/A2-B1
1857	Jul	5	15/B2-9
1857	Jul	17	15/B10-C3
1858	Jan	30	15/C4-6
1858	Aug	12	15/C7-10
1859	Apr	21	15/D4-7
1859	Apr	24	15/D12-E1
1859	Apr	29	15/E5-9
*1859	Aug	7	16/A3-6
1860	Jan	22	16/B12-C1
1860	Jan	23	16/C2-8
1860	Jan	24	16/C12-D1
1860	Jan	27	16/D2-5
1860	Apr	12	16/D6-11
1860	Apr	14	16/D12-E1
1860	Apr	19	17/A6-9
1860	Apr	25	17/A14-B5
1860	Apr	28	17/B12-C1
1860	May	2	17/C6-D1
1860	May	6	17/D2-9
1860	May	10	17/E4-9
1860	May	15	18/A3-6
1860	May	15	18/A7-14
1860	May	16	18/B1-6
1860	May	19	18/B7-14
1860	May	20	18/C5-12
1860	May	21	18/D3-8
1860	May	23	18/D13-E2
1860	May	26	18/E7-14
1860	May	29	19/A9-12
1860	May	31	19/A13-B4
1860	Jun	1	19/B9-12
1860	Jun	3	19/C3-14
1860	Jun	5	19/D1-6
1860	Jun	6	19/D7-14
1860	Jun	7	19/E1-4
1860	Jun	8	19/E5-6
1860	Jun	9	19/E7-8
1860	Jun	11	19/E9-12
1860	Jun	13	20/B3-6
1860	Jun	17	20/C9-D2
1860	Jun	19	20/D11-E12
1860	Jun	22	21/A11-B4
1860	Jun	24	21/C3-6
1860	Jun	26	21/C11-14
1860	Jun	27	21/D1-6
1860	Jun	28	21/D7-12
1860	Jun	29	21/D13-E4
1860	Jul	1	22/A3-9
1860	Jul	2	22/A10-13
1860	Jul	3	22/A14-B7
1860	Jul	6	22/C2-4
1860	Jul	7	22/C5-12
1860	Jul	8	22/C13-D1
1860	Jul	11	22/D14-E11
1860	Jul	15	23/A6-B1
1860	Jul	18	23/B10-C10
1860	Jul	20	23/C11-D4
1860	Jul	21	23/D5-10
1860	Jul	25	23/E1-6
1860	Jul	28	23/E7-9
1860	Jul	29	23/E10-13
1860	Aug	5	24/A12-B4
1860	Aug	8	24/B5-14
1860	Aug	9	24/C1-4
1860	Aug	10	24/C5-D2
1860	Aug	11	24/D3-8
1860	Aug	13	24/D9-E2
1860	Aug	14	24/E3-8
1860	Aug	16	24/E13
1862	Feb	11	25/C3-6
1862	Feb	12	25/C7-9
1862	Feb	14	25/C10-13
1862	Nov	17	25/E1-2
1862	Nov	19	25/E3-6
1862	Nov	20	26/A2-5
1862	Nov	21	26/A6-7
1862	Nov	23	26/A12-B1
1862	Nov	25	26/B2-9
1862	Nov	26	26/B10-C3
1862	Nov	30	26/C4-7
1862	Dec	1	26/C12-D3
1862	Dec	2	26/D4-11
1863			26/D14-E5
1863	Jan	28	26/E6-12
1863	Mar		27/A2-5
1863	Mar		27/A6-8
1863	Mar	10	27/A9-12
1863	Mar	13	27/A13-B4
1863	Aug	10	27/D9-12

1863	Sep	5	27/E1-4
1864	Feb	5	28/A13-B2
1864	Feb	9	28/B3-5
1864	Mar	3	28/B6-9
1864	Mar	3	28/B10-11
1864	Mar	4	28/B12-C1
1864	Mar	12	29/A2-B7
1864	Mar	16	29/B8-C1
1864	Oct	10	29/C5-10
1864	Oct	11	29/C11-13
1864	Oct	16	29/C14-D7
1865	Mar	24	31/A13-B1
1865	Mar	25	31/B2-7
1865	Mar	27	31/B8-13
1865	Mar	29	31/B14-C5
1865	Mar	30	31/C6-9
1865	Mar	31	31/C10-13
1865	Apr	2	31/C14-D7
1865	Jun	7	31/D8-11
1865	Aug	30	31/E2-5
1865	Sep	1	31/E6-8
1865	Sep	3	31/E9-14
1867	Feb	6	33/D13-E2
1867	Feb	12	33/E3-6
1867	Feb	15	34/A14-B3
1867	Feb	17	34/C4-9
1870	Oct	6	43/D4-7
1874	Mar	23	86/E5-6
1886-			
1887			56/B8-11
1893	Aug	5	79/A10-13
1893	Aug	16	79/B4-C1
n.d.			86/C7-9

to HOOKER, MARTHA (KILBOURNE),
MRS. EDWARD BEECHER

1880	Sep	8	55/A13-B2

to HOWARD, SUSAN RAYMOND

1870	Jan	2	43/A2-B5

to HUGO, VICTOR MARIE

1875	Apr	16	51/C14-D1
1875	Apr	16	51/D2-9

to JACKSON, ALICE (DAY),
MRS. PERCY

1875	Jun	8	51/D10-12
*1887	Oct	25	57/A10-B3
*1891	Jan	2	73/B3-6
1891	Aug	13	74/E4-7
1897	Feb	24	81/D4-6
1900	Jan	23	83/B2-5

to JARVIS, MISS

1877	Nov	22	53/D4-7

to LANGDON, OLIVIA (LEWIS),
MRS. JERVIS

1879	Apr	22	54/C12-D3

to LINCOLN, ABRAHAM

1861	Nov		25/A13-B4

to LIVERMORE, MARY RICE

1869	Nov	15	42/B12-C6
1869	Nov	15	42/C7-12
1869	Nov	15	42/C13-D6
1871	Mar	15	45/A2-B5
1871	Mar	15	45/B6-12

1871	Mar	17	45/B13-C4

to MILL, JOHN STUART

1869	Aug	9	41/D4-9

to MITCHELL, JOHN HIPPLE

1878	Mar	14	53/D13-14

to NEW HAVEN WOMAN
SUFFRAGE ASSOCIATION

1873			48/C10-D5

to PERKINS, EMILY

1875	Aug	7	51/E6-9

to PERKINS, MARY (BEECHER),
MRS. THOMAS CLAP

*1847	Feb	7	7/D2-5
1847	Feb	9	7/D9-12
b. 1853			11/E3-6
1859	Apr	29	15/E2-4
1870	Dec	1	44/B14-C7

to PERRY, CAROLINE GROSVENOR

1875	Mar	14	51/C8-10

to PHILLEO, ELIZABETH P.

1863	Aug	9	27/D5-8

to PHILLIPS, CURTIS and OTHERS

b. 1870	Jan	1	42/D11

to SANDS, JOHN L.

1872			46/D14-E-3
1872	May	24	47/E2-5

to SAVERY, ANNA C.

1871	Nov	12	46/C3-12

to SCOVILLE, HARRIET (BEECHER),
MRS. SAMUEL

1860	Feb	13	86/C11-D5

to SEVERANCE, CAROLINE SEYMOUR

1869	Aug	27	41/D10 -
			42/A2-9

to SHIPMAN, WILLIAM D.

1896	Feb	17	81/C2-5

to STANTON, EDWIN McMASTERS

1863	Apr		27/B5-8
1864 or			
1865			27/E9-12
1864	May		29/C2

to STANTON, ELIZABETH CADY

1870	Nov	25	44/B8-9
1870	Dec	21	44/C8-9
1870	Dec	29	44/C10-11
1871	Oct	18	46/A10-13
1872	May	12	47/D9-E1
1874	Mar	13	50/A2-B1
1875	Feb	28	51/B8-C7
*1892	Apr	26	77/A14-B3

to STEARNS, SARAH BURGER

1871	Spring		45/C12-D3

to STEBBINS, CATHARINE A. F.

1874	Dec	31	51/A10-B1

to STOWE, HARRIET (BEECHER),
MRS. CALVIN ELLIS

1849	Jul	31	8/E11-14
1869	a. Apr 27		136/D8-11

to TALCOTT, MARY KINGSBURY

1900	Feb b. 22		83/C6
n.y.	Feb	20	86/B9
n.y.	Jul	20	86/B10

to TALCOTT, MARY (SEYMOUR),
MRS. RUSSELL
1876-
1879   52/B9-12
1876   Aug 25   53/A14-B7
to UNDERWOOD, MR.
1889 *o.l.*   62/C4-5
to UNITED STATES CONGRESS
1878   Feb 13   86(a)/B2
to WAITE, CATHARINE VAN VALKENBERG
1880   Mar 23   54/E6-7
1880   c. Mar 23   54/E8-9
to WALLER, THOMAS MacDONALD
1890   Aug 7   71/C14-D1
to WARNER, CHARLES DUDLEY
1871   Nov 1   46/B4-7
1871   a. Nov 1   46/B8-11
1871   a. Nov 1   46/B12-C2
to WARNER, ELISABETH (GILLETTE),
MRS. GEORGE H.
1863   Oct 30   27/E5-8
1864   Dec 18   29/D8-E1
1866   Aug 22   32/B11-14
1870   Mar 19   43/B12-C1
to WARNER, GEORGE H.
1900   May 30   86(a)/C9-12
to WARNER, SUSAN (LEE),
MRS. CHARLES DUDLEY
n.d.   86/C5-6
to WELLES, MARY CROWELL
1904   Oct 7   85/D2-3
to WHITMORE, HARRIET GOULDER
1900   Jan 20   83/A13-B1
to WOODHULL, VICTORIA CLAFLIN
b. 1871   Feb 16   44/D5-6
1871   Oct 18   46/A14-B3
1872   Apr 10   47/C12-D1
1872   Jul 28   48/C4-9
c. 1876   52/B13-C2
c. 1877   53/B10-13
1888   Jul 19   60/B12-14
1888   Aug 19   60/C1-3
1888   Aug 24   60/C4-6
1889   Feb 4   63/B10-C3
1892   May 12   77/B12-C3
1904   Jan 8   85/B7-C11
1906   Sep 14   86/B5-7
to WOOLSEY, JANE STUART
1869   40/E2-5
to WRIGHT, MARTHA COFFIN
1871   Jul 23   45/E1-4
1872   Jan   46/E4-7
from ALLEN, GEORGE R.
*1872   May 16   135/A14-B4
from ANONYMOUS
*1872   Apr 2   114/A6-9
from ANTHONY, SUSAN B.
1869   Jun 11   114/A10-B1
1869   Jul 29   114/B6-9
1869   Aug 9   114/B10-C1
1869   Sep or
      Oct   114/C2-5

1869	Oct 15	114/C6-8
1869	Nov 3	114/C9-12
1869	Nov 8	114/C13-D4
1869	Dec	114/D5-8
1869	Dec 17	114/D9-E4
1869	Dec 29	114/E5-8
1870	Jan 10	114/E9-12
1870	Jan 12	115/A2-9
1870	Jan 27	115/A10-11
1870	Jan 30	115/A12-B6
1870	Feb 8	115/B7-8
1870	Mar 21	115/B9-C3
1870	c. May	115/C4-5
1870	May 2	115/C6-7
1870	Dec 2	115/C8-D1
*1871		115/D2-5
1871	Jan 5	115/D6-8
1871	Jan 21	115/D9-12
1871	Jan 29	115/D13-E3
1871	Feb 6	115/E4-9
1871	Mar 5	116/A2-10
1871	Mar 11	116/A11-B3
1871	Mar 21	116/B4-7
1871	Apr 22	116/B12-C5
1871	Apr 30	116/C6-9
1871	Jun	116/C14-D4
1871	Jun 6	116/D5-10
1871	Jun 11	116/D11-14
1871	Jun 12	116/E1-2
1872	Jan 29	116/E7-10
1872	Feb 6	116/E11-12
1872	May 19	117/A2-5
*1872	a. May 23	132/D3-6
1872	Jun 19	117/A10-13
1872	Jun 24	117/A14-B7
1872	Jul 20	117/B8-10
1872	Jul 24	117/B11-12
1872	Aug 5	117/B13-C2
1872	Aug 7	117/C3-5
1872	Sep 6	117/C12-D1
1872	Sep 10	117/D2-9
1872	Oct 9	117/D14-E3
1872	Oct 10	117/E4-6
*1873	Jan 7	117/E7-11
1873	Apr 21	118/A2-6
1873	May 12	118/A7-8
1873	Jul 11	118/A9-12
1873	Aug 5	118/A13-B2
1873	Aug 11	118/B3-6
1873	Sep 7	118/B7-10
1873	Sep 11	118/B11-14
1873	Sep 12	118/C1-3
1873	Sep 29	118/C4-7
*1873	Oct 4	121/C3-6
1873	Oct 13	118/C8-11
1873	c. Oct 15	118/C12-13
1873	Nov	118/C14-D1
1873	Dec 13	118/D2
*1873	Dec 15	118/D3-8
1874	Feb 17	118/D9-E2
1874	Feb 21	118/E5-8
1875	Jan 20	118/E9-14

1875	Sep	29	119/A2-7
1875	Oct	12	119/A8-10
1875	Oct	21	119/A11-14
1876	Aug	3	119/B5-6
1876	Sep	4	119/B7-14
1876	Dec	6	119/C1-4
1877	Jan	20	119/C5-11
1877	Sep	1	119/C14-D3
1877	Nov	11	119/D6-E1
1878	Jun	18	119/E2-5
1878	Oct		119/E6-9
1878	Oct	7	119/E10-13
1878	Oct	11	120/A3-4
1878	Oct	15	120/A5-8
1878	Nov	15	120/A9-10
1878	Dec	12	120/A11-14
1880	Dec	6	120/B1-4
1900	Mar	23	120/B5-6

from AVERY, RACHEL FOSTER

1879	Apr	6	120/B11-C4

from BARBER, JOHN

1876	Aug	31	120/C5-7
1879	Nov	10	120/C8
1880	Mar	24	120/C9-10

from BLACKWELL, HENRY BROWN

1869	Dec	1	120/C11-14
1869	Dec	16	120/D1-10
1870	Mar	16	120/E3-6
1870	Mar	28	120/E11 - 121/A5
1872	Jul	19	121/A11-14

from BLAKE, LILLIE DEVEREUX

1892	Dec	13	121/B10-12

from BRISTOL, AUGUSTA COOPER

b. 1879	Feb	21	121/B13-14
1879	Feb	21	121/C1-2

from BROWN, MARTHA McCLELLAN

1896	Oct	26	121/C7-9

from BROWN, OLYMPIA

1870	Mar	9	121/C10-11
1870	Apr	6	121/C12-14
1870	May	28	121/D1-6
1870	Jul	20	121/D7-12
1870	Jul	25	121/D13-E14
1870	Jul	27	122/A3-6
1870	Aug	15	122/A7-10
1870	Aug	29	122/A11-13
1870	Oct	5	122/A14-B3
*1870	Dec	8	122/B12-C1
1870	Dec	22	122/C2-11
1871	Mar	23	122/C12-D1
1871	Sep	25	122/D2-4
1871	Sep	26	122/D5-12
1871	Oct	20	122/D13-E1
1871	Oct	26	122/E2-5
1871	c. Oct 26		122/E6-7
1871	Dec	6	123/A2-11
1871	Dec	9	123/A12-B10
1872	Jan	2	123/B11-C2
1872	Jan	12	123/C3-6
1872	Jan	26	123/C7-10
1872	Feb	3	123/C11-D4

1872	Feb	7	123/D5-12
1872	Feb	9	123/D13-E5
1872	Sep	25	123/E6-9
1872	Oct	10	123/E10-12
1873	Feb	24	124/A2-5
1873	Mar	28	124/A8-11
1873	Apr	24	124/A12-B1
1873	May	9	124/B2-9
1873	Dec	31	124/D10-12
*1874	a. Jan 3		131/A13-B2
1874	Jan	6	124/D13-E8
1874	Jan a. 6		124/E9-12
1874	Jan a. 6		125/A2-10
1874	Mar	13	125/A11-B8
1874	Mar	30	125/B9-13
1874	Apr	9	125/B14-C7
1875-			
1876	Jun	26	125/C8-13
1875	Dec	27	125/C14-D10
1876	Jan	3	125/D11-14
1876	Jan	21	125/E1-4
1876	Jan	28	125/E5-6
1876	Feb	2	125/E7-10
1876	Mar	1	125/E11-12
1876	May	31	125/E13-14
1877	Feb	1	126/A3-10
1877	Mar	17	126/A11-12
1877	Apr	12	126/A13-B2
1877	Oct	19	126/B3
b. 1878			126/B4-5
b. 1878			126/B6-9
1878	Mar	16	126/B10-12
1878	Sep	15	126/C6-7
1878	Oct	15	126/C8

from BURR, FRANCES ELLEN

1874	Jan		126/C9-10
1874	Nov	1	126/C11-14
1878	Jul	17	126/D1-2

from BURRITT, ELIHU

1871	Oct	4	126/D3-5

from BUTLER, BENJAMIN F.

1871	Apr	14	126/D6
1871	Apr	30	126/D7
1877	Jan	25	126/D8-9
1884	Sep	22	126/D10

from BUTLER, JOSEPHINE

1874	May	22	126/D11-14

from CAMERON, KATE

*1875	Mar	16	131/A3-5

from CHASE, MARGUERITE B.

1878	May	15	126/E1-2

from CHENEY, MARY B.

1889	Jun	6	126/E3-10

from CHITTENDEN, LUCY B.

1880	Apr	5	127/A3-6

from COLEMAN, O. O.

1874	Apr	25	127/A10-12

from COMSTOCK, HANNAH

1871	Nov	20	127/A13-B4
1872	Dec	31+	
1873	Jan	6	127/B5-9
1873	Jan	23	127/B10-11

Hooker, Isabella Beecher
from Comstock, Hannah

1873	Jun	12	127/B12-C1
1873	Jun	19	127/C2-5
1873	Nov	11	127/C14-D3
1874	Feb	25	127/D4-7
1874	Apr	17	127/D8-11
1874	Apr	26	127/D12-14
1874	Jun	25	127/E1-6
1874	Aug	6	127/E7-10
1874	Sep	15	127/E11-14
1874	Dec	10	128/A3-6
1875	Feb	5	128/A13
1875	Nov	23	128/A14-B3
1876	Apr	1	128/B4
1876	Jun	8	128/B5-6
1876	Jun	16	128/B7-10
1877	Apr	19	128/B11-12
1877	Sep	22	128/B13-C2
1877	Oct	21	128/C3-7
1877	Nov	2	128/C8-11
1877	Dec	16	128/C12-D1
1878	Jul	10	128/D2-4
1878	Jul	25	128/D5-9
1878	Oct	3	128/D10-11
1878	Oct	8	128/D12-13
1878	Oct	16	128/D14-E2
1879	Jan	27	128/E3-5
1879	Oct	17	128/E6-9

from COOKE, HELEN M.

1877	May	4	128/E10-12
*1877	May	5	128/E13
1878	May	5	129/A3-5

from CROCKER, MRS. FRANK S.

1877	May	31	129/A6-B2

from DAVIS, EDWARD M.

1870	Apr	17	129/B7
1871	Mar	31	129/B8
1871	Apr	8	129/B9-12
1871	Jun	12	129/B13-C1
1874	Mar	14	129/C5
1874	Mar	26	129/C6-7
1875	Dec	9	129/C8-9
1876	Apr	2	129/C10-11
1876	Apr	3	129/C12-13
1876	Apr	9	129/C14-D1
1876	May	2	129/D2
1876	May	12	129/D3-4
1876	Oct	24	129/D5-6
1877	Dec	7	129/D7
1878	Feb	27	129/D8-9
1878	Feb	27	129/D10-11
1878	Mar	26	129/D12-13
1878	Apr	4	129/D14-E1

from DAVIS, PAULINA WRIGHT

c. 1869			129/E3-8
1869	Aug	17	129/E11-14
1869	Sep	27	130/A3-6
1869	Dec		130/A7-10
1869	Dec	4	130/A11-14
1869	Dec	23	130/B1-4
1870 or			
1871	Mar	12	130/B5-8
1870	May	23	130/B9-12

Hooker, Isabella Beecher
from Hawley, Harriet (Foote), Mrs. Joseph Roswell

1870	Jul	10	130/B13-C4
1870	Nov	29	130/C5-D1
*1870	a. Dec 8		122/B4-11
1871	Jan	1	130/D2
1874	Mar	1	130/E10-13
1875	Mar	16	131/A3-5
1875	Oct	26	131/A6-8

from DODGE, MARY ABIGAIL

1872	Mar	25	131/A9-10

from ELLIS, A. A.

1874	Apr	27	131/A11-12

from FIELD, M. E.

1870	May	5	131/B3-6

from FOSTER, JULIA

1878	Sep	18	131/B7-8
1879	Feb	18	131/B9

from FOSTER, JULIA MANUEL

1879	Apr	6	131/B10-11

from FULLER, SARAH E.

1877	May	28	131/B12-13

from GAGE, MATILDA JOSLYN

*a. 1872	Apr	2	114/A6-9
1872	Sep	16	131/C3-4
1875	Nov	22	131/C5-10
1875	Dec	11	131/C11-14
1875	Dec	23	131/D1-11
1876	Feb	1	131/D12-E1
1876	Feb	4	131/E2-7
1876	Feb	14	131/E8-13
1876	Feb	16	132/A3-4
1876	Mar	7	132/A5-8
1878	Oct	15	132/A9-10
1878	Oct	28	132/A11-12
1878	Dec	9	132/A13-14
1879	Feb	22	132/B1-2
1879	Feb	27	132/B3-4
1879	Feb	27	132/B5-6
1879	Mar	12	132/B7-8
1879	Mar	24	132/B9-10
1879	Jul	3	132/B11-12
1879	Jul	12	132/B13-14

from GARRISON, WILLIAM LLOYD, SR.

1869	Nov	12	132/C1-14

from GARRISON, WILLIAM LLOYD, JR.

1889	Feb	17	132/D1-2

from GIDDINGS, AMELIA

*1872	May	23	132/D3-6

from GRAVES, MRS. S. H.

1871	Oct	24	132/D7-10

from GRIFFING, JOSEPHINE

1870	Nov	27	132/D11-14
1871	c. Oct		132/E1-6

from HANAFORD, PHEBE

1870	Aug	29	132/E7-9
1871	Aug	9	133/A3-12
1871	Sep	13	133/A13-B1

from HARBERT, ELIZABETH BOYNTON

1878	Jul	29	133/B2-3
1878	Dec	29	133/B4-5

from HAWLEY, HARRIET (FOOTE), MRS. JOSEPH ROSWELL

1879	Mar	19	133/B6-9

from HEATH, S. ANNA
- 1880 Dec 12 133/B14-C3

from HICKORY, MRS. M. C.
- 1870 "28" 133/C4-8

from HIGGINSON, THOMAS WENTWORTH
- 1859 Feb 19 133/C9-12
- 1860 Mar 4 133/C13-D2
- 1898 Jan 15 133/D6-7

from HOLLOWAY, LAURA C.
- 1880 Apr 5 133/D8-11

from HOWLAND, MARIE
- 1873 Feb 14 133/D12-E3

from HUBBARD, JULIA A.
- 1874 Mar 23 133/E4

from JUDSON, MRS. M. J.
- 1875 May 4 133/E5-9

from KOONS, MRS. I. S.
- 1901 Apr 26 133/E10-11

from KRIFFIN, G. C.
- 1871 Apr 4 134/A3-6

from LIVERMORE, MARY RICE
- 1869 Oct 31 134/A9-10
- 1869 Nov 9 134/A11-14
- 1871 134/B1-2

from LLEWELLYN, W. H.
- 1874 Aug 5 134/B3-5
- 1874 Nov 2 134/B6-9

from LOCKWOOD, BELVA
- 1871 Jun 17 134/B10-13

from NEWMAN, FRANCIS W.
- 1874 May 28 134/C10-13

from NICOLL, CORNELIA COMSTOCK
- 1874 Dec 18 134/C14-D1

from PATTON, ABIGAIL HUTCHINSON
- 1874 Jul 31 134/D2-5

from PERRY, CAROLINE GROSVENOR
- 1878 Feb 22 134/D6-11
- 1878 Dec 20 134/D12-13

from PHILLEO, ELIZABETH P.
- 1869 Nov 1 134/D14-E1

from PILLSBURY, PARKER
- 1870 Mar 27 134/E2-5

from PRICHARD, SARA J.
- 1874 Mar 4 134/E6-13

from SANDS, JOHN L.
- *1872 May 16 135/A14-B4

from SARGENT, ELLEN CLARK
- 1873 Feb 2 135/B5-7
- 1873 Apr 3 135/B8-10
- *1877 Sep 25 136/B7-8
- 1877 Nov 12 135/B11-12
- 1878 Jul 22 135/C1-2

from SAYLES, LITA BARNEY
- 1878 Oct 23 135/C3-4

from SEVERANCE, CAROLINE
- 1869 c. Aug 17 135/C5-14
- 1869 Aug 17 135/D1-E2
- 1869 Sep 24 135/E3-6
- 1869 Nov 10 135/E7-14

from SHELDON, S. E.
- *1877 Apr 10 136/A9

from SLAYTON, HENRY L.

- 1878 Dec 2 136/A10-14

from SMITH, JULIA E.
- 1879 Apr 27 136/B1-3

from SMITH, MRS. L. M.
- 1874 Apr 7 136/B4-6

from SPENCER, SARAH J.
- *1877 Sep 25 136/B7-8
- 1877 Nov 18 136/B9-12
- 1877 Nov 22 136/B13-C4
- 1877 Dec 5 136/C5-6
- 1877 Dec 20 136/C7-10
- 1878 Mar 136/C11-12
- 1878 Mar 18 136/C13-D1
- 1878 May 8 136/D2-5
- 1879 Jul 30 136/D6-7

from STANTON, ELIZABETH CADY
- *1869 Apr 27 136/D8-11
- 1869 May 24 136/D12-E6
- 1869 Sep 136/E7-14
- 1869 Sep 1 137/B4-7
- 1869 Sep 8 137/B8-C3
- 1869 Sep 23 137/C4-9
- 1870 Mar 22 137/C14-D2
- 1870 May 29 137/D3-E10
- *1870 a. Jun 4 131/B14-C2
- 1870 Dec 1 138/A2-8
- 1870 Dec 28 138/A9-12
- 1871 Jan 3 138/A13-B2
- 1871 Mar 26 138/B3-5
- 1871 Apr 1 138/B6-9
- 1871 Apr 12 138/B10-11
- 1871 Apr 19 138/B12-C1
- 1871 Jun 10 138/C4-9
- 1871 Jun 30 138/C10-13
- 1871 Oct 138/D1-8
- 1871 Oct 15 138/D9-12
- 1871 a. Oct 15 138/D13-E2
- 1871 Nov 138/E3-5
- 1871 Nov 138/E6-8
- 1871 Dec 28 138/E9-12
- 1872 Jan 138/E13-14
- 1872 Feb 2 139/A2-11
- 1872 Feb 3 139/A12-B13
- 1872 May 2 139/B14-C3
- *1872 May a. 16 135/A14-B4
- 1872 Jun 14 139/C4-11
- 1872 Summer 139/C12-13
- 1872 Jun 25 139/C14-D7
- 1872 Sep 139/D8-11
- 1872 Sep 8 139/D12-E1
- 1872 Nov 19 139/E2-5
- *1873 Jan 7 117/E7-11
- 1873 Jan 21 139/E6-13
- 1873 Feb 20 140/A2-7
- 1873 Nov 3 140/A8-B2
- 1873 c. Dec 140/B3-6
- 1875 Nov 12 140/B7-12
- 1875 Nov 28 140/B13-C2
- 1876 Jul 1 140/C3-4
- 1876 Jul 5 140/C5-10
- 1876 Aug 6 140/C11-14
- 1877 Aug 30 140/D1-4

Hooker, Isabella Beecher
Documents

1896 May
  Two Autographed Quotes   109/B7
1898
  M.B.: Draft of *United
  States Citizenship ....*
  [Speech]   109/B8-E9
1900
  T.P.: *The Constitutional
  Rights of Women ... An
  Address before the
  International Council of
  Women ....*   109/E10
1900 Aug 5
  Hymns Sung at IBH and
  JH's 59th Anniversary   109/E11-12
1901-02
  Monday Afternoon Club
  Topics   109/E13
1901 Jan 3 - Dec 31
  Diary   110/A2-112/A7
1902
  T.P.: *An Argument on ...
  Citizenship before the
  Constitutional
  Convention ... Sitting in
  Hartford ....*   112/A8
c. 1902
  *Memorial of the
  Connecticut Woman
  Suffrage Association to
  the Constitutional
  Convention Assembled in
  Hartford ....*   112/A9
1903 o.l.
  Mem. re Married Women's
  Property Law   112/A10
1903 o.l.
  Autobiographical Note 112/A11-12
1903 Jun 20
  Autographed Quotation   112/A13
1905 May
  Magazine Cover and T.P.:
  "The Last of the
  Beechers, Memories on
  My Eighty-Third
  Birthday" from
  Connecticut Magazine   112/A14-B1
1905 Nov 23
  Instructions re
  Disposition of Several
  Bound Volumes   112/B2
1906
  Description of Birds   112/B3-9
1906 May 8
  Inscription   112/B10
1906 Jun 11
  Notes from the Spirit
  World   112/B11-C1
1906 Jun 29
  Notes from the Spirit
  World   112/C2-5
1906 Jul 1

  Notes from the Spirit
  World   112/C6-9
1906 Sep 16
  Instructions re
  Disposition of Bookcase 112/C10-11
n.d.
  Watts Poem: *How Doth
  the Little Busy Bee ....* 112/C13-D2
n.d.
  Poem: *Willie Winkie*   112/D3-5
n.d.
  Note re Fallen Women in
  Rochester   112/D6
n.d.
  Notes from the Spirit
  World   112/D7-8
n.d.
  Autographs Found in
  Envelope   112/D9-10
n.d.
  Recipes   112/D11-12
n.d.
  Misc. Envelopes   112/D14-E4

Hooker, Isabella Beecher
Mentioned
  by ANTHONY, SUSAN B.
    1871   Apr   2   116/B8-11
    1871   May 24   116/C10-13
    1871   Sep 10   116/E3-6
   *1871   a. Sep 16   130/D3-6
   *1872   Jan 25   47/A2-B1
    1872   May 29   117/A6-9
    1872   Sep   117/C6-11
    1872   Oct   9   117/D10-13
    1875   Nov   3   119/B1-4
  by BLACKWELL, HENRY BROWN
    1869   Dec 19   120/D11-12
  by BROWN, OLYMPIA
    1870   Dec   8   122/B4-11
    1873   Mar 18   124/A6-7
  by CHITTENDEN, LUCY B.
    1880   Mar 25   126/E11-13
  by COMSTOCK, HANNAH M.
    1873   b. Nov 11 127/C6-13
  by DAVIS, EDWARD M.
    1871   Dec   7   129/C2-3
  by DAVIS, PAULINA WRIGHT
    1872   Aug   5   130/D13-E2
  by HIGGINSON, THOMAS WENTWORTH
    1868   Oct 11   133/D3-5
  by REID, WHITELAW
    1871   Oct 13   135/A2-5
  by RUSSELL, FANNY ELDREDGE
    1870   Jan 24   135/A10-13
  by SEVERANCE, CAROLINE
    1870   Jan 25   136/A3-6
  by STANTON, ELIZABETH CADY
    1871   May 27   138/C2-3
  by STEARNS, SARAH BURGER
    1871   Jun 12   141/A3-10
    1871   Jun 20   141/A12-B1

Hooker, Isabella Beecher
Mentioned

1871	Jun	20	141/B2-5

by STEELE, FANNY

1874	Aug	21	141/B9-C2

Hooker, John

to BEECHER, FRANCES (JOHNSON),
MRS. JAMES

*1899	Jan	22	82/E1-4

to BURTON, MARY (HOOKER),
MRS. HENRY EUGENE

*1883	Aug	7	55/E1-4

to DAY, ALICE (HOOKER),
MRS. JOHN CALVIN

*1868	May	19	38/E1-4
*1880	Sep	2	55/A5-8
*1883	Jul	10	55/D7-10
*1885	Aug	3	56/A2-5
*1885	Aug	11	56/A6-13
*1885	Aug	14	56/A14-B3
*1885	Aug	31	56/B4-7
*1887	Oct	16	56/E2-5
*1887	Oct	19	57/A2-9
*1887	Nov	23	57/D2-9
*1887	Dec	1	57/D10-E3
*1887	Dec	11	58/A2-5
*1888	Jan	10	58/B12-C9
*1888	Feb	5	59/A2-13
*1888	Feb	13	59/A14-B11
*1888	Apr	22	60/A12-B11
*1888	Oct	5	60/C7-D4
*1888	Oct	22	60/E1-8
*1888	Oct	31	61/B4-7
*1888	Nov	3	61/B8-C7
*1888	Dec	7	61/E7-10
*1889	Jan	15	63/A2-13
*1889	Feb	5	63/C4-D1
*1889	Feb	20	64/A2-3
*1889	Mar	5	63/D12-E13
*1889	Jun	16	65/B12-C5
*1889	Jul	1	65/D2-13
*1889	Jul	11	65/E8-9
*1889	Jul	26	66/A2-5
*1889	Aug	4	66/B4-7
*1889	Aug	4	86(a)/B5-14
*1889	Aug	30	66/D4-7
*1889	Sep	8	66/D12-E1
*1889	Sep	19	66/E2-9
*1889	Oct	6	67/A2-9
*1889	Nov	18	67/B8-C5
*1889	Nov	28	67/C6-D3
*1889	Dec	14	67/D12-13
*1889	Dec	22	67/E6-11
*1890	Jan	31	68/C14-D7
*1890	Feb	7	68/D8-E8
*1890	Mar	14	69/A14-B9
*1890	Mar	19	69/B10-13
*1890	Mar	27	69/B14-C11
*1890	May	9	70/A2-9
*1890	May	13	70/A10-B7
*1890	May	23	70/B8-C5
*1890	Jun	13	70/D12-E7
*1890	Jun	27	70/E8-11

Hooker, John
from Beecher, Catharine E.

*1890	Jul	2	71/A2-B1
*1890	Jul	11	71/B2-5
*1890	Jul	27	71/C4-7
*1890	Jul	31	71/C8-13
*1890	Aug	12	71/D6-7
*1890	Aug	20	71/D8-E1
*1890	Aug	31	71/E2-9
*1890	Oct	12	72/A2-13
*1890	Nov	9	72/C6-13
*1891	Feb	16	73/C9-12
*1891	Apr	18	74/A13-B12
*1891	Sep	27	75/B5-12
*1891	Oct	5	75/B13-C3
*1891	Nov	1	75/D3-8
*1891	Nov	14	75/D9-E2
*1891	Nov	26	75/E3 - 76/A5
*1891	Dec	6	76/A6-13
*1892	Feb	21	76/D14-E3
*1892	Mar	3	76/E4-8
*1893	Oct	12	79/C4-7
*1893	Nov	18	79/C8-11
*1894	Jan	24	80/B5-8
*1894	Feb	22	80/B9-C2
*1894	Feb	28	80/C3-6
*1894	Mar	4	80/C7-10
*1894	Mar	11	80/C11-14
*1894	Mar	21	80/D1-4
*1894	Apr	22	80/D9-12
*1894	May	26	80/E7-14
*1894	Jul	15	81/B4-7
*1894	Jul	20	81/B8-11
*1897	Aug	7	81/D13-E6
*1897	Dec	6	82/A4-7
*1898	Jul	16	82/B14-C3
*1898	Jul	31	82/C4-7
*1898	Aug	23	82/C12-D1

to DAY, KATHARINE SEYMOUR

*1891	Jan	2	73/B3-6

to HOOKER, EDWARD BEECHER

*1874	Jul	21	50/C12-D5
*1875	Jul	18	51/E2-5
*1875	Dec	14	52/B5-8
*1876	Jan	16	52/C3-14
*1876	Feb	20	52/D9-E2

to HOOKER, ELISABETH (DAGGETT),
MRS. EDWARD

*1853	May	16	12/A2-B1

to JACKSON, ALICE (DAY),
MRS. PERCY

*1891	Jan	2	73/B3-6

to PERKINS, MARY (BEECHER),
MRS. THOMAS CLAP

*1847	Feb	7	7/D2-5

from ANTHONY, SUSAN B.

1873	Aug	11	118/B3-6
1874	Feb	19	118/E3-4

from BEECHER, CATHARINE E.

*1839	Oct	21	2/B12-C1
*transcript			1/A4-7

from BLACKWELL, HENRY BROWN			
1869	Dec	19	120/D11-12
1870	Mar	16	120/D13-E2
1870	Mar	30	121/A6
1871	Jan	28	121/A7-10
from BROWN, OLYMPIA			
1873	Mar	18	124/A6-7
1873	Sep	22	124/B10-C7
1873	Sep	22	124/C8-D9
from BURTON, MARY (HOOKER),			
MRS. HENRY EUGENE			
*1859	Aug	7	16/A3-6
from CHITTENDEN, LUCY B.			
1880	Mar	25	126/E11-13
1880	Apr	5	127/A3-6
from CLARK, CHARLES H.			
1889	May	31	127/A7-9
from COOKE, HELEN M.			
*1877	May	5	128/E13
from FULLER, SARAH E.			
1877	May	28	131/B12-13
from HAWLEY, HARRIET (FOOTE),			
MRS. JOSEPH ROSWELL			
1879	c. Mar 19		133/B10-13
from HAWLEY, JOSEPH ROSWELL			
*1857	Jun	28	15/A2-B1
from HIGGINSON, THOMAS WENTWORTH			
*1869	Aug	5	141/C5-6
from HOOKER, ISABELLA BEECHER			
1839	Jul	21	2/A8-11
1839	Jul	27	2/A12-13
1839	Aug	30	2/A14-B3
1839	Sep	12	2/B4-7
1839	Sep	25	2/B8-11
*1839	Oct	21	2/B12-C1
*transcript			1/A4-7
1839	Nov	9	2/C2-5
transcript			1/A8-12
1839	Dec	2	2/C6-9
transcript			1/A13-B3
1839	Dec	25	2/C10-13
transcript			1/B4-6
1840	Jan	22	2/D8-11
1840	Feb	22	2/D12-E1
1840	Mar	17	2/E2-5
1840	Apr	8	2/E6-9
1840	May	5	2/E10-13
1840	May	30	3/A3-6
1840	Nov	14	3/A7-10
1840	Nov	28	3/A11-14
1840	Dec	9	3/B1-4
transcript			1/B10-12
1840	Dec	18	3/B5-8
transcript			1/B13-C1
1841	Jan	2	3/B9-12
1841	Jan	16	3/B13-C2
1841	Jan	22	3/C3-6
transcript			1/C2-4
1841	Feb	7	3/C7-10
transcript			1/C5-7
1841	Feb	11	3/C11-14
1841	Feb	22	3/D1-4
1841	Mar	1	3/D5-6

1841	Mar	9	3/D7-8
1841	Mar	16	3/D9-11
1841	Apr	21	3/D12-E1
1841	Apr	22	3/E2-5
1841	May	16	3/E6-9
1841	May	27	3/E10-11
1841	Jun	7	4/A3-6
1841	Jun	12	4/A7-10
1841	Jun	19	4/A11-14
1841	Jun	25	4/B1-4
1841	Jun	29	4/B5-7
1841	Jul	2	4/B8-11
1841	Jul	9	4/B12-13
1841	Jul	12	4/B14-C2
1841	Jul	14	4/C3-6
1841	Jul	19	4/C7-10
1841	Aug	2	4/C11-14
1842	Jun	30	4/D5-6
1842	Jul	15	4/D7-9
1842	Aug	13	4/D14-E1
1842	Dec	2	4/E2-3
1842	Dec	4	4/E4-6
1842	Dec	30	4/E7-10
1843	Jan	2	4/E11-13
1843	Jan	4	5/A3-6
1843	Mar	25	5/A7-10
1843	Apr	6	5/A11-14
1843	May	6	5/B1-3
1843	Sep	6	5/B4-7
1843	Sep	7	5/B8-10
1843	Sep	19	5/B11-14
1843	Sep	22	5/C1-4
1843	Sep	26	5/C5-8
1843	Sep	28	5/C9-12
1843	Sep	29	5/C13-D2
1843	Dec	7	5/D3-4
1844	Feb	16	5/D5-7
1844	Apr	16	5/D8-10
1844	Aug	8	5/D11-13
1844	Aug	27	5/D14-E3
1844	Nov	11	5/E4-6
1844	Nov	14	5/E7-10
1844	Dec	5	5/E11-14
1844	Dec	11	6/A3-6
1844	Dec	25	6/A7-10
1845	May	22	6/A11-14
1845	May	28	6/B1-3
1845	May	29	6/B4-7
1845	Jun	11	6/B8-9
1845	Jun	12	6/B10-13
1845	Jun	13	6/B14-C1
1845	Jul	9	6/C2-4
1845	Sep	24	6/C5-8
1845	Sep	29	6/C9-11
1845	Nov	19	6/C12-14
1846	Mar	26	6/D1-4
1846	Mar	28	6/D5-6
1846	May	11	6/D9-10
1846	Jul	8	6/D11-14
1846	Oct	9	6/E10-13
1846	Oct	11	7/A3-5
1846	Nov	5	7/A6-7

1846	Nov	10	7/A8-9
1846	Nov	17	7/A10-13
1846	Nov	18	7/A14-B2
1846	Nov	19	7/B3-6
1846	Dec	9	7/B7-9
1847	Jan	21	7/B10-13
1847	Jan	22	7/C1-2
1847	Jan	29	7/C3-4
1847	Feb	2	7/C5-6
1847	Feb	3	7/C7-9
1847	Feb	4	7/C10-12
1847	Feb	5	7/C13-D1
1847	Feb	8	7/D6-8
1847	Feb	9	7/D13-14
1847	Feb	14	7/E1-4
1847	Feb	15	7/E5-7
1847	Feb	16	7/E8-11
1847	Feb	21	8/A3-6
1847	Feb	22	8/A7-10
1847	Feb	27	8/A11-13
1847	a. Feb 27		8/A14-B2
1847	Mar	23	8/B3-5
1847	Mar	29	8/B6-9
1847	Mar	30	8/B10-11
1848	Jun	29	8/C2-4
1848	Jul	11	8/C5-6
1849			8/C7
1849	Jan	11	8/C8-11
1849	Jan	16	8/C12-D1
1849	Mar	8	8/D2-3
1849	Mar	22	8/D4-8
1849	Mar	27	8/D9-12
1849	Jun	2	8/D13-E2
1849	Jun	18	8/E3-6
1849	Aug	15	9/A3-6
1849	Sep	11	9/A7-11
1849	Sep	12	9/A12-B2
1849	Sep	14	9/B3-7
1849	Sep	16	9/B8-C2
1849	Sep	18	9/C3-9
1849	Sep	20	9/C10-13
1849	c. Oct 2		9/C14-D3
1849	Oct	3	9/D4-7
1849	Oct	14	9/D8-14
1849	Oct	16	9/E1-4
1849	Oct	18	9/E5-8
1850	Jan	23	10/A2-4
1850	Jan	31	10/A5-7
1850	Feb	6	10/A8-12
1850	Mar	26	10/A13-B1
1850	May	3	10/B2-3
1850	May	27	10/B4-7
1850	Sep	20	10/B8-10
1850	Oct	8	10/B11-12
1851	Mar	5	10/B13-C1
1851	Apr	19	10/C2-3
1852	Jun	10	10/C4-7
1852	Jun	12	10/C8-11
1852	Jun	20	10/C12-D2
1852	Jun	25	10/D3-6
1852	Jun	26	10/D7-E2
1852	Jun	30	10/E3-14

1852	Jul	4	11/A3-B4
1852	Jul	7	11/B5-C2
1852	Jul	9	11/C3-10
1852	Jul	11	11/C11-D4
1852	Jul	17	11/D5-8
1852	Jul	18	11/D9-12
1852	Sep	9	11/D13-E2
1853	May	20	11/E7-10
1853	Jul		12/B2-3
1853	Oct	16	12/B8-C1
1853	Oct	26	12/C5
1854	Aug	2	12/C6-9
*1855	Jan	20	12/C10-D2
1855	Feb		12/D3-8
1856	Jun	17	12/E1-2
1857	Mar	28	12/E9-14
1857	Apr	2	13/A7-14
1857	Apr	8	13/B1-12
1857	Apr	18	13/C2-13
1857	Apr	23	13/C14-D7
1857	May b. 6		13/D8-E1
1857	May	6	13/E2-5
1857	May	16	14/A3-B6
1857	May	19	14/B7-14
1857	May	21	14/C1-4
1857	May	29	14/C5-D2
1857	Jun	4	14/D3-12
1857	Jun	11	14/D13-E2
1857	Jun	14	14/E3-10
1857	Jun	18	14/E11-13
*1857	Jun	28	15/A2-B1
1857	Jul	5	15/B2-9
1857	Jul	17	15/B10-C3
1858	Jan	30	15/C4-6
1858	Aug	12	15/C7-10
1859	Apr	21	15/D4-7
1859	Apr	24	15/D12-E1
1859	Apr	29	15/E5-9
*1859	Aug	7	16/A3-6
1860	Jan	22	16/B12-C1
1860	Jan	23	16/C2-8
1860	Jan	24	16/C12-D1
1860	Jan	27	16/D2-5
1860	Apr	12	16/D6-11
1860	Apr	14	16/D12-E1
1860	Apr	19	17/A6-9
1860	Apr	25	17/A14-B5
1860	Apr	28	17/B12-C1
1860	May	2	17/C6-D1
1860	May	6	17/D2-9
1860	May	10	17/E4-9
1860	May	15	18/A3-6
1860	May	15	18/A7-14
1860	May	16	18/B1-6
1860	May	19	18/B7-14
1860	May	20	18/C5-12
1860	May	21	18/D3-8
1860	May	23	18/D13-E2
1860	May	26	18/E7-14
1860	May	29	19/A9-12
1860	May	31	19/A13-B4
1860	Jun	1	19/B9-12

1860	Jun	3	19/C3-14
1860	Jun	5	19/D1-6
1860	Jun	6	19/D7-14
1860	Jun	7	19/E1-4
1860	Jun	8	19/E5-6
1860	Jun	9	19/E7-8
1860	Jun	11	19/E9-12
1860	Jun	13	20/B3-6
1860	Jun	17	20/C9-D2
1860	Jun	19	20/D11-E12
1860	Jun	22	21/A11-B4
1860	Jun	24	21/C3-6
1860	Jun	26	21/C11-14
1860	Jun	27	21/D1-6
1860	Jun	28	21/D7-12
1860	Jun	29	21/D13-E4
1860	Jul	1	22/A3-9
1860	Jul	2	22/A10-13
1860	Jul	3	22/A14-B7
1860	Jul	6	22/C2-4
1860	Jul	7	22/C5-12
1860	Jul	8	22/C13-D1
1860	Jul	11	22/D14-E11
1860	Jul	15	23/A6-B1
1860	Jul	18	23/B10-C10
1860	Jul	20	23/C11-D4
1860	Jul	21	23/D5-10
1860	Jul	25	23/E1-6
1860	Jul	28	23/E7-9
1860	Jul	29	23/E10-13
1860	Aug	5	24/A12-B4
1860	Aug	8	24/B5-14
1860	Aug	9	24/C1-4
1860	Aug	10	24/C5-D2
1860	Aug	11	24/D3-8
1860	Aug	13	24/D9-E2
1860	Aug	14	24/E3-8
1860	Aug	16	24/E13
1862	Feb	11	25/C3-6
1862	Feb	12	25/C7-9
1862	Feb	14	25/C10-13
1862	Nov	17	25/E1-2
1862	Nov	19	25/E3-6
1862	Nov	20	26/A2-5
1862	Nov	2	26/A6-7
1862	Nov	23	26/A12-B1
1862	Nov	25	26/B2-9
1862	Nov	26	26/B10-C3
1862	Nov	30	26/C4-7
1862	Dec	1	26/C12-D3
1862	Dec	2	26/D4-11
1863			26/D14-E5
1863	Jan	28	26/E6-12
1863	Mar		27/A2-5
1863	Mar		27/A6-8
1863	Mar	10	27/A9-12
1863	Mar	13	27/A13-B4
1863	Aug	10	27/D9-12
1863	Sep	5	27/E1-4
1864	Feb	5	28/A13-B2
1864	Feb	9	28/B3-5
1864	Mar	3	28/B6-9

1864	Mar	3	28/B10-11
1864	Mar	4	28/B12-C1
1864	Mar	12	29/A2-B7
1864	Mar	16	29/B8-C1
1864	Oct	10	29/C5-10
1864	Oct	11	29/C11-13
1864	Oct	16	29/C14-D7
1865	Mar	24	31/A13-B1
1865	Mar	25	31/B2-7
1865	Mar	27	31/B8-13
1865	Mar	29	31/B14-C5
1865	Mar	30	31/C6-9
1865	Mar	31	31/C10-13
1865	Apr	2	31/C14-D7
1865	Jun	7	31/D8-11
1865	Aug	30	31/E2-5
1865	Sep	1	31/E6-8
1865	Sep	3	31/E9-14
1867	Feb	6	33/D13-E2
1867	Feb	12	33/E3-6
1867	Feb	15	34/A14-B3
1867	Feb	17	34/C4-9
1870	Oct	6	43/D4-7
1874	Mar	23	86/E5-6
1886-			
1887			56/B8-11
1893	Aug	5	79/A10-13
1893	Aug	16	79/B4-C1
n.d.			86/C7-9

from HOWE, JULIA WARD

*1869	Aug	5	141/C5-6

from SEVERANCE, CAROLINE

*1869	Aug	5	141/C5-6
1870	Jan	25	136/A3-6

from SHELDON, ABBY B.

1878	Jan	19	136/A7-8

from STANTON, ELIZABETH CADY

1900	Apr	21	140/E11-12

from STONE, LUCY

*1869	Aug	5	141/C5-6
1877	Mar	25	141/C11-12

from VAN VOORHIS, JOHN

1873	Aug	6	142/A6-11

from VIBBERT, GEORGE H.

*1869	Aug	5	141/C5-6

Hooker, Martha (Kilbourne), Mrs. Edward Beecher
to DAY, ALICE (HOOKER),
MRS. JOHN CALVIN

*1880	Sep	2	55/A5-8
*1887	Oct	25	57/A10-B3
*1887	Nov	14	57/B14-C7
*1888	Feb	1	58/E4-12
*1888	Nov	3	61/B8-C7
*1889	Jan	8	62/D2-13
*1889	Nov	28	67/C6-D3
*1891	Nov	26	75/E3 -
			76/A5

to DAY, KATHARINE SEYMOUR

*1887	Oct	25	57/A10-B3

to JACKSON, ALICE (DAY), MRS. PERCY

*1887	Oct	25	57/A10-B3

Hooker, Martha (Kilbourne), Mrs. Edward Beecher
from Hooker, Isabella Beecher

    from HOOKER, ISABELLA BEECHER
        1880   Sep 8   55/A13-B2

Howard, Susan Raymond
    from HOOKER, ISABELLA BEECHER
        1870   Jan 2   43/A2-B5

Howe, Julia Ward
    to DAVIS, PAULINA WRIGHT
        *1869   Aug 5   141/C3-4
    to HOOKER, JOHN
        *1869   Aug 5   141/C5-6

Howland, Marie
    to HOOKER, ISABELLA BEECHER
        1873   Feb 14 133/D12-E3

Hubbard, Julia A.
    to HOOKER, ISABELLA BEECHER
        1874   Mar 23   133/E4

Hugo, Victor Marie
    from HOOKER, ISABELLA BEECHER
        1875   Apr 16   51/C14-D1
        1875   Apr 16   51/D2-9

Jackson, Alice (Day), Mrs. Percy
    from GILLETTE, HELEN (NICKLES),
    MRS. WILLIAM
        *1887   Oct 25   57/A10-B3
    from HOOKER, ISABELLA BEECHER
        1875   Jun 8   51/D10-12
        *1887   Oct 25   57/A10-B3
        *1891   Jan 2   73/B3-6
        1891   Aug 13   74/E4-7
        1897   Feb 24   81/D4-6
        1900   Jan 23   83/B2-5
    from HOOKER, JOHN
        1891   Jan 2   73/B3-6
    from HOOKER, MARTHA (KILBOURNE),
    MRS. EDWARD
        *1887   Oct 25   57/A10-B3

Jarvis, Miss
    from HOOKER, ISABELLA BEECHER
        1877   Nov 22   53/D4-7

Judson, Mrs. M. J.
    to HOOKER, ISABELLA BEECHER
        1875   May 4   133/E5-9

Koons, Mrs. I. S.
    to HOOKER, ISABELLA BEECHER
        1901   Apr 26   133/E10-11

Kriffin, G. C.
    to HOOKER, ISABELLA BEECHER
        1871   Apr 4   134/A3-6

Langdon, Olivia (Lewis), Mrs. Jervis
    from HOOKER, ISABELLA BEECHER
        1879   Apr 22   54/C12-D3

Mott, Lucretia Coffin
from Wildman, J. K.

Lincoln, Abraham
    from HOOKER, ISABELLA BEECHER
        1861   Nov   25/A13-B4

Livermore, Daniel Parker
    to ANTHONY, SUSAN B.
        1870   Jan 20   134/A7-8
    from ANTHONY, SUSAN B.
        1870   Jan 25   134/A7-8

Livermore, Mary Rice
    to HOOKER, ISABELLA BEECHER
        1869   Oct 31   134/A9-10
        1869   Nov 9   134/A11-14
        1871   134/B1-2
    from HOOKER, ISABELLA BEECHER
        1869   Nov 15   42/B12-C6
        1869   Nov 15   42/C7-12
        1869   Nov 15   42/C13-D6
        1871   Mar 15   45/A2-B5
        1871   Mar 15   45/B6-12
        1871   Mar 17   45/B13-C4

Llewellyn, W. H.
    to HOOKER, ISABELLA BEECHER
        1874   Aug 5   134/B3-5
        1874   Nov 2   134/B6-9

Lockwood, Belva
    to HOOKER, ISABELLA BEECHER
        1871   Jun 17   134/B10-13

Lucas, Margaret B.
    to DAVIS, PAULINA WRIGHT
        1873   May 28   134/B14-C6

Manning, Emily S.
    to BROWN, OLYMPIA
        1871   Dec 6   134/C7-9

McManus, Ella Burr
    DOCUMENT:
    b. 1905 Apr
        Draft of Article on IBH 144/A10-B1

Merritt, Isabel (Hooker), Mrs. Walter G.
    to DAY, ALICE (HOOKER),
    MRS. JOHN CALVIN
        *1888   Feb 1   58/E4-12
        *1891   Nov 26   75/E3 -
                               76/A5

Mill, John Stuart
    from HOOKER, ISABELLA BEECHER
        1869   Aug 9   41/D4-9

Mitchell, John Hipple
    from HOOKER, ISABELLA BEECHER
        1878   Mar 14   53/D13-14

Mott, Lucretia Coffin
    from WILDMAN, J. K.
        *1869   Dec 6   142/C13-D2

Photographs

w/unidentified women 113/C2
1902
IBH, age 80 113/C3
1902
IBH, age 80 113/C4-5
c. 1905
IBH, c. age 83 113/C6

Pillsbury, Parker
to HOOKER, ISABELLA BEECHER
1870 Mar 27 134/E2-5

Prichard, Sara J.
to HOOKER, ISABELLA BEECHER
1874 Mar 4 134/E6-13

Reid, Whitelaw
to WARNER, CHARLES DUDLEY
1871 Oct 13 135/A2-5

Rogers, Sadie M.
to ANTHONY, SUSAN B.
*1871 May 8 135/A6-9

Russell, Fanny Eldredge
to ANTHONY, SUSAN B.
1870 Jan 24 135/A10-13

Sands, John L.
to ANTHONY, SUSAN B.
*1872 May 16 135/A14-B4
to HOOKER, ISABELLA BEECHER
*1872 May 16 135/A14-B4
to STANTON, ELIZABETH CADY
*1872 May 16 135/A14-B4
from HOOKER, ISABELLA BEECHER
1872 46/D14-E3
1872 May 24 47/E2-5

Sargent, Ellen Clark
to HOOKER, ISABELLA BEECHER
1873 Feb 2 135/B5-7
1873 Apr 3 135/B8-10
*1877 Sep 25 136/B7-8
1877 Nov 12 135/B11-12
1878 Jul 22 135/C1-2
to STANTON ELIZABETH CADY
*1877 Nov 23 135/B13-14

Savery, Anna C.
from HOOKER, ISABELLA BEECHER
1871 Nov 12 46/C3-12

Sayles, Lita Barney
to HOOKER, ISABELLA BEECHER
1878 Oct 23 135/C3-4

Scoville, Harriet (Beecher), Mrs. Samuel
from HOOKER, ISABELLA BEECHER
1860 Feb 13 86/C11-D5

Severance, Caroline
to DAVIS, PAULINA WRIGHT

*1869 Aug 5 141/C3-4
to HOOKER, ISABELLA BEECHER
1869 c. Aug 17 135/C5-14
1869 Aug 17 135/D1-E2
1869 Sep 24 135/E3-6
1869 Nov 10 135/E7-14
to HOOKER, JOHN
*1869 Aug 5 141/C5-6
1870 Jan 25 136/A3-6
from HOOKER, ISABELLA BEECHER
1869 Aug 27 41/D10 -
42/A9

Sheldon, Abby B.
to HOOKER, JOHN
1878 Jan 19 136/A7-8

Sheldon, J. E.
to HOOKER, ISABELLA BEECHER
*1877 Apr 10 136/A9

Shipman, William D.
from HOOKER, ISABELLA BEECHER
1896 Feb 17 81/C2-5

Slayton, Henry L.
to HOOKER, ISABELLA BEECHER
1878 Dec 2 136/A10-14

Smith, Julia E.
to HOOKER, ISABELLA BEECHER
1879 Apr 27 136/B1-3

Smith, Mrs. L. M.
to HOOKER, ISABELLA BEECHER
1874 Apr 7 136/B4-6

Spencer, Sarah J. Andrews
to HOOKER, ISABELLA BEECHER
*1877 Sep 25 136/B7-8
1877 Nov 18 136/B9-12
1877 Nov 22 136/B13-C4
1877 Dec 5 136/C5-6
1877 Dec 20 136/C7-10
1878 Mar 136/C11-12
1878 Mar 18 136/C13-D1
1878 May 8 136/D2-5
1879 Jul 30 136/D6-7

Stanton, Edwin McMasters
from HOOKER, ISABELLA BEECHER
1863 Apr 27/B5-8
1864 or
1865 27/E9-12
1864 May 29/C2

Stanton, Elizabeth Cady
to ANONYMOUS
1870-
1871 137/C10-13
to ANTHONY, SUSAN B.
1871 May 27 138/C2-3

to BROWN, OLYMPIA
*1873	Jan	7	117/E7-11
*1892	Apr	26	77/B4-7

to DAVIS, PAULINA WRIGHT
1869	Jul or		
	Aug		137/A2-B3

to HOOKER, ISABELLA BEECHER
*1869	Apr	27	136/D8-11
1869	May	24	136/D12-E6
1869	Sep		136/E7-14
1869	Sep	1	137/B4-7
1869	Sep	8	137/B8-C3
1869	Sep	23	137/C4-9
1870	Mar	22	137/C14-D2
1870	May	29	137/D3-E10
*1870	a. Jun 4		131/B14-C2
1870	Dec	1	138/A2-8
1870	Dec	28	138/A9-12
1871	Jan	3	138/A13-B2
1871	Mar	26	138/B3-5
1871	Apr	1	138/B6-9
1871	Apr	12	138/B10-11
1871	Apr	19	138/B12-C1
1871	Jun	10	138/C4-9
1871	Jun	30	138/C10-13
1871	Oct		138/D1-8
1871	Oct	15	138/D9-12
1871	a. Oct 15		138/D13-E2
1871	Nov		138/E3-5
1871	Nov		138/E6-8
1871	Dec	28	138/E9-12
1872	Jan		138/E13-14
1872	Feb	2	139/A2-11
1872	Feb	3	139/A12-B13
1872	May	2	139/B14-C3
*1872	May a. 16		135/A14-B4
1872	Jun	14	139/C4-11
1872	Summer		139/C12-13
1872	Jun	25	139/C14-D7
1872	Sep		139/D8-11
1872	Sep	8	139/D12-E1
1872	Nov	19	139/E2-5
*1873	Jan	7	117/E7-11
1873	Jan	21	139/E6-13
1873	Feb	20	140/A2-7
1873	Nov	3	140/A8-B2
1873	c. Dec		140/B3-6
1875	Nov	12	140/B7-12
1875	Nov	28	140/B13-C2
1876	Jul	1	140/C3-4
1876	Jul	5	140/C5-10
1876	Aug	6	140/C11-14
1877	Aug	30	140/D1-4
1877	Nov	28	140/D5-6
1880	Dec	18	140/D7-10
*1892	Nov	28	140/D11-E4
1892	Dec	24	140/E5-10
n.y.	Jun	20	140/E13-14

to HOOKER, JOHN
1900	Apr	21	140/E11-12

to TILTON, THEODORE
1871	c. Oct		138/C14

from ALLEN, GEORGE R.
*1872	May 16	135/A14-B4

from ANTHONY, SUSAN B.
1871	Apr	2	116/B8-11
1871	Sep	10	116/E3-6
*1871	a. Sep 16		130/D3-6
1872	May	29	117/A6-9
1877	Sep		119/C12-13
1877	Oct	5	119/D4-5
*1892	Nov	27	140/D11-E4

from BLACKWELL, HENRY BROWN
1872	Jul	27	121/B1-2
*1872	Aug	6	121/B3-4

from DAVIS, EDWARD M.
1872	Aug	31	129/C4

from DAVIS, PAULINA WRIGHT
1872	Jul	13	130/D7-12
1872	Aug	5	130/D13-E2

from GAGE, MATILDA JOSLYN
1870	Jun	4	131/B14-C2

from HOOKER, ISABELLA BEECHER
1870	Nov	25	44/B8-9
1870	Dec	21	44/C8-9
1870	Dec	29	44/C10-11
1871	Oct	18	46/A10-13
1872	May	12	47/D9-E1
1874	Mar	13	50/A2-B1
1875	Feb	28	51/B8-C7
*1892	Apr	26	77/A14-B3

from SANDS, JOHN L.
*1872	May	16	135/A14-B4

from SARGENT, ELLEN CLARK
*1877	Nov	23	135/B13-14

from STANTON, MARGARET
*1877	Nov	24	135/B13-14

from STONE, LUCY
*1872	Aug	6	121/B3-4

from TRAIN, GEORGE FRANCIS
1870	May	22	141/D13-E1

from WRIGHT, MARTHA COFFIN
1872	May	20	142/E5-8
1872	Jun	21	142/E9-12

Stanton, Margaret
to STANTON, ELIZABETH CADY
*1877	Nov	24	135/B13-14

Stearns, Sarah Burger
to GRIFFING, JOSEPHINE W.
1871	Jun	12	141/A3-10
1871	Jun	15	141/A11
1871	Jun	20	141/A12-B1

to HOOKER, ISABELLA BEECHER
1875	Mar	17	141/B6-8

to WOODHULL, VICTORIA CLAFLIN
1871	Jun	20	141/B2-5

from HOOKER, ISABELLA BEECHER
1871	Spring		45/C12-D3

Stebbins, Catharine A. F.
from HOOKER, ISABELLA BEECHER
1874	Dec	31	51/A10-B1

Sumner, Charles
    to HOOKER, ISABELLA BEECHER
        1871   Jan 9   141/D6-7
        1871   Apr 27   141/D8-10

Talcott, Mary Kingsbury
    from HOOKER, ISABELLA BEECHER
        1900   b. Feb 22   83/C6
        n.y.   Feb 20   86/B9
        n.y.   Jul 20   86/B10

Talcott, Mary (Seymour), Mrs. Russell
    from HOOKER, ISABELLA BEECHER
        1876-
        1879   52/B9-12
        1876   Aug 25 53/A14-B7

Tilton, Theodore
    from STANTON, ELIZABETH CADY
        1871   c. Oct   138/C14

Tingley, Annie H.
    to BROWN, OLYMPIA
        1871   Dec 4   141/D11-12

Train, George Francis
    to STANTON, ELIZABETH CADY
        1870   May 22 141/D13-E1

Trimble, Kate
    to HOOKER, ISABELLA BEECHER
        1878   Apr 8   141/E2-3
        1878   May 12 141/E4-7
        1878   Nov 21 141/E8-10
        1879   Feb 10 141/E11-12
        1879   Mar 14 141/E13-14

Trimble, Mary F.
    to HOOKER, ISABELLA BEECHER
        1879   Jan 2   142/A3-5

Underwood, Mr.
    from HOOKER, ISABELLA BEECHER
        1889 o.l.   62/C4-5

United States Congress
    from HOOKER, ISABELLA BEECHER
        1878   Feb 13 86(a)/B2

Van Voorhis, John
    to HOOKER, JOHN
        1873   Aug 6   142/A6-11

Vibbert, George H.
    to DAVIS, PAULINA WRIGHT
        *1869 Aug 5   141/C3-4
    to HOOKER, JOHN
        *1869 Aug 5   141/C5-6

Vinton, A. H.
    from DALGHREN, SARAH
    MADELINE VINTON
        1870   Apr 11 129/B3-6

Waisbrocker, Lois
    to HOOKER, ISABELLA BEECHER
        1878   Mar 11 142/A12-B2

Waite, Catharine Van Valkenberg
    from HOOKER, ISABELLA BEECHER
        1880   Mar 23 54/E6-7
        1880   c. Mar 23 54/E8-9

Walker, Miss C. C.
    to ANTHONY, SUSAN B.
        *1871   115/D2-5

Walker, Francis A.
    to HOOKER, ISABELLA BEECHER
        1873   Mar 22 142/B3-5
        1890   Jan 7   142/B6-13

Waller, Thomas MacDonald
    from HOOKER, ISABELLA BEECHER
        1890   Aug 7   71/C14-D1

Warner, Charles Dudley
    to HOOKER, ISABELLA BEECHER
        1868   Nov 22 142/B14-C7
    from HOOKER, ISABELLA BEECHER
        1871   Nov 1   46/B4-7
        1871   a. Nov 1 46/B8-11
        1871   a. Nov 1 46/B12-C2
    from REID, WHITELAW
        1871   Oct 13 135/A2-5

Warner, Elisabeth (Gillette), Mrs. George H.
    from HOOKER, ISABELLA BEECHER
        1863   Oct 30 27/E5-8
        1864   Dec 18 29/D8-E1
        1866   Aug 22 32/B11-14
        1870   Mar 19 43/B12-C1

Warner, George H.
    from HOOKER, ISABELLA BEECHER
        1900   May 30 86(a)/C9-12

Warner, Susan (Lee), Mrs. Charles Dudley
    from HOOKER, ISABELLA BEECHER
        n.d.   86/C5-6

Welles, Mary Crowell
    from HOOKER, ISABELLA BEECHER
        1904   Oct 7   85/D2-3

Wheeler, F. G.
    to HOOKER, ISABELLA BEECHER
        1880   Mar 10 142/C8-9
        1880   Mar 18 142/C10-12

Whitmore, Harriet Goulder
    from HOOKER, ISABELLA
        1900   Jan 20 83/A13-B1

Wildman, J. K.
    to MOTT, LUCRETIA COFFIN
        *1869 Dec 6 142/C13-D2

Wood, Emma A.
>   to HOOKER, ISABELLA BEECHER
>> 1874   Nov 27   142/D3-7

Woodhull, Victoria Claflin
>   to HOOKER, ISABELLA BEECHER
>> 1871   Oct 12   142/D8-9
>> 1871   Oct 19   142/D10-13
>   from ANONYMOUS
>> 1871   Apr 18   114/A2-5
>   from DAVIS, PAULINA WRIGHT
>> 1874   Feb b. 27   130/E3-9
>   from HOOKER, ISABELLA BEECHER
>> b. 1871   Feb 16   44/D5-6
>> 1871   Oct 18   46/A14-B3
>> 1872   Apr 10   47/C12-D1
>> 1872   Jul 28   48/C4-9
>> c. 1876   52/B13-C2
>> c. 1877   53/B10-13
>> 1888   Jul 19   60/B12-14
>> 1888   Aug 19   60/C1-3
>> 1888   Aug 24   60/C4-6
>> 1889   Feb   4   63/B10-C3
>> 1892   May 12   77/B12-C3
>> 1904   Jan   8   85/B7-C11
>> 1906   Sep 14   86/B5-7
>   from STEARNS, SARAH BURGER
>> 1871   Jun 20   141/B2-5

Woolsey, Jane Stuart
>   from HOOKER, ISABELLA BEECHER
>> 1869   40/E2-5

Wright, Martha Coffin
>   to BLACKWELL, HENRY BROWN
>> 1870   Jan   2 142/D14-E4
>   to STANTON, ELIZABETH CADY
>> 1872   May 20   142/E5-8
>> 1872   Jun 21   142/E9-12
>   from ANTHONY, SUSAN B.
>> 1871   Mar 21   116/B4-7
>   from HOOKER, ISABELLA BEECHER
>> 1871   Jul 23   45/E1-4
>> 1872   Jan   5   46/E4-7

ANNE THRONE MARGOLIS is an Assistant Professor of English at Williams College, where she teaches courses in American literature and American Civilization. She holds an M. Phil. in American Studies from Yale University and is currently completing her doctoral dissertation, Henry James and the Problem of Audience.

MARGARET GRANVILLE MAIR, a Research Librarian at The Stowe-Day Foundation, received her A. B. degree from Smith College. In 1977 she published *The Papers of Harriet Beecher Stowe*, a bibliography of the author's manuscripts in The Stowe-Day Library.